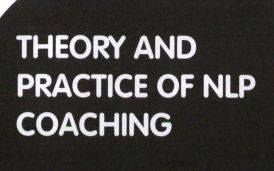

THEORY AND PRACTICE OF NLP COACHING

SAGE has been part of the global academic community since 1965, supporting high quality research and learning that transforms society and our understanding of individuals, groups and cultures. SAGE is the independent, innovative, natural home for authors, editors and societies who share our commitment and passion for the social sciences.

Find out more at: **www.sagepublications.com**

THEORY AND PRACTICE OF NLP COACHING

A PSYCHOLOGICAL APPROACH

BRUCE GRIMLEY

Los Angeles | London | New Delhi
Singapore | Washington DC

Los Angeles | London | New Delhi
Singapore | Washington DC

SAGE Publications Ltd
1 Oliver's Yard
55 City Road
London EC1Y 1SP

SAGE Publications Inc.
2455 Teller Road
Thousand Oaks, California 91320

SAGE Publications India Pvt Ltd
B 1/I 1 Mohan Cooperative Industrial Area
Mathura Road
New Delhi 110 044

SAGE Publications Asia-Pacific Pte Ltd
3 Church Street
#10-04 Samsung Hub
Singapore 049483

Editor: Alice Oven
Assistant editor: Kate Wharton
Production editor: Rachel Burrows
Copyeditor: Gemma Marren
Proofreader: Sharon Cawood
Indexer: Avril Ehrlich
Marketing manager: Tamara Navaratnam
Cover design: Jennifer Crisp
Typeset by: C&M Digitals (P) Ltd, Chennai, India
Printed by MPG Books Group, Bodmin, Cornwall

Library of Congress Control Number: 2012938455

British Library Cataloguing in Publication data

A catalogue record for this book is available from
the British Library

ISBN 978-1-4462-0171-8
ISBN 978-1-4462-0172-5 (pbk)

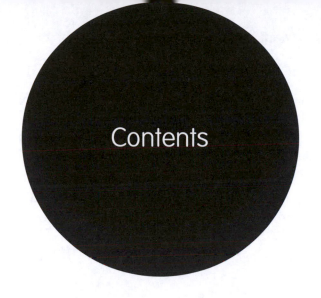

Contents

A glossary is available online at www.sagepub.co.uk/Grimley

This book is dedicated to my father, Frank, who taught me to appreciate the magnificence of 'NOW' and to my mother, Josephine, who taught me to appreciate the magnificence of a good party.

About the Author

Bruce Grimley is Managing Director of Achieving Lives Ltd and an Associate Fellow of the British Psychological Society (BPS). He is a practicing Chartered Psychologist who is registered with the Health Professions Council (HPC) in the UK. His speciality since qualifying as a psychologist has been one-to-one work, a subject on which he has written, consulted, lectured and passionately spoken about on the national and international scenes.

Bruce was one of the Association for Coaching's (AC) first accredited coaches and presently works with the AC assessing coaches. He also assesses and supervises psychologists within the Division of Occupational Psychology in the BPS as well being a founder member of the Special Group in Coaching Psychology.

Bruce Grimley is an accredited NLP trainer with the Association for NLP in the UK and internationally trains for the International Association of NLP Institutes and Coaching Institutes for which he is the UK president. Bruce is also a registered psychotherapist with the NLPtCA which is affiliated to the United Kingdom Council of Psychotherapists (UKCP).

Bruce believes the first application of NLP is to oneself. He enjoys life with his wife and two grown-up children in the Cambridgeshire countryside, making use of NLP principles to ensure he and those close to him remain in the most productive emotional state possible. From that place it is a matter of feeding forward all that NLP has to offer in terms of a perspective that puts the individual in charge of their life rather than the other way around.

Acknowledgements

There are many people who have helped me write this book, too numerous to put into one paragraph. A big thank you to John Grinder and Richard Bandler who got the ball rolling. I would like to thank Steve Andreas, Rodger Bailey, Bill O'Hanlon and Robert Dilts who were there around the beginning and who through email have supported my endeavours and have been wonderfully cooperative. Of course, a thank you to all of my NLP colleagues who have been instrumental in helping me develop my map of NLP and a special thank you to Dr Ho Law who expedited the idea of writing a book about NLP from the perspective of a registered psychologist. I would like to thank Professor Karl Nielsen, Dr Suzanne Henwood, Dr Frank Bourke, Dr Michael Hall and Dr Paul Tosey who have helped me develop an ability to be more accurate in my observations and recording. I would like to say thank you to SAGE and their great team who have assisted me in getting this book to you, the reader, in the most professional format. Finally, and in fact most importantly, I would like to acknowledge Jackie, my long-suffering and beautiful wife, and Matthew and Hayley, my wonderful grown-up children who resorted to putting salt in a cup of tea they made me when I was on a Skype call so as to get my attention and register a protest. Thank you to all of you who have helped me write this book and have made 2011–12 so enjoyable.

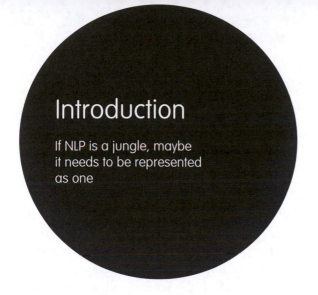

Introduction

If NLP is a jungle, maybe it needs to be represented as one

I went through the ritual of my advanced practitioner, master practitioner and train the trainer with John Seymour, co-author of *Introduction to NLP*. In the preface, Grinder tells us O'Connor and Seymour show us glimpses of an English rose garden, trimmed and proper (O'Connor & Seymour, 1990).

However, in this book you will find little such systemization; if NLP is a jungle, as Grinder suggests it is in his preface, maybe it needs to be represented as one. In the summer of 2008 John Grinder told me and a group of students that what passes as NLP around the world today is something he does not recognize as NLP.[1] I remember once waiting to listen to a well-known NLP speaker, Shelle Rose Charvet, talk. I was quite hungry and was delving into my cheese and pickle sandwiches as I waited about eight rows back in the auditorium. Shelle happened to be walking up, so I said 'Hello'. Shelle, in her sprightly way, said hello back and then in mock horror showed amazement that before such a prestigious key note I would be chomping away at cheese and pickle sandwiches, rather than engaging in the more appropriate behaviour which would have been to take luncheon at the restaurant. I looked up at her and in my best Cockney said, 'Shelle, I am hungry'. She laughed and said, 'Yup, sometimes a cigar is just a cigar'. What NLP is very good at is helping people see that as soon as we begin to interpret we begin to move away from 'reality' and when we move away from 'reality' we move away from each other. In a time-oriented world we start conversations filtered through generalized maps and we find the generalizations which we thought would save time end up costing us time as misunderstandings escalate and frustration increases. We all create personal maps of the world to which we are emotionally committed and we often walk around this planet as though these road maps were the only ones in existence and represented 'the only truth'.

---

[1] A three-day workshop with John Grinder and Carmen Bostic St Clair in Brighton about NLP modelling. The outcome of the training session was to assist participants in accessing the 'know nothing' state in order to effectively model.

The reason for writing this book is that I believe NLP has an untapped potential. However, rather than capitalizing on that potential, it is in danger of degenerating into a mere set of useful coaching techniques assimilated into other paradigms which are politically and academically more organized and astute.

The purpose of this book is not to take the reader through a set of NLP techniques and suggest that once they can master the 'Swish' pattern or the 'Meta Model' they will become more effective coaches. The purpose of this book is to introduce the modern coach or aspiring coach to an adventure, and assist them to understand that the key to sustaining this adventure is not in the techniques of NLP, but in the spirit of NLP. This spirit is to be found in the underlying conceptual assumptions, the ontology and epistemology, which generate the techniques. From the figure below, the reader will see that NLP lies firmly to the left of the table. It is this ontological orientation which could well be a key reason as to why NLP has not been systemized ... yet. By the end of this book the reader will understand why the next key step in the NLP story *has* to be an appropriate systemization, if it does not wish to be remembered in the archives as an interesting branch of pop psychology led by charismatic evangelists who fell out of love.

The ultimate frame

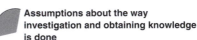

Assumptions about the grounds of knowledge and how one might begin to communicate this knowledge to others

Anti-positivism ──────── **EPISTEMOLOGY** ──────── **Positivism**

The social world is relativistic and constructed via individual frames of reference

NLP

Explanation of the social world is sought through regularities and general laws of causal relationships between variables and elements

Assumptions about the way investigation and obtaining knowledge is done

Ideographic ──────── **METHODOLOGY** ──────── **Nomothetic**

Emphasis is placed on subjective accounts; the meaning for the participant/actor

NLP

Importance of doing research based on systematic procedures, rules and protocols. Surveys/tests are preferred methods

Assumptions about the very essence of the phenomena under investigation

Nominalism ──────── **ONTOLOGY** ──────── **Realism**

External reality/structures do not exist. Names and labels simply act as concepts individuals/societies create which are particular and idiosyncratic

NLP

There is an objective, tangible reality which is, and can be established empirically.

NLP is not a set of techniques or iterations which can be applied to a problem and the reason for this is that the 'problem' is never the same. If the problem – and therefore the solution – is never the same, what *is* the solution? NLP shows us it is by moving to different levels of perception and organization of thought. NLP suggests that as we learn to do this, we learn to learn. Consequently, whatever situation we find ourselves in, either professionally or personally, we can learn how the systemic interrelations work and where the leveraged points of intervention are. This way we can maximize a solution for all parties within that system. I will suggest in the following chapters that left-brain rote learning of NLP patterns which become proprietary brands is not a viable way forward for NLP. The way forward for NLP is a deeper appreciation of the psychological strands from which NLP draws and a concerted effort to bring those strands into NLP education.

I am hoping the reader will finish reading this book with a sense of excitement concerning how much can be achieved through adopting NLP as a way of life, and also as a coaching modality. NLP at present certainly may be a bit of a jungle, but like most jungles it is full of energetic life, diversity, complexity and resourcefulness. To systemize this may be to rob it of some of these characteristics. However, to develop it in such a way as to be consistently accessible, ethical and professional is what this book seeks to do.

PART 1

The Development of NLP and Coaching Psychology

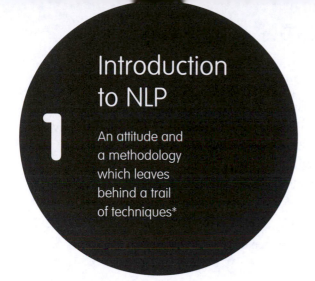

Introduction to NLP

An attitude and a methodology which leaves behind a trail of techniques*

Definition

… Now I would like you to take a few deep breaths and relax. Welcome to NLP … As you now sit reading these words, you are breathing lightly … and you can enjoy a wonderful relaxing experience … as you do, you will find the three single letters N … L … P written in front of you … It may be as you take a breath you discover you are curious, you have heard many stories and you would like to hear for yourself what NLP is really about … Maybe you would like to see it in action … and now, you have a sense by reading this book your questions will be answered … You may not be aware of it, however your heart has quickened, just slightly as you anticipate a journey of learning which means you are going to see improvement as you read this book … as you continue to read, you might be aware that a crude attempt at employing one of the NLP models has been directed at you. The Milton Model, of which you will learn much more in Chapter 7, was created by Bandler and Grinder after spending time modelling Dr Milton Erickson, founder of the American Society of Clinical Hypnosis. 'An attitude and a methodology which leaves behind a trail of techniques' is probably the most well-known definition of NLP but like so much in NLP it is hard to track down in writing. In NLP folklore this definition is attributed to Richard Bandler, however my research over two years could not source any extant publication. It is characteristic of NLP that people are polarized into two camps, a bit like Marmite – love it or hate it. One of the possible reasons for this is that the two founders of NLP were highly charismatic and, according to John Grinder, arrogant people. They were both educators in the Human Potential movement era, located in the highly experimental Kresge College of the University of California, Santa Cruz, where no grades were given (Gilligan, 2011). On the first meeting between these two people, there was immediate rapport. Grinder explains the characteristics he believed he and Richard Bandler shared:

---

*attributed to Richard Bandler

- Arrogant.

- Curious.

- Unimpressed by authority or tradition.

- Strong personal boundaries – a well-defined sense of personal responsibility for their own experiences and an insistence that others do likewise.

- Willingness to try nearly anything rather than be bored (or boring).

- Utterly lacking in self-doubt – egotistical.

- Playful.

- Full capability as players in the acting as if game.

- Full behavioural appreciation of difference between form and content.

    (Bostic St Clair & Grinder, 2001: 121).

As we will see throughout this book, the above characteristics permeate the practice of NLP to date, and do so in such a way that those who do not share at least some of the above characteristics find the practice of NLP an unpleasant experience. Conversely, those who do have a quantity of the above characteristics find resonance at such a deep level they seem convinced they have found the Holy Grail of psychological 'truth'.

The letters NLP stand for Neuro Linguistic Programming. What this means is described in one of the first text books on NLP:

> 'Neuro' (derived from the Greek *neuron* for nerve) stands for the fundamental tenet that all behaviour is the result of neurological processes. 'Linguistic' (derived from the Latin *lingua* for language) indicates that neural processes are represented, ordered and sequenced into models and strategies through language and communication systems. 'Programming' refers to the process of organizing the components of a system (sensory representations in this case) to achieve specific outcomes. (Dilts, Grinder, Bandler & DeLozier, 1980: 2)

Nobody seems absolutely certain as to when the term NLP came into existence or who created it; however, it did not appear in published form until 1979 in *Frogs into princes* (Bandler & Grinder, 1979). One story is that NLP was coined by Bandler and Grinder in an intentionally mischievous way, possibly poking fun at its quasi academic status (Tosey & Mathison, 2009: 12). Another story is Bandler made up the name when a traffic policeman asked for his profession (Brown, 2007: 173). Terrence McClendon, who was a part of the original research group at Santa Cruz, says the name appeared on Richard Bandler's new office shortly after the Meta Model group started in 1974. He goes on to say that at this time business cards were printed up with MM for Meta Model, which was later to become the logo for Richard Bandler and John Grinder's publishing company, Meta Publications (McClendon, 1989). Frank Pucelik says the original name for NLP during the first three years was 'Meta' (Pucelik, 2010).

However, if I am going to introduce you to something we need to know what it is I am introducing you to. For instance, is NLP 'the study of the structure of subjective experience' (Dilts, Grinder, Bandler & DeLozier, 1980)? If it is then there are already paradigms which do this, for example phenomenology, which like NLP talks about sensation as the unit of experience (Merleau-Ponty, 1962: 3). Psychodynamic psychology in its different guises has language full of nominalizations which seek to describe the structures and interrelations of subjective processes in such a way that we have an explanatory frame which is valid. Cognitivism seeks to put thinking at the foundation of the structure of subjective experience and through well conducted research attempts to persuade us they have hit the button. It would seem that if NLP is the study of the structure of subjective experience, then many others have been there before and such a definition, which seeks to demonstrate the provision of something new, is redundant.

It we take another popular definition of NLP, 'An attitude with a methodology which leaves behind it a trail of techniques', I believe we have something more substantial. However, we need to understand what the attitude is, what the methodology is and what the trail of techniques is. I believe there is within the NLP community as agreed an understanding as one will ever get concerning this.

The NLP Attitude

Curiosity and adventure seem to be the two attitudes which spring to mind when one considers this question. Interestingly the encyclopedia of NLP does not use the criterion of attitude to define NLP and describes it as 'a behavioural model, and set of explicit skills and techniques' (Dilts & DeLozier, 2000: 849). I would like to argue that attitude is core to NLP, its practitioners and its researchers, and indeed attitude is one of the variables which sets NLP apart from other paradigms. I would argue the key attitudes are arrived at through assimilation of the NLP presuppositions. If people assimilate these presuppositions, they themselves become very different people compared to those who they were before. Tony Grant (2001a: 234) in critiquing the Neuro-Associative Conditioning method of Anthony Robbins puts it well: 'if an individual in fact had the required high levels of these attributes (personal commitment, cognitive flexibility and insight), he or she would probably be likely to adopt the new behaviour anyway, regardless of the techniques employed'. What Tony Grant is saying here is if we have the right attitude we actually do not need the techniques. A cognitive behavioural approach would predict change in behaviour and language if a person assimilated such beliefs/attitudes as:

- The mind and body are part of one system.
- The meaning of your communication is the response you get.
- You have all the resources you need.
- If something does not work, keep changing until it does.
- The map is not the territory.
- There is no failure only feedback … and so on.

I would suggest the extent to which a person demonstrates through their behaviour and language that they run these beliefs is the extent to which someone can call themselves a practitioner of NLP. In a similar vein Linder-Pelz tells us she aims to reduce NLP coaching 'to basics and principles rather than tools' (2010: 53). From a systemic point of view, these basics and principles are of a different logical type and level compared to that of the tools which are generated as a function of such principles. We will look at the important part presuppositions play in the psychology of NLP in Chapter 5.

NLP Methodology

The NLP community generally accepts that the methodology of NLP is modelling, whether this be the analytical modelling of Dilts (1998) or the more bottom-up approach of Grinder (NLP Academy, 2001–2003: 9). Again the extent to which one's coaching methodology can demonstrate the use of either of these two modelling processes is the extent to which one can be said to be practicing NLP coaching. This key NLP skill will be discussed in detail in Chapter 12.

NLP Techniques

Again the NLP community seems to be in agreement here: the techniques refer to patterns and models generated by modelling projects. NLP coaches make good use of such NLP models as the Meta Model (1975) and the Milton Model (1975). Clean Language and Symbolic Modelling are coaching models created by Penny Tompkins and James Lawley (1997a & 1997b) as a result of modelling David Grove, a New Zealand psychotherapist. How NLP has developed within the popular coaching industry through the development of such coaching models will be discussed in detail in Chapter 14.

Beginnings

So we now have a basic frame within which we can get to understand and practice NLP coaching. We need to develop a certain attitude which was present in the co-founders and formalized in the NLP presuppositions; using this attitude we engage in modelling, and as a result of modelling develop patterns of excellence that hitherto have not been available for conscious scrutiny, testing or use. We also make use of those models which have been created and written up by previous NLP modelling projects.

Throughout this book this is the definition I will use to describe NLP. My intention is to suggest that if NLP is to begin to have a place in history and develop from 'a small experimental-research therapy group' (Lewis & Pucelik, 1990: i), it needs to begin to standardize its definitions and processes.

In my introduction to date we understand NLP is 'charismatic', we know what the letters stand for, and we have a working definition of what those letters mean. How did it all start? It started because an undergraduate mathematics and computer science student wanted an Associate Professor in linguistics to provide a model of how he did Gestalt therapy.

NLP began in the early 1970s at the University of Santa Cruz when Richard Bandler contacted John Grinder, an Associate Professor of linguistics, and invited him to attend a Gestalt workshop with the aim of observing his self-taught expertise of Fritz Perls and developing a model. NLP makes no commitment to theory but is regarded as having the status of a model. A model is a set of procedures whose usefulness and not 'truthfulness' is the measure of worth. These patterns are sometimes even presented as lies, systematic misrepresentations of what is actu-

> NLP needs to standardize its definitions and processes so that those interested in the discipline can recognize:
>
> - What NLP is.
> - How it is different from other approaches.
> - It is capable of falsification.
> - It is capable of empirical validation.
> - And consequently it is capable of real development rather than superficial popularism.

ally occurring. The idea is we never have access to objective reality. The 'truth' is scorned in NLP; what is important is whether what we consistently do is useful or not.

One of the main assumptions here, and the one that underpins NLP, is the presence of a consistent internal ordering and structuring of individual experience. By modelling experts such as Fritz Perls and Virginia Satir, this tacit ordering and structuring can be made available and transferred to others.

The model was based upon John Grinder's observation of Richard Bandler and Frank Pucelik as they performed their 'miracle groups' on a Monday, with John then conducting his own 'miracle group' on the following Thursday to see if he could replicate the results. After several months Grinder found he could. This modelling process was repeated after Bandler returned from attending a month-long seminar in Cold Harbor, Canada, with Virginia Satir. Again Grinder modelled Bandler, making use of the Satir verbal patterns. After these two modelling projects, Bandler and Grinder between them wrote up the first NLP model called the Meta Model in *The structure of magic* (Bandler & Grinder, 1975b). A second book, *The structure of magic 2* (Grinder & Bandler, 1976), looked at some of the other strategies of Perls and Satir, such as the 'empty chair technique', 'making the rounds', 'Satir categories' and the 'parts party', as well as the second model to come out of NLP, that of representational systems. However, at this time and in both of these publications NLP is not mentioned.

The NLP Context

The world was ripe for change. NLP started and consisted of small group situations where participants learned from their own interactions and experiences.

An appreciation of the context of this time is useful to understand the beginnings of NLP. The prevailing Zeitgeist was that the whole world was going to change as a result of efforts in the Santa Cruz area. When Bandler and Grinder wrote up the Meta Model, they were going to change the world with it; when they discovered representational systems they were going to change the world with that. It was at this time that Jobs and Wozniak were building the personal computer revolution out of a garage. The unpopular Vietnamese war, which Frank Pucelik had experienced at first hand, was coming to an end and young students were passionate about creating a better world for their future. Carlos Castaneda, dubbed the Godfather of the new age, was being lauded by the *New York Times* and Michael Murphy, a founder of the Esalen Institute, for his writings. Castaneda's writings included a central tenet of NLP and that is the ability to access a 'know nothing' state, an ability to 'stop the world'. It is only when we can do this that we truly see without the distortion of personal filters. In this state we see, hear and feel sensory experience as sensory experience. There are no instant associated meanings or feelings created in this state, just an appreciation of sensory experience which can mean anything we choose it to mean. In this way we learn to run our brain, rather than have our brain run us. R.D. Laing, the psychiatrist whose teachings were continued at Esalen and who was famous for being anti-psychiatrist – a term he hated (Gordon, 2009: 10) – was at the height of his fame and popularity. Laing himself was an excellent natural modeller. The world was ripe for change, and the students at Santa Cruz University and the participants of the Esalen Institute 50 miles down the coastline were going to deliver it.

In a very similar way to the early T groups which came out of the Research Center for Group Dynamics (RCGD, established in 1945) in Connecticut led by Kurt Lewin, NLP consisted of small group situations where participants learned from their own interactions and experiences. The evolving dynamic led to various experiments which created change in their personal lives and the lives of others. Grinder seemed to be the cohesive glue and if it was not for him NLP would not have come about according to Pucelik.[1] Pucelik was a broken man after his involvement in the Vietnam war and was looking to find personal answers; Bandler was the Jewish kid from the other side of town who was not averse to getting into scraps and would have ended up dead was it not for Virginia Satir (Dilts & Hallbom, 1990). Other members of the group who were also from the university and contributed much to the beginnings of NLP

[1]From notes taken by B. Grimley from the NLP Academy workshop in London, UK on 22 September 2010.

were Jeff Paris, Patrick and Terri Rooney, Marilyn Moskowitz, Ilene McCloud, Devra Canter and Treveleyan Houck. The team worked and played with modelling projects for more than 30 hours each week, unpaid, and together they developed what they first called Meta and was later to become NLP. These people had never been publicly recognized, until Frank Pucelik chose to speak of them in London in 2010 (Morris, 2010).

What Really Did Go on in Those Early Days?

It is difficult to obtain similar accounts of precisely what did go on in the early 1970s because different participants have different memories. Richard Bandler points out in the forward of Terrence McClendon's book *The wild days: NLP 1972–1981* (1989) that McClendon's recollections did not match his own exactly. *The wild days* is a colourful book and talks of the context in which NLP developed. Richard Bandler is described on one occasion as getting all red in the face and hyped up, shouting, hollering and storming out of Professor Bert's class in 1972. He was frustrated because psychology was so impractical; he believed what should be happening was that something practical like Gestalt therapy should be in place at Santa Cruz. Richard Bandler had transferred to Santa Cruz from Los Altos Hills after two years to major in mathematics and computer science. After transferring again to behavioural sciences, it transpired that Santa Cruz was sufficiently flexible to allow Richard to get his way. As a fourth-year student he was allowed to create his own courses. According to McClendon, students who attended would receive the same credits as though they were being tutored by a full professor. In the spring of 1972 Richard Bandler held his first Gestalt course at Kresge College, Santa Cruz. In order to do this he needed a supervisor for his course and this was John Grinder. Typically Richard's courses were highly experiential and even though some encounter groups at Kresge College were apparently conducted nude, Richard's were strictly a clothes-on event (McClendon, 1989: 9). McClendon's book amusingly talks about interesting activities in the wild days, which on one occasion involved tying a blindfolded group member to a cross, pouring lighter fluid at the bottom and setting it ablaze. When it was clear she could smell the smoke from the fire that John Grinder had lit, Richard Bandler asked the member if she would like her gift. This happened to be a knife with which she could cut herself loose (McClendon, 1989: 46). McClendon recounts other strange encounters in those days, for instance he talks of the group experimenting with negative hallucinations at the Alba Road training. McClendon describes using the deep trance phenomenon of developing negative hallucinations to partially undress

In researching for *The Gestalt approach & eye witness to therapy* (Perls, 1973), Spitzer says Bandler used to come away from the headphones and films sounding and acting just like Fritz Perls, to such an extent that Spitzer found himself calling Bandler Fritz on several occasions.

women and then tell them what colour their underwear was (McClendon, 1989: 81). It is clear from McClendon's book that the youthful experimenters did deviate from traditional academia in their course work and it is this departure which can be equivocally interpreted as either bold, Esalen-type experimentation with fun consistently textured into the activities, or irresponsible, unethical and unprofessional behaviour with no place within scientific investigation.

A Chronology of NLP Development

Until 1975 what developed from Meta into NLP had not been put into book form. It seems to have been a frenzy of unorthodox, playful and creative therapeutic experimentation and discovery in the Santa Cruz hills. However, there was one book Richard Bandler used to carry all the time (McClendon, 1989: 7), and that was a copy of *The Gestalt approach & eye witness to therapy* (Perls, 1973). Robert Spitzer, who owned Science and Behaviour Books, had hired Richard to edit the materials entrusted to him by Fritz Perls who died in 1970. It was through editing the films and transcripts that Bandler developed his fascination with Gestalt therapy. Spitzer talks of Bandler learning to play music by listening to the music of someone he admired over and over again until he sounded just like them. This process was replicated by Bandler with both Virginia Satir and Fritz Perls. In researching for *Eye witness to therapy*, Spitzer says Bandler used to come away from the headphones and films sounding and acting just like Fritz Perls, to such an extent that Spitzer found himself calling Bandler Fritz on several occasions (Spitzer, 1992: 2).

Gregory Bateson, the well-known anthropologist, who wrote the introduction for *The structure of magic*, introduced Bandler and Grinder to a psychiatrist he had consulted when working on the subject of Balinese trance. After modelling this psychiatrist, Milton Erickson in Phoenix, Arizona, further volumes were published. Between 1975 and 1980 much of the phenomenal energy of the initial therapeutic group at Santa Cruz, which developed from Bandler and Grinder's Gestalt course, began to transfer to alternative partnerships and further publications. It might be useful at this stage to look at a timeline of NLP to date:

1967: Bandler introduced by Becky Spitzer to Robert Spitzer (owner of Science and Behaviour Books) and lives on their property as caretaker (Spitzer, 1992: 1).

1968: Bandler introduced by Robert Spitzer to Virginia Satir and then sent to Canada to audio-tape a one-month-long workshop. He then spends several months transcribing the audio tapes (Spitzer, 1992: 2).

December 1969: Fritz Perls leaves transcripts of films and lectures with Robert Spitzer (Perls, 1973: x). Bandler starts looking at these materials and films of Fritz Perls, in order to write *Eye witness to therapy*.

Winter 1969: Grinder assigned to be the faculty sponsor for a T group Bandler was a part of at Santa Cruz (Bostic St Clair & Grinder, 2001: 142).

Spring 1970: Bandler asks John Grinder to observe the Gestalt therapy group he and Frank Pucelik were running, with the aim of understanding what Bandler and Pucelik were doing in order to produce training materials so Bandler and Pucelik could then train others. Grinder agrees and makes it explicit he will use the underlying strategy on which transformational grammar was founded (Bostic St Clair & Grinder, 2001: 143).

Summer 1970: After several months Grinder can reproduce, in the same time frame, the same outcomes as Bandler and Pucelik. Grinder then, based upon his new set of intuitions and his observations, maps his new competency into a formal represen-tation. This results in the beginning of the Meta Model (Bostic St Clair & Grinder, 2001: 145).

1971: After Grinder returns from East Africa Bandler approaches him and asks to repeat the process, but this time modelling the patterns he had learned from Virginia Satir. Grinder agrees. After the project they note significant overlaps between the verbal patterns of Perls and Satir. The verbal patterning of both performers are combined into the Meta Model (Bostic St Clair & Grinder, 2001: 146).

1974: The manuscript for *The structure of magic* is drawn up (Bostic St Clair & Grinder, 2001: 148).

1975: *The structure of magic* is published (Bostic St Clair & Grinder, 2001: 148).

1975–77: *Patterns of the hypnotic techniques of Milton H. Erickson, M.D.* Volume 1 (Bandler & Grinder, 1975a) and Volume 2 (Grinder, DeLozier & Bandler, 1977) are published.

1976: Bandler, Grinder and Satir publish *Changing with families*.

1978: The Division of Training and Research (DOTAR) is set up by Richard Bandler after Leslie Cameron-Bandler speaks about the need for a 'home' for NLP. David Gordon, Richard Bandler and Leslie Cameron-Bandler set up the practitioner and master practitioner formats and train participants in NLP. These participants disperse to their parts of the world and set up their own training institutes (Swingle, 2006).

1978: David Gordon published what Tosey and Mathison (2009: 63) describe as the earliest explicit discussion of sub-modalities in the field in his book *Therapeutic metaphors* (Gordon, 1978).

1979: Steve Andreas's publishing company Real People Press edits into book form Bandler and Grinder's seminars, *Frogs into princes* (1979). This is the first time NLP is mentioned in book form.

1980: One of the first 'textbooks' on NLP is published: *Neuro-linguistic programming. Volume 1. The study of the structure of subjective experience* (Dilts, Grinder, Bandler & DeLozier, 1980).

This timeline brings us to the 1980s when Bandler and Grinder acrimoniously split and went their own ways. Bandler later filed a suit against Grinder and other members of the early NLP community in 1997 claiming trademark infringement among many others. This legal action was settled in court and a covenant not to sue dated 3 February 2000 is published in the Appendix of Bostic St Clair and Grinder (2001).

Between 1982 and 1987 Grinder developed New Code NLP with Judith DeLozier. In 1986 they provided a five-day seminar entitled 'Prerequisites for personal genius' and the book *Turtles all the way down* (1987) was a transcript of the seminar. New Code NLP developed from an appreciation of ecology and systems and was heavily influenced by Gregory Bateson, to whom the book was dedicated. With New Code NLP, Grinder and DeLozier wanted to bring the wisdom of the unconscious mind back into the dance with consciousness and language. We will explore this in Chapters 12 and 13 when we look at modelling and systems thinking. Bandler during this time went on to develop his own brands which were Design Human Engineering® (DHE) and Neuro-Hypnotic Repatterning™. In 1982 Robert Dilts co-founded the dynamic learning centre with Todd Epstein. Both later went on to develop the first NLP 'University' in 1991 with Teresa Epstein and Judy DeLozier.

Space prevents a fuller exploration of how the NLP diaspora developed into the international presence we have today. However, hopefully the reader can appreciate that NLP in practice can take many different forms depending upon which stream you fish in.

Traditionally in order to become a part of the NLP community, one will start the journey by completing an NLP practitioner course. Suffice to say there is no government or legal affiliation nor standard certification level. Neither is there any official course content or level of competency. NLP World put this state of affairs nicely:

> There are a number of groups, organisations, associations, boards and bodies who have set up their own standard by creating certification/affiliation schemes in order to reflect how they believe NLP should be taught and practiced. These organisations often differ in their opinion. Each organisation has a different judgment and none are mandatory to join or achieve training through. Many training providers choose not to affiliate themselves with any certification or affiliation bodies. (NLP World, 2012)

In Chapter 17 I provide a list of these associations, courses, recommended readings and so forth for those who wish to begin to take their first steps into the NLP world.

> NLP today continues to be a loosely woven fabric, refusing to be tied down, refusing to close its mind to the possibility of new discoveries.

NLP today continues to be a loosely woven fabric refusing to be tied down, refusing to close its mind to the possibility of new discoveries. For many this is what makes it so exciting. NLP practitioners, whatever their age, talk like undergraduate students who are on the verge of some great discovery. I sincerely hope as you continue your journey with me through this book, you too will discover there are some useful items you can put in your shopping basket to take home and play with as you develop your coaching practice.

BRAIN TEASERS

1 Do you think Richard Bandler is right? Is psychology an impractical science? What is your evidence?

2 If NLP is so fantastic why do you think that after 40 years it has not got a foothold in mainstream psychology, which is the science of human thinking and behaviour?

The History
of Coaching

2

The enquiry shifted from
documenting the roots
of coaching … to identifying the
influences each of the root
disciplines have on coaching.
(Vikki Brock, 2008: vi)

When the modern coaching phenomenon started will depend upon what your
definition of coaching is. The quote from Brock's PhD dissertation suggests
there was never a specific date, but rather an emergence as various root disciplines converged to create a very specific way of interacting late in the twentieth century. Coaches from around the world daily discuss the still very open
questions concerning exactly the nature of coaching as they struggle to form
individual and collective identities. For example: Is
coaching a profession or an industry? Do you need
any training or qualifications to be a coach? Should
coaches be accredited? What is the difference between
coaching and counselling? What do different types
of coaches do? Is there any robust evidence that coaching provides a good return on investment? The list
really does go on. From a legal point of view the title
coach is not protected. So any person who can demon-
strate the basic skills, let us say listening, rapport building and questioning skills,
could legally call themselves a coach. Yet since the Stone Age is this not exactly
what all right-minded people seek to do when they converse with another
human being? In bringing up our children do we not seek to be coaches? In
working within a team do we not seek to be a coach? In listening to our
friend's woes over a drink do we not seek to act as coach? When discussing
boardroom strategy does not the CEO seek to coach the team of directors?
Why should we need a profession to do what we are actually doing in our
everyday business and social activities? In this section I will seek briefly to
answer the above questions. As I do this the reader might appreciate that in
the early twenty-first century we entered into a time of unprecedented change.
Brock (2008) makes the point that coaching came into existence in order to fill
an unmet need in a new interactive, fluid world of rapid change and complexity. Presently in Western society traditional havens of security have been

> Coaching came into
> existence in order to fill
> an unmet need in a
> new interactive, fluid
> world of rapid change
> and complexity.

swept away. Many marriages now fail. Even though spirituality is regarded as important for a rounded and quality life, attendance in places of formal worship has declined drastically. The idea that you can have a job for life has now been replaced by portfolio careers. Local communities have been decimated as whole industries have been shut down, and modern globalization has facilitated a move to distant shores where productivity and further development can be more economically assured. Resultant anxiety has been calmed by fast food and flashy media, quicker than the mind can follow edits and promises. Obesity and addiction are the consequences of quick fixes in emotionally traumatized citizens who reel in unbelief as yet another headline seems to substantiate the possibility that, despite rhetoric to the contrary, Gordon Gekko actually is the new messiah in a modern world directed by targets and driven by markets. As the markets favour those who have the means to invest, the gap between poor and rich increases, those who need help fall between the cracks of an increasingly stretched public sector and an underclass emerges creating moral panic in those who have something to lose. For some, coaching has come into its own in the late twentieth century/early twenty-first century in order to assist those who do not yet have a *Diagnostic and statistical manual of mental disorders* (DSM) label; for others this new territory is now the norm and they embrace it, so coaching is a way of helping move one's career and life quickly forward. In 2003 organizations worldwide were spending $1 billion on coaching and this was expected to rise to $2 billion by 2005 (Hamlin, Ellinger & Beatti, 2009: 13). It could well be that coaching is here to stay. These figures seem to be corroborated through an online search where I found that in the USA alone, 'The business demand for coaching is nearly doubling each year. Out of the $80 billion being currently spent on corporate education, FLI Research estimates that $2 billion is spent on executive coaching at senior executive levels in Fortune 500 companies' (Business Wire, 2011).

> The business demand for coaching is nearly doubling each year.

Is Coaching a Profession or Industry?

Many would argue that this is just a matter of semantics, however words and the meanings we give them are a key component of NLP, and the ability to effectively use language as a separate representational system is what distinguishes us from the lower animals … So what is the difference?

Grant and Cavanagh (2004: 3) have summarized professional status as defined by several key criteria:

1 Significant barriers to entry.

2 A shared common body of knowledge rather than proprietary systems.

3 Formal qualifications at university level.

4 Regulatory bodies with the power to admit, discipline and meaningfully sanction members.

5 An enforceable code of ethics.

6 Some form of state-sanctioned licensing or regulation for certain professions, or parts of professions.

Clearly at present this is not the case for coaching, with Jonathan Passmore telling us five years ago, 'At present becoming a coach is as easy as saying the word' (Passmore, 2006: 3). In the UK it is illegal to call yourself a doctor, a clinical psychologist or an architect, for instance, without undergoing under-graduate training, postgraduate training and then extensive supervised practice. For the majority of such professions, the equivalent NVQ qualification is at professional Doctorate level. Going through such procedures is indeed a sig-nificant barrier to entry, meaning not only do participants have to have the aptitude to become a professional, but they also have to have the ambition, motivation and dedication too.

Klass (1961: 698) points out that historically there were three professions: medicine, divinity and law. The earliest universities were founded primarily to prepare students for the professions. Klass says that when this relationship between university preparation and professional practice has been breached the standards have fallen to a very low level. He describes an example at the turn of the century when doctors in the USA were turned out by diploma mills not associated with an accredited university. He says that only when the Flexner Commission corrected this state of affairs did the standards of medical practice recover from being at their lowest ebb. An added complication in the professionalizing of coaching is that already existing practitioners of human resource development (HRD) and organizational development (OD) claim that coaching is an extant core component of what they have been doing for decades (Hamlin, Ellinger & Beatti, 2009: 13). Many psychologists would add their profession as well, so the earnest plea would be why re-invent the wheel?

When one looks at the many definitions of industry, one often finds words which remind us of the industrial revolution, when wealth was created through heavy machinery involved in such activities as mining and manufac-turing. The word summons up economic activity which has at its heart a very much more hands on and physical essence. In terms of economic evolution it also suggests infancy. Clark's basic sector model, developed in 1950 (Nagle, 1999: 13), makes the point that this image of 'industry' is tied up with primary and secondary sectors – raw materials and the working of those materials into more refined products. As countries develop there is a tendency to move away from primary and secondary sectors to tertiary and quaternary sectors. These sectors are to do with service and knowledge. In these tertiary and quaternary terms it is easy to see how coaching fits in well with a definition of industry.

The words industry and profession, as far as coaching is concerned, can therefore usefully be seen as a continuum rather than a difference. The coaching industry gradually is developing professional credentials. Links with universities are being made, ethical practice and professional standards are being created and qualifications which seek to educate and differentiate professional coaches from other professionals are becoming available. The interested reader can look at Chapter 17 for a list of associations and universities offering these credentials.

> Based upon the evidence, it seems clear coaching is somewhere between being an industry and becoming a profession.

Professor Stephen Palmer alluded to this evolution as he confidently claimed coaching is now worthy of being called a profession in his address to the Special Group in Coaching Psychology (SGCP) annual conference in 2008. He demonstrated how coaching now has postgraduate courses at universities throughout the world with coaches studying and developing the profession at PhD level. There are many coaching associations which insist on adherence to a code of ethics, there are professional standards which coaching associations insist on, there are accreditation schemes which have at their core well-defined competencies against which to evaluate would-be coaches. Finally, there is a vibrant international coaching community which communicates constantly and seeks to raise the bar.

Based upon the evidence, it seems clear coaching is somewhere between being an industry and becoming a profession.

Qualifications to Coach

Given the present evolution of coaching, it would not surprise the reader to know that one does not need a qualification to professionally coach. This can be contrasted with other professions such as teaching, nursing, law, medicine, architecture, finance and psychology, where in order to practice you must obtain qualifications and in some cases titles are protected by law. For some it is this differentiation which means coaching is not yet a profession. Coaching psychology is a discipline within psychology, in a similar way that clinical, educational or occupational psychology is. In the UK, the SGCP formed as a result of lobbying the Coaching Psychology Forum (CPF). The CPF founded in 2002 did so in response to concerns about untrained or poorly trained coaches. In this sense coaching psychology stemmed from the proliferation of coaches who were poorly trained and thus post-dated coaching in the UK. Vikki Brock points out that psychology as a profession currently has by far the greatest influence over coaching and its development (19.4 per cent), compared with the next professions in the table: consulting (11 per cent) and OD (10.9 per cent) (Brock, 2006: 26). Even though coaching psychologists tend to emphasize the psychological roots of coaching more than other coaches, they also emphasize the need for a rigorous scientific approach. The SGCP does not accredit any coaching courses nor does it 'gatekeep' membership to its specialist organization. Coaches who wish to understand the psychological background of many coaching models do not have to possess a psychological qualification to join the SGCP as affiliate members. Pauline Willis, a past chair, writes: 'It is worth bearing in mind that most established coaching psychologists do not have a qualification that is specific to "coaching psychology" because existing forms of accreditation do provide psychologists with a skill set that is appropriate to this kind of practice. Interesting and valuable continuing professional development (CPD) options are available for seasoned psychologist practitioners to address a range of specific interests and skills gaps' (Willis, 2011). This very much seems to be the perspective of many coaches who formerly existed in backgrounds other than psychology. Just as psychologists point to the psychological nature of many coaching models, so other professionals point to the various competencies from their backgrounds which they believe are transferable to the coaching endeavour.

> **COACHING IS:**
> A human development process that involves structured, focused interaction and the use of appropriate strategies, tools and techniques to promote desirable and sustainable change for the benefits of the coachee and potentially for other stakeholders.

'Qualifications' from this perspective would mean a demonstration of CPD, for example reading books, attending workshops, and obtaining certification on adjunctive disciplines such as psychometrics and specific coaching skills.

What seems to be certain is that as more organizations and individual buyers make use of coaching and develop their understanding of what coaching has to offer, when they look at tenders, they will look too for people who are qualified in coaching to a high degree. It makes sense that in order to be qualified in a discipline, then that discipline itself must be differentiated from others and needs a specific definition. Cox, Bachkirova and Clutterbuck (2010: 1) describe coaching as 'a human development process that involves structured, focused interaction and the use of appropriate strategies, tools and techniques to promote desirable and sustainable change for the benefits of the coachee and potentially for other stakeholders'. I would argue that in the modern era, one increasingly needs to be qualified in order to compete effectively and demonstrate one has mastered the skills which naturally flow from the above definition.

Should Coaches Be Accredited?

It would seem to me that if there are coaching associations which seek to raise the bar by offering accreditation in order to demonstrate a more professional approach, any coach wishing to succeed would miss a trick by not taking this up. At present most major coaching organizations offer individual accreditation to coaches. If any coach or potential coach would like to look further into this they can look up the coaching organization of their choice in Chapter 17.

What is the Difference Between Coaching and Counselling?

This is a very interesting question and key because different professionals are keen to 'mark' their territory, frame the terms of reference and reap the benefits. The common quip is that they are the same; it is just that for coaching you double or treble your fee. However, the debate is deeper and more complex than this and has at its heart ethical considerations, theoretical orientation and professional practice. There is also a political element as counsellors have often undertaken a considerable amount of training and supervision and resent those with much less training charging more than them for doing one-to-one work.

A good starting point is the difference between helping relationships, as seen by Frank Bresser and Carol Wilson (2006: 21), using the metaphor of driving a car.

- A therapist will explore what is stopping you driving your car.
- A counsellor will listen to your anxieties about the car.
- A mentor will share tips from his or her own experiences of driving cars.
- A consultant will advise you on how to drive the car.
- A coach will encourage and support you in driving the car.

Even though the above is an excellent set of generalizations, it is feasible each of the helping relationships above will employ elements of the other relationships to some degree and possibly in some sessions exclusively depending upon the circumstances.

It is also feasible that helpers from other disciplines would object to such simplifications. Bachkirova and Cox (2004: 1–2) point out that coaching sees counselling as a remedial activity, working on problems (Carroll, 2003), that it is problem and crisis centred with an emphasis on diagnosis, healing or analysis (Parsloe & Wray, 2000: 12) or a focus on poorer performers (Stone, 1999: 3), while coaching is seen as proactive and counselling as reactive (Whitmore, 1997). Bresser and Wilson talk about the primary focus of coaching being to move the client forward and build desire, whereas the primary focus in counselling is about dealing with distress, and in psychotherapy dealing with damage and needing a period of time before moving on (2006: 21). There are other putative differentiators such as counselling being theoretical and coaching being practical. However, key to these points is that counsellors who work from a positive psychology perspective, a solution focused perspective or a strength based perspective, just to name a few, would vigorously challenge these generalizations made by coaches. Bachkirova and Cox (2004: 2) quote Berglas (2002: 5): coaches have found a niche in the market with an 'anti-counselling orientation', which, in some cases, has been bolstered by 'the promise of quick and painless improvement of performance'.

Another difficulty in making distinctions between helping relationships is an ethical one. Bachkirova and Cox (2004: 5) point out that Grant (2001b) suggests counselling supports a pathological population, while coaching supports a normal population. To clinically label someone when the definition of mental health is still an area of academic debate, they argue, is unsustainable. It is also questionable to suggest that people who have a clinical label are somehow not normal. Bachkirova and Cox say it is a sign of mental health that someone has sufficient self-awareness to recognize all is not well and seek redress. Coaching that seeks to differentiate itself from 'non-normal' populations succeeds in making itself more attractive with less of a stigma attached to it; however, it does so at the expense of stigmatizing those who seek counselling or psychotherapy even further. The famous David Rosenhan experiment of 1973 showed how easy it is to provide someone incorrectly with a clinical label when eight normal participants in an experiment were diagnosed by expert professionals with seven cases of schizophrenia and one case of bipolar disorder. When they were finally 'released' two months later, the psychiatric community was a bit upset and challenged Rosenhan to replicate the experiment, to which he agreed. After a month, the major hospital which participated proudly announced they had spotted 41 fake patients. Rosenhan replied that he had in fact sent no patients to the hospital at all. Robert Spitzer (not to be confused with the owner of Science and Behaviour Books who introduced Richard Bandler to Virginia Satir), who appears in Adam Curtis's BBC documentary 'The Trap' (2007), was the chair of the third version of the *Diagnostic and statistical manual of mental disorders* (DSM-III, 1980). He pointed out the psychiatric response to this Rosenhan effect was to focus only on behaviour. In the DSM-III professionals would provide lists of observable behaviours and in order to meet clinical caseness a certain amount of boxes needed to be ticked. However, in doing this, normal sadness, for instance, was often mistaken for depression because it did not take into account the context and circumstances, which meant it was a very normal response to be sad. The result was that many 'normal' people became medicalized and labelled as belonging to a clinical population. Another excellent critique of the DSM is voiced by Paula Caplan (1995). She puts forward the argument that the contents of this highly influential volume are created socially and not scientifically.

Space necessitates brevity on this interesting topic. However, a final ethical consideration is in contrast to the previous paragraph, where individuals have sufficient self-awareness and emotional intelligence to seek counselling or coaching, and concerns those employees and individuals who see no need for counselling or coaching. It is known that within the echelons of high potential executives, there is a significantly higher proportion of 'psychopaths' than in the general population (Babiak & Hare, 2006: 193). There is also a significantly higher proportion of 'narcissists' in management positions (Babiak & Hare, 2006: 131). Angela Mansi hypothesizes that narcissists in particular are resistant to coaching (2009: 22–5). With the Hogan Development Survey (HDS) surfacing well-known derailing behaviours in executive positions, the ethical consideration is at what stage should an organizational culture be challenged because it is covertly supporting such destructive behaviours, and at what stage should we accept the creative tension within the organization is just right and underperforming managers just do not have the 'right stuff', are not responding to coaching and need the 'softer' counselling option or quietly to let go? In other words, is the coaching intervention a systemic one or an individual one? Nigel Sargent, in his award winning MSc dissertation, quotes one of his partici-

> It is known that within the echelons of high potential executives, there is a significantly higher proportion of 'psychopaths' than in the general population.

pant coaches who he calls Sandra. She says: 'Very rarely does an individual show signs of derailing unless there is a problem with the whole system' (2010: 7). These are all rhetorical questions which hopefully will stimulate the reader's mind and help them appreciate that the line between coaching and counselling is far from clear.

What Do Different Types of Coaches Do?

As the coaching industry develops many professionals are seeking to find their market niche. One will therefore find sales executives offering sales coaching, entrepreneurs and senior managers offering business coaching, marketing executives offering marketing coaching and counsellors offering life coaching. The list is literally as long as your imagination chooses to make it. Fitness, flirt, voice, media, communication, assertiveness, dress, group all act as adjectival words which describe the type of coaching you can purchase in the twenty-first century, with fees ranging from £50 to £500 per hour (Association for Coaching, 2004).

Is There Any Evidence Coaching Works?

At present, coaching is building an evidence base as the industry develops into what it hopes will become a fully grown profession in due course. Much of the evidence of coaching efficacy at present comes from small-scale studies. Many good MSc and PhD projects also provide robust small-scale studies offering rich qualitative findings and calling for further research into unanswered questions. The difficulty with such small-scale studies, however well they are done, is that because of the small samples used one cannot generalize the findings to other populations. This is because the findings might be a function of the sample rather than a function of coaching per se. The more the researcher can ensure the sample represents the whole population for which it seeks to make predictions, the more it can generalize to that population. Good research also needs to control for other variables which could produce good results in the particular study conducted. For instance, in working with traders under stress in the city a good result could have been caused by the time of year, the culture of the organization, the fact that participants were self-selecting or that rewards were given for participation, etc. The small-scale nature of much of the research to date in coaching means it is difficult to generalize the results to larger populations and also categorically say it is coaching that has created the positive difference rather than other influences which could be accounted for, but have not been, because of time and budgetary considerations.

Conclusion

Most coaches will accept that if we take the more formal concept of coaching as an activity where one person pays another for coaching services, then coaching started in the mid-twentieth century and 'took off' in the early twenty-first century. At present, even though we may not have a coaching profession, the mature coaching industry is certainly in a position where it can offer professional coaching services.

BRAIN TEASERS

1 What do *you* think the difference between coaching and counselling is?
2 Have you ever been to see a professional coach? If you have, what was the difference between that experience and everyday conversation?

3

What is NLP Coaching?

NLP and coaching are both unregulated activities: caveat emptor

In Chapter 1 we discovered our working definition of NLP is: 'An attitude with a methodology which leaves behind it a trail of techniques'. In Chapter 2 we discovered our working definition of coaching is: 'A human development process that involves structured, focused interaction and the use of appropriate strategies, tools and techniques to promote desirable and sustainable change for the benefits of the coachee and potentially for other stakeholders'. NLP coaching is an amalgam of these two definitions.

At present there is no independent NLP coaching association. This is to be contrasted in the UK with the fact there is an independent psychotherapy association, the Neurolinguistic Psychotherapy and Counselling Association (NLPtCA) which formally sits within the College of Constructivist Psychotherapies (CCP) in the United Kingdom Council for Psychotherapy (UKCP). This state of affairs represents the fact that counselling and psychotherapy are more developed in their organization and practice compared with coaching, indeed many coaching techniques come from counselling and psychotherapy models. From reading the previous chapters the reader might well notice not only is NLP an unregulated activity, but so is coaching. I mean by unregulated there is no protection to the titles, so any Tom, Dick or Harriet can set themselves up as an NLP coach with the minimum of training. As with all coaching providers, it is therefore very much the case that the buyer needs to research the experience, qualifications and claims of any NLP coach or NLP coaching organization they choose to make use of.

In this chapter I would like to explore, with the aid of our definitions, what NLP brings to the coaching relationship which other approaches may not and what the consequence of this is for both the coach and the coachee.

The NLP Attitude

The importance and primacy of attitude has already been alluded to in previous chapters. Here I would like to expand on the NLP presuppositions. It seems clear that in order to practice as an NLP coach one needs to think and perceive in a way that is different; I would suggest this way is guided by the NLP model of the human being.

The APET Model

At the heart of any psychological modality has to be an underlying model of human functioning. NLP would suggest this model is never 'true'; however, it is either useful or not to a degree. The APET model (Activating trigger, Pattern matching, Emotional arousal, Thought and conditioned beliefs), which was developed in part by a psychologist who was an NLP trainer in the mid-1990s, is a very good modern model which goes a long way in understanding the attitude of an NLP coach (Griffin and Tyrrell, 2000). The reason it is good is that not only does it explain human processing well from an NLP perspective, but also it differentiates NLP from its cognitive counterpart.

In Table 3.1 below, the reader can see the basic difference between the ABC of cognitive coaching and the APET from Human Givens which characterizes how an NLP coach would perceive the coachee.

The main difference is that for the NLP coach compared with the cognitively oriented coach, human thinking is dependent upon an unconscious patterning of information, which then gives rise to emotion that occurs in less than 1/10th of a second. This happens so rapidly one cannot consciously appreciate our thinking is in fact a product of previous processes. For the coach who comes from a more cognitive perspective, the leverage in the coaching process is often in the thinking. The beliefs which arise from thinking are what a cognitively oriented coach would hone in on, for they believe that if they can facilitate a change here, they will then facilitate a change in the emotions and behaviour of the coachee.

> For sustainable change to occur the unconscious mind *must* support the conscious mind.

The NLP coach recognizes that the beliefs of the coachee are only the end part of a set of systemic relationships which reach deep into the unconscious and into the rudimentary maps of the world that an individual carries around and often confuses with 'the real world'. However much the coachee changes,

Table 3.1   A comparison of APET with cognitive behavioural coaching

APET	ABC
• Activating trigger	• Activating trigger
• Pattern matching	• Belief (thinking)
• Emotional arousal	• Consequence (behavioural and emotional)
• Thinking (belief)	

or claims a change, at the level of belief, unless this is accompanied by appropriate changes in the underlying pattern of perception and emotion, the coachee will experience no lasting change in their behaviour. Essentially the unconscious mind will not be supporting the conscious mind and relapse will occur when the coachee tires of putting in the conscious effort to behave and think in a way that is not supported at deeper levels.

We will look at the NLP presuppositions and how they affect the coaching relationship in more detail in Chapter 5. However, suffice to say at present the way in which an NLP coach does think and perceive stems from an understanding of the human being which flows from the APET model, or a model that is very similar.

What is at the heart of the APET model is the belief humans are pattern-matching machines, thus 'programming' in NLP, which comes from an age when the personal computer was taking off. Each coachee will have unique sets of patterns which give rise to emotion, described by Daniel Goleman as feelings that create distinctive psychobiological states which lead to a propensity for action and simplified thinking styles (Griffin & Tyrrell, 2000: 15). For the NLP coach the nature of these patterns is of great significance as it sets the frame for a complex interaction between perception, emotion and thought, which in turn is directly related to language and behaviour. What NLP brings to the coaching endeavour is a rich appreciation for complex interactions of equally complex internal processes which are configured at different levels of neurology and are of different types. At this point it is not necessary to understand what these processes are, as all will be revealed in Part 2, for instance in the chapters on Meta Programs and Systems Thinking. However, what is useful for the reader to understand is that when operating from an NLP perspective, their coachee is simultaneously communicating to them at many different levels, and recognizing these multitudinous communications is key. It is often said in NLP circles that NLP coaching consists of 95 per cent observing and listening and 5 per cent intervention. One could be forgiven for thinking that with this rich appreciation for the incredible complexity of human functioning NLP coaching is a very complicated process. However, the intention of everything NLP is to reduce the models it makes use of to their simplest, workable components – this is known in NLP as 'elegance'. A nice description of NLP coaching comes from an unknown source and is provided in metaphor form demonstrating the primacy of the emotional state, as would be expected when considering the APET model:

> NLP coaching consists of 95 per cent observing and listening and 5 per cent intervention.

A boy asks his mother, 'What is NLP?'

His mother replies, 'I will tell you in a moment, but first you have to do something so you can understand. See your granddad over there in his chair?'

'Yep,' said the boy.

'Go and ask him how his arthritis is today.'

The boy went over to his grandfather. 'Granddad,' he said, 'how's your arthritis today?'

'Oh, it's a bit bad, son,' replied the old man. 'It's always worse in the damp weather. I can hardly move my fingers today.' A look of pain crossed his face.

The boy went back to his mother. 'He said it was bad. I think it hurts him. Are you going to tell me what NLP is now?'

'In a minute, I promise,' replied his mother. 'Now go over and ask Granddad what was the funniest thing that you did when you were very young.'

The boy went over to his grandfather. 'Granddad,' he began, 'what was the funniest thing I ever did when I was very young?'

The old man's face lit up. 'Oh,' he smiled, 'there were lots of things. There was the time when you and your friend played Father Christmas and sprinkled talcum powder all over the bathroom pretending it was snow. I laughed – but I didn't have to clean it up.' He stared into the distance with a smile.

The boy went back to his mother. 'Did you hear what Granddad said?' he asked. 'Yes,' his mother replied. 'You changed how he felt with a few words. That's NLP.'

The attitude of the NLP coach is one that can easily be deconstructed and understood in terms of the APET model. The metaphor above shows how the NLP coach is acutely aware of the emotional state of the coachee and seeks to shift this from negative or neutral to positive. In terms of the standard 'presuppositions' of NLP, this could be understood from the recognition that the mind and body are part of one system. Irrespective of what one is thinking, if one can shift the body so it feels good, this inevitably will have an effect on the mind when one returns to thinking. Because the body is connected to the mind and the mind is connected to the body, you shift one and the other has to move. GP surgeries throughout the world are recognizing the tremendous benefits of exercise. Because as you exercise you move into a different 'distinctive psychobiological state' and as you do this your thinking inevitably will change too. As mentioned I will be discussing all the other presuppositions in Chapter 5; however, for now it is important to recognize that an NLP coach is different from others in that when they first meet their coachee their attitude is greatly directed by the presuppositions of NLP, which fit nicely into the APET model of Griffin and Tyrrell.

The NLP Methodology

Modelling is the key methodology of NLP. If an NLP coach wishes to understand or learn about his coachee, he believes the most direct and effective way of doing this is by modelling them. Robert Dilts, who is known in NLP circles to be more cognitively oriented than many other practitioners, tells an interesting story. He says that when he went to talk to Milton Erickson to understand how he managed to do hypnosis to such a high standard, Erickson would invariably answer, 'I don't know'. Erickson recognized that, like many, he could create a personal story or theory to satisfy the conscious mind; however, whether this truly reflected the complexity of his perception, thinking and behaviour was doubtful. Dilts made the point that Erickson never treated the symptom, always the patient. For Erickson every person was different so every person needed a different model – the idea you could take a standard process and apply it across patients was not the way Erickson worked; Erickson met his patients at their model of the world. Frank Pucelik, another early developer of NLP, talks about how Richard Bandler and other early NLP modellers could get the same results as Fritz Perls in a fraction of the time. This was because Fritz Perls had to satisfy a conscious and theoretical model in order to practice. Rather than just practice, Perls, as all good reflective practitioners do, sought to build a conscious understanding of what he did, in order to develop and build on previous activity. However, as he did this, such a model became a filter, reducing the amount of sensory information available to him. In an interview with Michael Carroll of the NLP Academy (2010), Frank Pucelik told the audience that what people who are really good at something say they do, is not it. Their conscious understanding is 'smoke'. The question the early NLP modellers were after was what was the critical behaviour, what was the critical observation and what was the critical reaction to that observation ... what is really doing the magic? Pucelik says 90 to 95 per cent of what Perls did was 'smoke'. The question was whether we could extract the key variables and work without the 'smoke'. Pucelik said in the interview he could perform in 45 minutes what it would take Fritz Perls 10 to 15 sessions to perform. It is these kinds of claims which we will look at more carefully in Chapter 16 when we look at the scientific validation of NLP as a methodology and a set of techniques.

For me it is clear that in order to professionally and ethically coach, one must have a psychological model from which to work and that model needs to be empirically validated as clearly as possible. However, NLP would still hold true to the belief that the more we can, in our professional activity, learn to suspend our own models of the world, the more we can truly appreciate the models of other people. Once we have this appreciation it is then much easier to facilitate the required changes because when those models

> NLP is a practical activity not a theoretical one.

are the focus of our attention our matching and pacing is exquisite. This means it is much easier to lead the coachee from his existing model, to a model which supports his stated outcome. The idea of 'stopping the world' in this fashion is elucidated in *Turtles all the way down* (DeLozier & Grinder, 1987: 76) and comes also from Carlos Castaneda (1970). The concept suggests that internal dialogue is a way of sustaining our own models of the world, which means we only process incoming information in such a way that it fits with that model.

In other words we learn nothing new. In NLP coaching, to engage in this practice is to distort what our client says and does, in such a way that it fits into what we think, rather than to truly understand what they think. The more the NLP coach can 'stop the world', the more they can truly be 'present' and attend to what it is the client is experiencing and communicating. Tim Hallbom makes the point that when Bandler and Grinder were asked what the theory behind NLP was, they replied they did not wish NLP to have a theory as they wanted it to be a practical activity and not a mental one (Dilts & Hallbom, 1990).

The other form of modelling which is used in NLP coaching is modelling where the coachee is encouraged to develop greater self-awareness using the existing patterns of NLP. This is called analytical modelling because in a top-down fashion it is imposing a structure and process upon the perceptual and cognitive activity of the coachee. The coach could therefore encourage the coachee to ask themselves Meta Model questions in order to obtain a fuller representation of what they are talking about, and consequently provide them with greater choice. Alternatively the coachee could engage in multi-level modelling and develop awareness at the different levels of environment, behaviour, strategy, belief, identity and mission. A final example for the present moment is where the coachee could be encouraged to develop an understanding of how they represent their problem and solution in a sensory fashion. This modelling would take the form of sensory units such as: I see my boss (V^e), I get a terrible feeling (K^{i-}) and I say to myself I can't do this (A^{i-}). The coach could experiment with the coachee in building a different representation: 'Notice what happens if when you see your boss you make him much smaller, you then delete any feelings and say to yourself this is going to be a piece of cake, and find you then experience positive feelings in this context? (V^e—V^{i+}—A^{i+}—K^{i+})'. Here we can see the coachee is asked to experiment with taking the original trigger, the sight of their boss ($V_{isual}^{external}$), creating a smaller internal visual representation which looks positive for them ($V_{isual}^{internal\ positive}$) then *saying* something positive to oneself ($A_{uditory}^{internal\ positive}$) and then obtaining a positive feeling ($K_{inaesthetic}^{internal\ positive}$). Modelling is a skill set which R.D. Laing had. He was a contemporary of Bandler and Grinder and was admired by them. Like them he was known for his unorthodoxy and charisma, no doubt a child of his time. Leon Redler (2001) says of him: 'He was very plastic and mimetic, so he could imitate and get into other people's moods, thoughts, language, and world, including those of so-called "mad" people. And he was able to bring back and speak of what it was like to be "mad" (more or less). This gave "mad" people an enormous sense of relief. Someone heard them. They were not alone. Madness was not unreason, a total unintelligibility, a total difference between the sane and the insane. Ronnie showed that we're all in it together'. Again it is not necessary to understand modelling in its totality here as we are going to explore and discuss it much more in Chapter 12. Suffice to say at present an NLP coach will use both types of modelling to consistently get excellent results.

The Trail of Techniques

The trail of techniques will refer to the models which the NLP coach will make use of in the coaching intervention. The first three NLP models were the Meta Model, representational systems and the Milton Model (Bostic St Clair & Grinder, 2001: 142–84). Strictly speaking representational systems was more of a design than a model as it was not developed from modelling one particular person. We will look at the difference between design and modelling in Chapter 12. We will also explore whether NLP has in fact ever created a model. The move away from modelling, as a methodology, and the use of design is a trend that has continued as there are some techniques in NLP which quite clearly have not come from modelling projects at all but have been either borrowed or developed from more theoretical streams. Examples would be the TOTE (Test, Operate, Test, Exit) model which is taken from Miller, Galanter and Pribram (1960). Another example would be that of Robert Dilts's logical levels model which was adapted from the work of Gregory Bateson (Dilts, 1990). Other non-NLP writers are regularly being associated with NLP and taught in some NLP programs, such as Clare Graves – Spiral Dynamics (Beck & Cowan, 1996); Ken Wilbur – integral theory AQAL (All Quadrants All Levels) (Wilber, 2000); and Peter Senge – systems thinking (Senge, 1990). These developments show how after 40 years NLP is a mixture of many strands and could be accused of being all things to all men. The encyclopedia of NLP (Dilts & DeLozier, 2000) is a fine volume that starts with Abductive Thinking and ends with Zero Sum Interactions, but also demonstrates that in practice NLP is anything but that which it consistently purports to be, a discipline that has modelling as its core activity. This tension between NLP as a discipline which develops models through modelling methodology, and NLP as a disparate group of people seeking to improve their lot by whatever means, will probably continue for the foreseeable future. I think Tosey and Mathison (2009: 14) very nicely sum up how this entirety can be formulated in their six faces of NLP. They see NLP as a Practice, a Philosophy and a Product. These three Ps give rise to six faces of NLP:

1 Practical magic: communication in action.
2 Methodology: modelling core of the practice.
3 Philosophy: epistemology and presuppositions.
4 Technology: framework techniques.
5 Commodities: consumables, self-help products.
6 Professional services: coaching, consulting and psychotherapy.

Tosey and Mathison make the point that the NLP coach who experiences NLP for the first time will probably encounter the products of NLP and adopt a somewhat technical approach as they learn to come to terms with and deliver the plethora of techniques and frameworks available. However, the substance of

NLP is in the everyday practice, methodology and philosophy which are below the surface of the water. These are less obvious but comprise the main substance of the field.

As the reader you will encounter many of the various NLP techniques and frameworks in Part 2. At this juncture if you can satisfy yourself with the understanding that the trail of techniques does not just come from NLP modelling projects, this will save confusion at a later time in your NLP journey. Many NLP techniques come from a very broad church which may not methodologically share NLP's stated passion for modelling. We will see how this makes evaluating NLP as a distinct coaching methodology very difficult in Chapter 16.

BRAIN TEASERS

1 So actually you can get away with being an NLP coach and not even bother with modelling because it has 'stolen' frameworks and techniques from many other disciplines without modelling. Discuss.
2 Surely by trying to formalize NLP in an 'academic' way one is going to create this 'smoke' which is the very antithesis of NLP. Is this desirable?

PART 2

Understanding NLP and Supporting Psychological Principles

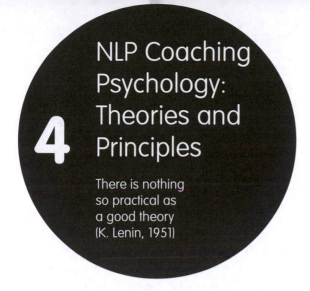

NLP Coaching Psychology: Theories and Principles

4

There is nothing
so practical as
a good theory
(K. Lenin, 1951)

Many regard NLP as atheoretical, however, as Linder-Pelz and Hall (2007) point out, 'solid theoretical foundations, along with empirical efficacy data are widely accepted criteria for an evidence-based coaching practice' (Cavanagh, Grant & Kemp, 2005; Stober & Grant, 2006). As Kurt Lenin suggests a good theory generates a multitude of good practical solutions in the real gritty world, and in psychology this is evidenced through well conducted validity and reliability studies. However Kurt Lenin also recognized in his T group encounters that theories often emerge from the dynamic interplay of individuals. Theory and practice thus are in constant flux as practice informs and textures theory and vice versa. In this chapter I will look at the four main theoretical strands that inform NLP: modelling, transformational grammar, systems theory and general semantics.

Modelling

NLP can be seen as the psychological equivalent of reverse engineering, using modelling as its methodology. In Chapter 1 you might have recognized a couple of key NLP principles as I explained the early history.

The first principle is you do not learn by understanding, you learn by imitation and much of that imitation is carried out unconsciously. When Bandler was audio-recording Virginia Satir, he was listening to Virginia Satir in one earphone, and in the other earphone was listening to Pink Floyd. In the training a time arrived when Virginia Satir was trying, in a left-brain way, to explain to the participants what was needed in order to do some work. When she was evidently not succeeding, Bandler just came down into the classroom and said you do this, then you do that, and finish with this, OK? And returned to his Pink Floyd. Satir was very impressed that Bandler had somehow encapsulated what she was trying to explain theoretically in just a

> You do not learn by understanding, you learn by imitation and much of that imitation is carried out unconsciously.

few behavioural steps (Dilts & Hallbom, 1990). In NLP coaching one of the first things we want to know is: Who does your coachee seek to emulate, who is their model, their inspiration? It maybe that your coachee is creative and they want to be the best *they* can be, not an imitation of someone else … OK, what would that person look like, what would they do, how would they do it? Without answers to these questions how can a coaching intervention possibly succeed? It cannot. Often when a coachee understands this process in a right-brain way it is job done. You see the 'Ah ha' come on in their eyes; they realize all the time they have been *analysing the problem* and what is required for progress is to *model the solution*.

The second principle is that imitation is always done within a context. When Grinder was observing Bandler and Pucelik, he was observing them in a context, and that context was with other people, in this case specifically in a therapy group. In order to test the extent to which Grinder was learning he needed to test the model in a similar context. This is why he held his groups the following Thursday. As Robert Spitzer said, Bandler became so similar to Fritz Perls that he often by mistake called him Fritz. Bandler could have come away from that one month in Canada, made transcripts of the audio tape and carried on being Richard Bandler. However, he did not, he tested out the patterns he was assimilating and when he recognized the feedback he was getting was not the same feedback that Virginia Satir was getting, *he knew* he had not learned.

> Human beings have an emotional commitment to the solutions which they discover, and it is this psychological commitment that makes them rigid in operation and blind to alternative patterns of operating.

The reason so many coaches struggle at this stage is that they do not have the tools nor an appropriate model to assist the coachee to recognize that there is no such thing as failure, there is only feedback. In the coaching space, where the coachee feels supported, the coach can often take the coachee through steps so they can get glimpses and experiences of their new model succeeding; however, they then get into the world outside of the coaching space and revert back to the patterns which do not provide them with the outcome they want; they are afraid that if they try something new they will fail, and they do. This is nicely alluded to by Gregory Bateson, when he pointed out that the difference between Von Neumann's robots and humans is in learning. To be infinitely intelligent implies to be infinitely flexible, and Von Neumann's robots could never experience the pain which human beings feel when continually proven wrong when previously they had been wise. Human beings have an emotional commitment to the solutions which they discover, and it is this psychological commitment that makes them rigid in operation and blind to alternative patterns of operating (Bateson, 1972: 241–2). Think of it, your coachee comes into coaching with a perfect model of the world. The difficulty is this model of the world does not provide them with what they desire. They intellectually get what you are telling them … in your coaching exercises they even get an experience of what it must be like to actually have a different model of the world, a model which makes it *easy* for them to get what they want. However, when they go into the world, rather than *apply* the cognitive, affective, linguistic and behavioural strategies you have rehearsed, they revert to the old model of the world and find that the coaching is not working. To use yet another NLP presupposition, they think their old map of the world is the territory and will not let go of it. Modelling is a skill the NLP coach will pass on to their coachee and we will find out more about it in Chapter 12.

EXERCISE 1 (30 MINUTES)

NLP is about doing, not talking about, so put the book down now and do this exercise, please. If you cannot do it now, commit to doing this exercise in the next 24 hours.

Set an alarm for 20 minutes. Make sure you will not be disturbed for 20 minutes and think of someone who has a skill that you would love to have, but do not. At this point set yourself a reminder that if any emergency arises you can attend to it *immediately* and have access to *your old model* of the world in order to deal with it, using all of your sensory equipment and strategic awareness. However, for now I want you to relax and think about that person, think about the context they operate in. They may be a male or they may be a female, however use all of your senses to immerse yourself in *their* world, let yourself relax and attend to *their* model of the world. Notice how they move, notice how they look, notice how they dress. See how they interact with other people. Become more aware of what they say, how they say it, when they talk, when they stop, what it is they pay attention to. How do they know when to act and when not to act? Look at the muscle tone, notice their breathing, micro-muscle everything they do and say. Throughout the whole of this 20-minute period, you will go into a light trance experience. Remember it is always *you* who controls the depth of your trance experience, so just go into a state which is comfortable for you and one which *you know* you can come safely out of. As you stay there, ensure that you do not second-guess your model, but you simply imitate them as you sit there watching them, listening to them, feeling what it is like to be like them. Continue doing this for 20 minutes. When your alarm goes off allow yourself to wake up and continue your day. After 24 hours, notice how you are different. If you have done this exercise effectively you will change in a significant way.

Albert Bandura in social learning theory developed the term 'model' to describe the person whose behaviour is being observed, and suggested there were five major functions involved in modelling (Gross, 1987: 70).

- The learner must attend to the pertinent clues in the stimulus situation and ignore incidentals which do not affect the performance of the behaviour which they seek to learn.
- They must record in memory a sensory-based or semantic code for the modelled behaviour for storage purposes.
- Rehearsal of this stored memory is important.
- The learner has to reproduce the motor activities accurately. This will involve as many trials as needed in order to get the 'muscular feel' of the behaviour through feedback.
- The learner must value the consequences related to that behaviour in order to learn through modelling.

Social learning theory developed from behaviourist psychology which had already developed the concepts of classical (anchoring in NLP) and operant conditioning, and the idea of mental maps later on with Edward Tolman. Grinder regards behaviourism as the closest paradigm to NLP because it denies the need for involving the consciousness of coachees undergoing the change process (Bostic St Clair & Grinder, 2001: 208). I have taken some time to emphasize modelling in the first part of this chapter as it is a key principle of NLP coaching according to our definition. In the remainder of this brief chapter I would like to touch on the other psychological theories and principles which are responsible for the NLP presuppositions and directly relate to how the NLP coach operates. The following chapters in Part 2 will look at practical exercises and talk of case histories which demonstrate the delivery of NLP coaching and suggest ways you can integrate NLP more easily into your existing practice or start up as an NLP coach yourself.

Transformational Grammar

John Grinder believes the single most pervasive influence in NLP is the paradigm of transformational grammar (TG) (Bostic St Clair & Grinder, 2001: 66). When the co-founder of a discipline makes such a statement it would seem prudent to sit up and take notice. After modelling Bandler who had assimilated models of both Perls and Satir, Grinder noticed a similarity between the patterns of the model and what TG was saying. One of the similarities was a distinction between competency and performance. This was a distinction which social learning theory made too. Social learning theory says that we learn all the time, because all the time we are alive we cannot help but observe what goes on. In this sense we are implicitly building maps of behaviour and are competent in that behaviour. However, we do not necessarily perform according to that behaviour unless there is a very good reason to do so. TG similarly made the point that we all have an underlying competency to correctly speak the language we have modelled (competency), however, if we get a bit boozy down the local pub, or get rather upset, the peculiar words that come out of our mouths do not mean we need a new grammar or model to explain them. Such language is much more effectively explained by saying the performance has been distorted by the state of the operator in such a way as to produce a unique performance. Edward Tolman found that rats who were just left to run around in a maze without any reinforcement would not find their way to the end, compared with rats who were reinforced with each success with a food box at the end of the maze. However after ten trials with no reinforcement, when reinforcement was introduced on the eleventh trial, the rats became as proficient as those who had reinforcement all along in getting to the end at an exponential rate. Tolman explained this by pointing out you do not need reinforcement to learn, as you are learning all the time – what the rats needed was a reason to demonstrate their underlying competency. We will see the relevance of TG to NLP coaching when we look at the Meta Model in Chapter 6. There we will discover how through the basic modelling processes of deletion, distortion and generalization we create secondary linguistic maps of the world. These linguistic maps are often very different to the deep sensory structure from which they are derived. We will see the relevance of social learning theory to NLP coaching when we look at the psychodynamic concept of secondary gain in Chapter 12 which is all about modelling.

As a challenge to you, the reader, I ask: What is it that you *know* you are already competent in, however you refuse to perform? So often for people, the words 'I could never do that' become a self-fulfilling prophesy, and the competency we possess becomes limited by a linguistic prison.

Systems Theory

If John Grinder was the glue which held NLP together in the early days, Gregory Bateson was the mentor and inspiration for both Bandler and Grinder. When attempting to understand NLP at a deeper level I asked Grinder what I could read to take my NLP journey further; he told me to read *Steps to an ecology of mind* (Bateson, 1972) so I did. Bateson had been sending students to Milton Erickson since 1953 when he arranged for Jay Hayley to attend a seminar in hypnosis given by him (Hayley, 1986: 9). Clearly Erickson was doing something that fascinated Bateson and maybe it was something to do with an appreciation of the systemic interrelations between the conscious mind and the unconscious mind. Bateson, as Aldous Huxley, felt that humans had lost the grace of the lower animals because of the deception that self-consciousness brings with it. The reason of the heart needs to be integrated with the reason of the mind, however with humans this is rarely the case. The evidence is DSM-IV-TR (2000), with a DSM-V in the pipeline. Not only was it possible that Erickson had an appreciation of intra-systemic relations, but also of inter-systemic relations. Hayley tells us that during this period a revolution occurred in the field of therapy and what once were called symptoms or individual problems, began to be redefined as products of personal relationships … it began to seem possible to place individual therapy within a broader framework of family therapy (Hayley, 1986: 11). In *Steps to an ecology of mind* Bateson describes his own theory of schizophrenia, called the double bind. This is based upon the theory of logical types and points out that in communication people can say one thing with their

> The heart has its reasons which the reason does not at all perceive.

body and a contradictory thing with their language. This puts the recipient of such a communication into a double bind, a context where they cannot win whatever they do. A politician telling you, 'Let's be honest about it, to do this

job you have to lie', would be a nice example of a double bind. If they are telling the truth they must be lying because they are a politician, but if they are
lying they must be telling the truth. New Code NLP returned very much to
an appreciation of Bateson's work and recognized that NLP was becoming too
clunky and technical; a hardening of the categories was setting in. New Code
NLP will be discussed throughout the rest of the book and, particularly in
Chapter 13, it addresses the nice state of affairs put so eloquently in French:
'Le Coeur a ses raisons que la raison ne connait point' (The heart has its reasons which the reason does not at all perceive).

General Semantics

General semantics is probably best known for providing the signature NLP
presupposition: 'The map is not the territory'. A fuller representation comes
from Korzybski:

> **A map is not the territory it represents but if correct it has a similar structure to the
> territory which accounts for its usefulness. (Korzybski, 1994: 58)**

If you can imagine a London underground map, it deletes a tremendous
amount of information. As a general rule the 'territory' is far richer than any
map. For Korzybski the territory was spinning with
electrons, highly interconnected and never the same in
any one moment. What the map does is extricate
those bits of importance and delete everything else.
What makes the underground map useful is not any
faithful reproduction of the underground content,
such as the colour of the trains, or the number of
benches on a station, but the fact that the relationship of the stations to each
other is the same on the map as it is under the ground of London. If I am in
Brixton and I want to get to Kings Cross this information is really useful. What
Korzybski argues is that natural language, which he says is based upon
Aristotelian systems, is not structured in a similar way to our nervous system,
nor the world we live in, and so we end up responding not to the world but to
our own faulty linguistic representations. We might say if my 'linguistic map of
the world is wrong', I will simply get another one which is right, one which
has a similar structure to the territory. Only if that were true the world would
be a better place, or in Korzybski's terms a saner place. What actually happens
is these distorted and emotionally laden linguistic representations are mistaken over and over again for the actual territory. It is a bit like going into a
restaurant and mistaking the menu for the actual food. Korzybski argues that
the structure of the nervous system and of the world of objects is such that

> It is a bit like going into
> a restaurant and
> mistaking the menu for
> the actual food.

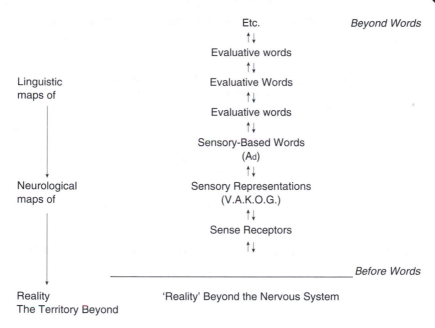

Figure 4.1   Korzybski's Levels of Abstraction from Hall (2011d)

only in mathematics do we find a language of similar structure (Korzybski, 1994: 47, 50). Above is Michael Hall's explanation of Korzybski who showed why the map is not the territory.

What we need to ensure is that the relationships of objects out there in the world are represented structurally in a similar way by us. The fundamental mistake humans make is to confuse their many levels of evaluative representing for the actual world and thus develop an 'is' reality based upon faulty logic and confusion of levels of representation. Korzybski developed the structural differential in order to visually instruct people as to how to disentangle themselves from this semantic mess. Sometimes NLP practitioners seem to confuse the threads which come from Korzybski's work with the psychological writings of constructivist and constructionist writings. John Rowan (2008: 160) does make a good case that from a *psychological* perspective NLP does not really have its roots in constructivist psychology. One of his main arguments is that within the NLP literature there is no mention of classic contributions to constructivist psychology such as Danziger (1997), Gergen (1997) or Greer (1997). Hall in his reply does clarify for the reader and cites Korzybski as the basis for calling NLP constructivist.

Kurt Lewin of T group fame, who we mentioned in Chapter 1, suggested there is nothing so practical as a good theory. Throughout the rest of this book you will discover how NLP practice flows naturally from these four theories.

BRAIN TEASERS

1 The psychological principles of NLP are modelling (behavioursim), transformational grammar, systems theory and general semantics (constructivism). Without falling into the trap of developing a Jackdaw epistemology, can you think of any other major psychological school that is not represented in this chapter that should be? Discuss.

2 Emotion is one of the ties that keeps us attached to models of the world which do not work. Korzybski's answer is to build a mathematical type of language which is more similar to the structure of the territory. To what extent would emotion be diminished if we did this? Discuss the advantages and disadvantages of emotional responses.

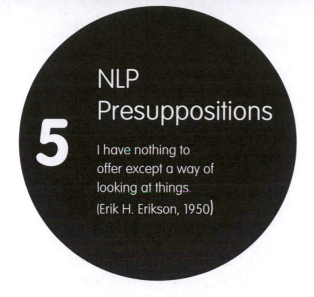

NLP Presuppositions

5

I have nothing to offer except a way of looking at things.
(Erik H. Erikson, 1950)

NLP, like any other 'way of looking at things', is a map. It has been estimated there are 200 to 400 different types of therapy (Edelstien, 1990: 1). From an NLP coach's perspective, all these 'therapies' are simply maps – they are not true, they are not false, they are simply ways of looking at things. Erik Erikson, who is probably best known for his life cycle theory, recognized this when he spoke about only offering a way of looking at things. Implicit in his statement is that there are many other ways of looking at things. For the NLP coach the key question is 'do such maps provide the observer with greater utility, do they help the coachee move more elegantly towards their outcome?' Of course, from an NLP coaching perspective the question is, are they useful and do they do what they say they do? Jay Hayley says of Milton Erickson that he was the first major clinician to concentrate on how to *change* people; previously clinicians were content simply to *understand* the mind, they were explorers then, and changing people was of secondary interest (Hayley, 1985: vii). I talk about maps of therapy or ways of looking at things because, as we discovered in Chapter 2, coaching is still in its infancy and maps of coaching have not really been developed, and where they have, it is an easy task to trace their genesis back to counselling or psychotherapy. It is an equally easy task to note how such maps have been modified for use on a 'non-clinical' population and how small-scale studies shout from the roof tops: 'Coaching works, a new profession is born'. A talented mix of marketers, academics and professionals from diverse backgrounds feed forward the good news through their networks and media outlets, and 'coaching' is the revitalized word on linguistic maps around the world in those who want to build effective teams or seek to be all they can at an individual and group level.

However, any system of knowledge has to have a point at which it accepts something at face value because it cannot prove what it accepts. Dilts gives the example of Euclidean geometry which presupposes the existence of a point (Dilts & DeLozier, 2000: 998). Without acceptance of this presupposition you cannot have Euclidean geometry. This is very different from the acceptance of an assumption. Take the following sentence:

'The manager agreed to coaching as he really liked Tom.'

One can assume a lot, but presuppose little. For instance, we can *assume* the manager thinks coaching is effective and it will help Tom. We could assume the manager thinks coaching is ineffective, but the culture of the organization is such that a coaching intervention will help Tom's career. We can assume Tom wants a break from work and coaching provides that on a regular basis. We could assume the manager is agreeing to coaching for himself as he likes Tom. The list goes on, but none of these is necessarily true. Conversely, however, we can *presuppose* coaching has been proposed to the manager, otherwise the sentence just cannot make sense. One can more clearly see why our assumptions are only assumptions and not presuppositions if we retain the structure of the sentence but only change one word:

'The manager agreed to coaching as he really hated Tom.'

We can see, hear or feel how even though the structural relationships remain the same and are expressed in the presupposition 'coaching has been proposed to the manager', the assumptions we did have are now probably changed. We might think it is the manager who is having the coaching and he wants to improve his performance to help him get one up on Tom. We could assume the manager thinks coaching is not just ineffective, but destructive and it will be the end for Tom if he has it. We learned from Korzybski (1994) in the previous chapter that when we use natural language to create maps of the world which are very different from the world as it is, we can quickly get into trouble, especially when we treat those linguistic maps of the world as though they were the world itself.

> These statements have to be true if the coaching we perform is to be called NLP coaching.

When we think of NLP as a coaching methodology, the presuppositions of NLP form the basic epistemology of our coaching intervention. These statements have to be true if the coaching we perform is to be called NLP coaching. If these presuppositions cannot be seen in our work, then we may be doing great coaching, but we are not doing NLP coaching. The NLP presuppositions are to NLP coaching what the point is to Euclidean geometry.

Many will say, 'Hang on, Bruce, the NLP presuppositions actually are assumptions'. Such people are absolutely right, but miss the point. To be an NLP coach you exist 'as if' the presuppositions are incontrovertibly true; you do not hang about for 'proof', whatever form that may take. The air you breathe, the words you speak, the sights you see, the sounds you hear and the steps you take are all filtered unconsciously through these NLP presuppositions, and the elegance you display as an NLP coach, and as a human being, has more to do with that process than any technical ability to perform say a six-step reframe, or deliver an appropriate metaphor. I remember going past a church in South London once and I saw a poster which read, 'If you were arrested for being a Christian would there be enough evidence to convict you?' You could replace Christian with NLP coach and the jury would be testing you against the NLP presuppositions.

John Grinder calls these presuppositions a pedagogical device to assist people new to NLP in making the required transitions in their thinking, and when talking about the NLP presuppositions he sometimes calls them 'organizing assumptions'. However, what does not change is the purpose, which is that there are several organizing assumptions which NLP coaches use to put themselves into an emotional and physiological state which is useful to operate in and from (Bandler & Grinder, 1979: 137).

Michael Hall makes a similar point and talks of the NLP presuppositions as devices to suggest the kind of attitude or a meta-state frame that transforms us so that our practice of NLP moves to a higher level of mastery (Hall & Bodenhamer, 2003: 40).

As mentioned, this is one of the distinguishing features of NLP coaching and is a key element in the definition of NLP coaching. It may be useful to note that the other co-founder of NLP is on exactly the same page here; he believes there is one thing that delineates when someone knows what NLP is and it is not a set of techniques but an attitude (Bandler, 1985: 155). When Grinder developed New Code NLP which went back to the more systemic roots of NLP, his chain of excellence model was designed to produce a content-free high performance state (Bostic St Clair & Grinder, 2001: 233). The model points out that any *performance* is a function of *state* and the best way to obtain the correct state is to manipulate your *physiology* and the best way to do this is through modulation of your *breathing*. Nowhere in this model is there mention of the use of technique in order to maximize performance. When you are in the appropriate state you have access to your vast reservoir of unconscious resources and one of the NLP presuppositions suggests this is all you need to perform effectively (Bandler & Grinder, 1979: 137).

> NLP is about being in a resourceful state.

COACHING SESSION 1

I had performed the initial free-of-charge introductory session and the 'chemistry check' seemed to work out. The coachee (Jerry) liked the way I coached and we developed and agreed a psychological contract. Jerry came in to the first session red in the face and using expletives to tell me how useless everyone in his organization was. At this time two of the NLP presuppositions came to my mind: (a) every behaviour has a positive intention and (b) the individual is doing the best he can with the resources he has. This enabled me to check my state, which initially was quite anxious at this outburst. After Jerry had come to a natural finish, I calmly stated: 'That is really interesting. What are you intending to achieve with that language and that particular state?' Jerry explained he was just venting his frustration that people were not doing as he asked and it was really annoying him, to which I asked

(Continued)

(Continued)

at the appropriate time, 'Is there another way of communicating so you could convey your intention in another manner?' I took Jerry to a third perceptual position so he was like a fly on the wall. From there he was looking at himself in his organization interacting with other people, noting his language and behaviour and the responses he was generating. We began to explore communication styles and one of the other NLP presuppositions: 'the meaning of your communication is the response you get'. Jerry really enjoyed this exercise and calmed down significantly. When he left this session 90 minutes later he was relaxed and motivated to try out new ways of communicating.

In this session even though use of perceptual positions helped tremendously, as did some Milton Model language patterns, what allowed both of those 'techniques' to work so well was my recognizing two of the NLP presuppositions and consequently achieving an optimal coaching state where I could access both the resources of my own unconscious mind and also the unconscious mind of the coachee. In this instance I remember it being a very relaxed yet assertive state, and as I remained relaxed at both a conscious and unconscious level the coachee gradually learned to model me and obtain that state as well, which meant he could engage productively in the coaching session. It also meant I could observe and listen to the key markers in the coachee's language and behaviour to notice where the drivers were in this ineffective model of his. For example, when he spoke about the others in his organization *they* were marked out. He was deleting his portion in the interaction which was partially responsible for the responses he was getting. In this instance too an NLP presupposition was effectively used within the coaching space to assist the coachee in recognizing he was not currently communicating effectively.

NLP is about being in a resourceful state. If something happens in the world, like Jerry coming in all hot and bothered, it is *essential* that the NLP coach has the requisite variety to make the necessary alterations to ensure he remains in that optimal state. In the coaching example above, access to two NLP presuppositions allowed me to do this.

Requisite variety is a term from systems theory and Tosey and Mathison suggest that many of the NLP presuppositions actually come from systems and cybernetics thinking that preceded NLP and only one is an original NLP creation … and yet even this could be traced to Bandura, as discussed in Chapter 4. Like much of NLP there is no standardization here and lists vary from author to author. However, the below list is taken from Tosey and Mathison (2009: 98) and is a translation from the German (Walker, 1996: 111):

1 Every behaviour is potentially communication (Bateson, Perls, Satir, Erickson).

2 Mind and body are part of the same cybernetic system (Bateson, Perls, Satir, Erickson).

3 People have all the resources they need to make changes (Perls, Satir, Erickson).

4 People orientate themselves by their internal maps, their model of the world and not to the world itself (Korzybski).

5 The map is not the territory (Korzybski).

6 People make the best choices that present themselves to them (Satir).

7 Choice is better than no choice (Satir).

8 Every behaviour is generated by a positive intention (Satir).

9 The meaning of a communication is the response it elicits, not the intention of the communicator (Erickson).

10 Resistance is a message about the communicator (or therapist) (Erickson).

11 If what you are doing isn't working, do something different (Erickson).

12 There is no failure, only feedback (Erickson).

13 The most flexible variable controls the system (Ashby's law of requisite variety).

14 Everything that a human being can do can be modelled (Bandler and Grinder).

From an NLP coaching perspective it is easy – these 14 statements are true and you act in your work as a coach 'as if' they are true.

So if the coachee whines, 'I can't help myself', presupposition number 6 suggests an answer: 'Of course I fully appreciate that, and you are doing a great job at present', possibly followed by presupposition number 8: 'And of course this behaviour has been very useful for you at some level'. This could then be followed by a Meta Model challenge, of which we will learn more in Chapter 6: 'But what would it be like if you could help yourself?' … Milton Model language … leading into presupposition number 7: 'This would then provide you with choice, you can still behave like you used to, but now you also have many other ways of behaving too which means you take control'.

What I would like to emphasize though is that what is going to make the above verbal communication effective is not just the words, but the way in which they are delivered, the pace, the timing, the pitch, the volume. Unless it is delivered by someone who has the above 14 presuppositions running automatically in their mind and body, the communication will be proportionately ineffective. For instance, an NLP coach could well, after the sentence, 'But what would it be like if you could help yourself?', notice light trance develop as the coachee begins to imagine such a scenario. The NLP coach could anchor that trance state just as they begin their Milton Model part of the communication; this anchor could then be used at other portions of the communication to take the person back into trance if needed. I believe that in training NLP coaches, development of this attitude, which flows from acceptance of the above 14 presuppositions as true, is absolutely key and is also the most problematical in terms of 'installation' and in terms of measurement. We can talk more about this in Chapter 16 when we look at research into NLP.

The fact that NLP has much of its epistemology rooted in systemic and cybernetic thinking is both a strength and a weakness. A weakness is that NLP coaching cannot be measured in the traditional way. Robert Dilts explains that cybernetic models are different from statistical or linear models in that they deal with feedback of total systems; a particular cause and effect cannot be isolated from its context. Therefore each part must be considered and measured in terms of the whole (Dilts, 1983: 20). For Milton Erickson every client was different. If he was presented with 10 people with 10 phobias, he would not 'treat' them with the NLP phobia cure, he would recognize that each of these 10 phobias is very different because the 10 individuals coming to him are very different. They are coming to him from contexts which are very different, and consequently with models of the world which are very different. To take a set of procedures, which the NLP phobia cure is, and apply them irrespective of the individual in front of him would be to disrespect the creativity and resourcefulness of that person who already has all the resources they need within themselves to make the change they want (presupposition 3). The astute reader will recognize, however, in coaching this orientation is also a considerable strength as it puts the emphasis not on technical delivery of a protocol, but on an ability to develop a deep understanding of and to work with the coachee's model of the world, which is the source of both their excellence and their limitation. It is this model the NLP coach works with, not the model which comes from their cognitive understanding developed at university. As we will discover in Chapter 7 one of the first steps in applying the Milton Model to coaching is keeping your sensory apparatus *externally* focused on your coachee and not *internally* focused on what you think you should be doing according to your coaching model.

> Your sensory apparatus should be *externally* focused on your coachee and not *internally* focused on what you think you should be doing according to your coaching model.

You will also recognize a paradox within NLP here, and there are many. Surely to accept these 14 or so presuppositions as true and to work from them is to limit the scope of our work. If at the heart of modelling, which is the methodology of NLP coaching, we find it necessary to access a 'know nothing' state, then surely in this state we know nothing of these 'presuppositions'. This indeed is so, and like all good paradoxes points to a solution at a different level of understanding. One might at this point be reminded that one of the characteristics of an NLP coach is to have a positive response to ambiguity and vagueness. Others are enumerated by Bostic St Clair and Grinder (2001: 123):

1 A hypnotic fascination with competency/excellence.

2 A clean behavioural distinction between form and substance, process and content.

3 A positive affinity for what others call risk taking.

4 A recognition of the value of formalization and explicit representations.

5 A positive response to ambiguity and vagueness.

6 A sharpened alertness for unusual events.

The paradox alluded to above is satisfied by point 4. As humans natural language is what sets us apart from the other animals. We can through language represent to ourselves and others that which is not present. The key is ensuring that through that medium the representation accurately maps the unspeakable in such a way that Korzybski would regard it as useful. The co-founders of NLP would probably agree that these presuppositions are badly in need of revision and reorganization; the interesting and contentious presupposition here is that NLP was ever organized in the first place. However, as is often said 'we are where we are', and the NLP presuppositions as they stand are key to making the necessary cognitive and perceptual transition so as to perform as an NLP coach.

Often NLP is associated with the humanistic and third wave of psychology which developed into the Human Potential movement. This movement was eminently represented in the Santa Cruz area in the 1960s and 1970s (Hall, 2011a).

Carl Rogers, a founder of that movement, believed that no approach which relied upon knowledge, upon training or upon the acceptance of something that was taught, was of any use; he believed such methods were futile and inconsequential. The most they could accomplish, according to Rogers, was some temporary change, which soon disappeared, leaving the individual more than ever convinced of their inadequacy (Rogers, 1961: 32). What is of course needed is rapport and we will explore that in Chapter 7 when we look at the work of Milton Erickson.

BRAIN TEASERS

1 If at the heart of NLP coaching you have presuppositions which flow from a systemic and cybernetic perspective, how can you ever effectively have an *individual* coaching solution and at the same time remain true to NLP's systemic presuppositions?
2 From the 14 NLP presuppositions listed in this chapter which one is your favourite? Why? Also, which one is your least favourite? Again, can you discover why?

The Meta Model

6

Language both connects us
to the world and isolates
us from it

For the NLP coach the Meta Model is a key linguistic tool in the coaching tool box; it is also the first model to emerge from NLP.

Theory

Transformational grammar is the theory supporting the Meta Model. Bandler and Grinder tell us their first NLP model is designed to make the insights of transformational grammar available and *usable* to those people who work with complex human behaviour (Bandler & Grinder, 1975b: 2). Grinder had written a book with Suzette Elgin entitled *Guide to transformational grammar* which was published in 1973, two years before *The structure of magic* (1975b) which leaves us in a bit of a quandary. If the Meta Model is simply the product of a modelling project why is TG so often referred to? What the reader would do well to understand is that the Meta Model does not rest upon the 'truth' of TG and generative grammar. The patterns which emerge from NLP are the outcome of modelling projects and not theoretical and experimental musings. Even though the Meta Model may have been very influenced by Grinder and Elgin's understanding of transformational grammar, from an NLP perspective the Meta Model was the result of a modelling project. Jackendoff (2002: 107), for instance, suggests linguistics has moved on and the syntactocentric architecture of TG is a mistake and talks of both semantics and phonology as being generative as well as syntax. If TG is now redundant as an explanatory frame, that does not mean the Meta Model no longer has utility as a linguistic tool in the NLP coach's tool box.

In the early part of *The structure of magic* (1975b: 6), which is the book form of the Meta Model, Bandler and Grinder talk about Vaihinger's concept of 'the logical

We cannot interface with the 'real' world without dramatically changing it into a personal map of that world.

function'. Vaihinger[1] makes the same point as Korzybski and that is: 'Where the logical function actively intervenes, it alters what is given and causes it to depart from reality' (Vaihinger, 1924: 159). Where Vaihinger seems to differ from Korzybski is in the belief that objective reality does not consist of any logical function and the real clue to the development of religion, ethics, science and mathematics is rather to be found in the development of fictions, rather than a mathematically based language (Morris, 1932: 280). What all these authors are saying is we cannot interface with the 'real' world without dramatically changing it into a personal map of that world, and each of our maps is different from the world and different from the maps of other people. The basis of all our behaviour therefore is to be found in these *maps* of reality, not in reality itself. Both linguistic and non-linguistic maps are built through three fundamental modelling processes: deletion, distortion and generalization.

Deletion is the process whereby we pay attention to some aspects of our experience but exclude others. For instance, a teenager may be playing on the Xbox when 'dinner is ready' is shouted out. This is not ignored, it is actually not even heard, it is deleted. This hypothetical teenager's map of the world is so constructed that anything not Xbox related does not even enter conscious awareness.

Distortion is the process whereby we creatively change our sensory experience to either develop or hinder our development. Our teenager, if they heard the suggestion 'dinner is ready', could have creatively and unconsciously actually heard 'dinner is nearly ready'. An artist when seeing a landscape can creatively distort the shapes put onto canvas to create something new. An athlete can distort the experience of pain so it is bearable and can run that extra mile, or lift that extra weight. A golfer can see the hole on the green as much closer than it really is. A mathematician can see connections between numbers in a way many others cannot and consequently can make predictions others cannot. A factory worker can distort time so it appears their shift is not as long as it really is. Our ability to distort means our ability to make life better or worse for ourselves. When humans a long time ago noticed a spark come off a piece of flint and imagined a fire, to when Einstein imagined riding a beam of light, our ability to distort sensory experience is our ability to discover science, art and culture and consequently grow, or become trapped in dogma, rigidity and pathology and consequently reduce. For Einstein, the only factor that separates empty fantasy from scientific 'truth' is the degree of certainty to which our sense experience is combined with our conceptual maps of the world to create validated experience. Concepts without connection to sense experience are meaningless – it is only when our concepts find certainty through application in the real world of sense data do we find meaning and 'truth' (Schilpp, 1979).

Generalization is the process where elements of a person's model become detached from the original experience and come to represent the whole category

---

[1]Bandler and Grinder (1975b: 225) say Fritz Perls claimed Vaihinger provided the philosophical foundations for Gestalt therapy.

of which the original experience is an example. So a student gets their sums wrong in a maths exam, and they develop a model where there is no point in taking exams as they are bound to fail. Conversely, they are successful in asking a member of the opposite sex out and so it is clear every member of the opposite sex will want to go out with them in the future.

In *The structure of magic* (1975b: 8) Bandler and Grinder describe three levels of departure from 'reality'. Firstly, there are *neurological filters*. If someone blows a dog whistle, a human will not hear it as it is outside of their sensory range, however a dog will. This therefore is the first set of filters which demonstrates that our maps of the world do not replicate the real world. Secondly, there are *social filters*. The most obvious may be that of language. See Box 6.1 for experimental support that language acts as a map which distorts our sensory experience to accord with our verbal labels. It also shows how when we change our language, we then begin to experience the world differently. We will discuss *individual filters* later, which is the third departure from reality.

BOX 6.1   TESTING FOR THE SAPIR WHORF HYPOTHESIS

Brown and Lenneberg (1954, cited in Gross, 1987: 181) demonstrated that we can more easily recognize colours for which we have words. This was tested by asking participants of three languages (which linguistically divide up the visible spectrum very differently) to identify colours. Colours for which there was no verbal representation could not easily be seen. When there is 'colour blindness' due to no verbal representation it was shown that by creating a word for that part of the colour spectrum, that part of the visible spectrum became easier to identify. Research has supported the idea that language does not prevent sensory experience, but simply codes it for storage, identification and recollection at some later time. For example, Carmichael, Hogan and Walter (1932) provided two separate groups of participants with identical visual stimulus figures but different verbal labels for each figure. After a period of time participants were asked to reproduce the stimulus figures. It was shown that they distorted the visual stimulus in accordance with the verbal label they had received.

Not only does language act as a filter, but it also prevents any further exploration of sensation. As soon as we 'name' something we begin to enter into the false belief that we are acquainted with that which we have named, and we stop exploring the sensory properties of that which is named. Through this process we limit the choices we have in any given circumstance. The Meta Model is a set of questions that seeks to test the accuracy of our naming function. NLP sees the mind at large as potentially limitless, however, in order to survive, it needs to act as a reducing valve and help us attend to only those things which experience has shown are important to us. As every human has

> Not only does language act as a filter, but it also prevents any further exploration of sensation.

had different experiences, these reducing valves which are our maps of the world are as unique as fingerprints. However, when we treat them as *reality* we reduce the choices available to us. We refuse to give them up because we are emotionally attached to them and consequently blind to alternatives. As Korzybski noted, we identify too strongly with our maps and become entwined in an 'is' reality. We mistakenly believe that to give up our map of the world is to give ourselves up. Besides sharing a common language, different cultures also share common beliefs and customs. There are as many of these social filters as the mind can create. Berger and Luckmann (1966: 49) call these objectifications and regard them as enduring indices of the subjective process of their producers. They give as an example a black cross being painted on someone's door. This symbol could represent someone intending to kill. Culturally, however, the shared belief of what a black cross represents means that there is no need for anyone to be killed. The cross by itself has come to represent that the owners of the door are officially in a state of enmity. Not only do different cultures have their own objectifications, but also subcultures within cultures develop their objectifications too. The more a person becomes enmeshed within these objectifications and mistakes them for 'reality', the more they become limited in the choices they can make. Box 6.2 provides a popular metaphor for the process of objectification.

BOX 6.2   OBJECTIFICATION (MICHAEL MICHALKO, 2011)

Start with a cage containing five chimpanzees. In the cage, hang a banana on a string and put stairs under it. Before long, an ape will go to the stairs and start to climb towards the banana. As soon as he touches the stairs, spray all of the chimpanzees with freezing cold water.

After a while, another chimpanzee makes an attempt with the same result – all the chimpanzees are sprayed with freezing cold water. This continues through several days. Pretty soon, when another chimpanzee tries to climb the stairs, the other chimpanzees all move to prevent it.

Now, turn off the cold water. Remove one chimpanzee from the cage and replace it with a new one. The new chimpanzee sees the banana and wants to climb the stairs. To his horror all the other chimpanzees attack him. After a few days, and further attacks, he knows that if he tries to climb the stairs, he will be assaulted.

Next, remove another of the original five chimpanzees and replace it with a new one. The newcomer goes to the stairs and is attacked. The previous newcomer takes part in the punishment with enthusiasm. Again, replace a third original chimpanzee with a new one. The new one makes for the stairs and is attacked as well. Two of the four chimpanzees that beat him have no idea why they were not permitted to climb the stairs nor why they are participating in the beating of the newest ape.

After replacing the fourth and fifth original chimpanzees, all the chimpanzees which have been sprayed with cold water, have been replaced. Nevertheless, no chimpanzee ever again approaches the stairs: Why not? Because that's the way they've always done it.

For these chimpanzees the stairs, which essentially are a neutral stimulus, like the black cross, have come to be associated with the unconditional stimulus of being sprayed with freezing water and consequently being attacked by peers. Each new chimpanzee that enters goes through the ritual of being socialized into the shared map of what trying to ascend the stairs means. The stairs have become objectified so for this subculture they have an idiosyncratic meaning which would not be the case for stairs in any other subculture. So just like words, objects too within our culture can represent something they are not. However, these 'representations' become our personal reality and a part of our individual map and we feel, behave, think and speak as though they are the things they represent … just like eating the words on the menu rather than the food or salivating when a bell goes off.

> So just like words, objects too within our culture can represent something they are not.

As mentioned above, the third departure from reality for humans is the *individual level*. Each and every one of us within the cultures and subcultures we have grown up in has experienced relationships with the outside world in a unique way. We have developed maps which may share common themes with others of our culture and subculture, however these maps will have many idiosyncratic and personal differences too.

Besides coding sensory experience for later identification and recollection, language also operates as the medium through which we justify our maps, and consequently prevents change in our lives. So when a coachee comes into the coaching session and says, 'It is hopeless; I really can't see a way forward', they will distort and delete aspects of their experience to fit their linguistic generalization. If someone gives this coachee an opportunity to move forward, the coachee will distort that interaction and delete aspects of it, until for them phenomenologically it is experienced as a barrier rather than an opportunity.

Transformational Grammar

Noam Chomsky, a linguist, argued that even though we are not aware of it, underlying the competency to speak our natural language is a very definite structure. He developed his theory of transformational grammar that suggests we generate specific sentences, which are known as the surface structure. We generate these sentences from our sensory experience, which is known as the deep structure, using a set of generative rules. Deep structure is the fullest linguistic representation of the coachee's experience. Judith Green tells us that for Chomsky the purpose of generative rules was simply to distinguish between grammatical and ungrammatical utterances. What was special about Chomsky was that before him linguists had only focused on the processing of single words because they had no method for the representation of larger units like sentences and whole texts (Green, 1986: 67).

Chomsky was interested about the role of syntax in sentence understanding and argued that our intuitive ability to distinguish grammatical from ungrammatical sentences is evidence we must 'know' the rules of grammar. Chomsky proposed that his generative rules consisted of re-write rules because they re-write any particular sentence into its constituent parts. For instance, the sentence 'they are measuring cups' is ambiguous. Is someone telling us a set of cups are 'measuring cups' for the purpose of quantifying a certain measure of liquid, or is someone measuring the dimension of cups with a measure of some kind?

In Figure 6.1 below the re-write rules make it clear both measuring and cups belong to the noun phrase (NP^2) section of the verb phrase (VP). However, in Figure 6.2 measuring is clearly the verb (V) within the verb phrase (VP). The Meta Model effectively is a set of verbal patterns designed to challenge sentences which are limited in the sense that they have either deleted or distorted the deep structure from which they have been derived in order to accord with some generalization from the past. For instance, even though both sentences above are grammatical sentences the first noun phrase is not specified. So a Meta Model challenge would be: 'Who are measuring devices?' Another Meta Model challenge to the verb phrase of Figure 6.2 would be: 'How are they measuring cups?' These Meta Model challenges would clear up the semantic

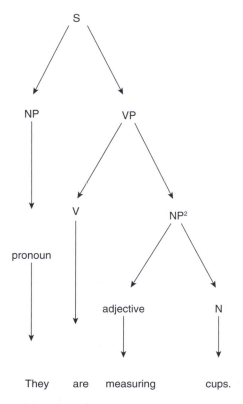

Figure 6.1 Two syntactic tree structures

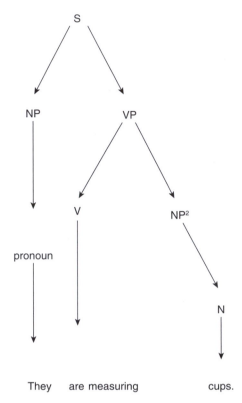

Figure 6.2   Two syntactic tree structures

ambiguity and provide a richer model of the world in that afterwards unspec-
ified noun and verb phrases become specified.

Bostic St Clair and Grinder describe the purpose of the Meta Model as 'a
challenge which is designed to create a context in which the client will expand
his or her map of possibilities or discover they have no idea what they are talking about'. Both of these are useful experiences in coaching to motivate the
client to change their mental maps 'which contain the limitations that are the
source of their dissatisfaction' (Bostic St Clair & Grinder, 2001: 148).

Application

In Table 6.1 you can see how the Meta Model identifies then challenges the
deletion, distortion or generalization used to create the individual map of the
coachee. I created this explanation for training Senior Specialist Advisors and
Personal Advisors conducting welfare-to-work coaching. In this figure the
reader can see how the Milton Model (Chapter 7) is essentially the opposite
of the Meta Model in that the Milton Model provides violations of the Meta
Model. This allows the recipient to distort the interpretation according to their
personal map, and is a very good model for developing rapport. You will learn
why this is useful in coaching in the next chapter. Dilts points out humorously

(1990) that when Bandler and Grinder came back from modelling Milton Erickson in Phoenix, they told the Santa Cruz group that everything they had been doing (the Meta Model) was wrong, it was all the total opposite. What Dilts goes on to say is that when teaching Meta Model patterns to others in the early days, the enthusiastic Meta Modellers would go out and alienate every person they came across by effectively challenging everything others said. Students loved it as they had a pattern whereby they could challenge their professors: 'Tell me professor, *how*, precisely, do you know that? *What* is your evidence? *Where* can this be found?' When using the Meta Model it is essential you develop rapport with your coachee first, otherwise your questions will have the effect of an inquisition. Rather than recover important information your coachee will become defensive and inflexible.

Table 6.1 How the Meta Model clarifies and the Milton Model confuses

Language Pattern	Description	Meta Model *Clarifying questions*	Milton Model *Pacing and leading language*
Deletions			
Unspecified Noun	What or whom is not specified	'Who specifically?' 'What specifically?'	'Enjoy!'
Unspecified Verb	How is not specified	'How specifically?'	'... and you can learn'
Nominalisation	Process words turned into nouns	'How am I understanding?'	'You have new understandings ...'
Lack of Referential Index	Does not specify who it refers to	'Who gets jobs?'	'People get jobs, you know!'
Simple Deletion	Information is deleted	'Do what?'	'Simply do it!'
Comparative Deletion	To whom or what is it being compared?	'John's a lot better than what or whom?'	'John's a lot better!'
Distortions			
Complex Equivalence	Implying two things are equal	'How does x mean y?' or 'So x is the same as y?'	'Being late means you don't care ...'
Lost Performative	Value judgement – by whom?	'Who says so?'	'And it's good to get people into work ...'
Mind Reading	Claiming to know someone's thoughts	'What leads you to believe that?'	'I know you are considering leaving ...'
Cause and Effect	Implying one thing causes another	'How does me being curious cause me to listen to you?'	'If you are curious then you will listen to me ...'
Presuppositions	Basics that must be true in order for the sentence to make sense	'How do you know I can learn this?' or 'What leads you to believe I will enjoy learning this?'	'You will enjoy learning this'
Generalisations			
Universal Quantifiers	All, every, etc.	'Always?' 'Counter example'	'It's always good to drink ...'
Modal Operator of Necessity	Identifies basis of personal rule	'What would happen if I didn't?' 'How do you know?'	'You should find it very easy to get a job ...'
Modal Operator of Possibility	Identifies basis of limitation or possibility	'What would happen if you could?' 'How do you know?'	'You can't get him to start a job'

Is Your Current Linguistic Map Relevant to Your Outcome? ____

The benefit of using the Meta Model is that it helps the coachee recognize whether or not their current model of the world in a particular context is still relevant. Take the simple statement, 'I am useless'. Effectively the coachee is verbally doing a 'mind read' on themselves in order to maintain and keep solidly in place a map of the world which possibly was created in early childhood. By maintaining this map of the world the coachee effectively deletes and distorts all interactions in the present so as to create a self-fulfilling prophesy. As a result of such distortion this state of uselessness is consistently 'proven' every day of the coachee's life. This is an unconscious process and the coachee will not even be aware of it. When rapport has been established and when appropriate, the simple Meta Model challenge 'And what leads you to believe that?' is the first step in recovering the fullest linguistic representation of this map of the world and the recognition that it is no longer appropriate for modern day use. It is at this stage that often the coach can begin to understand whether this is a coaching or counselling intervention, as per Bresser and Wilson in Chapter 2. If you remember, they talk about the primary focus of coaching to be to move the client forward and build desire, whereas the primary focus in counselling is about dealing with distress, and in psychotherapy it is about dealing with damage and needing a period of time before moving on. A coachee at this stage might recognize that actually there is nothing substantial that supports having such a model of the world. They will then set to work immediately revising their outdated model with a new one and proceed, now filtering for evidences that demonstrates how effective and useful they are. However, if at this stage there is distress and an orientation to the past and an unhealthy identification with such a limiting map of the world, this could be an indication that a counselling or therapeutic intervention is called for. The NLP coach will need at this stage to be aware of their level of expertise and act accordingly.

COACHING SESSION 2

A manager wished to have a session of coaching to help her overcome nerves in talking to other people about her work. She had no difficulty in talking if she sat down, however as soon as she stood up she began to shake uncontrollably. She said she could not explain it, and it was just bizarre. At this time it was about 60 minutes into the session and we had done the 'chemistry check', the development of a psychological contract and built rapport. As an NLP coach I had been listening, observing and modelling how the coachee managed so excellently to put herself in this predicament. I noticed as she was talking to me she had gone into a light trance. I said to her, I want you to just remain in that state looking over there. I touched her on the shoulder and asked her, 'What do you see?' She said, 'I am with my mother. Every time I get up she tells me to sit down. I am remonstrating with her but she is

(Continued)

(Continued)

adamant'. I Meta Modelled the whole scene, 'How do you know you are remonstrating? What are you sitting on? How do you know your mother is adamant?' I finally asked how old she was. She said around 13. Using the Meta Model had allowed the coachee to develop a full linguistic representation of her limitation. When this had been done I asked her whether this was an appropriate model to carry around if she wished to stand up and speak in public. She became tearful and said no. I then asked her if she would like to change this representation. She said she would. I asked her what she needed and what her mother needed in order to change. She said her mother needed to accept she was growing up and had her own voice, and she needed to believe in herself. I asked if all parties were prepared to accept these alterations and they were. As the coachee remained in a light trance she 'saw herself' stand up and get bigger, while her mother accepted this and became smaller. Ecology checks were performed, as was future pacing. Finally the coachee was ready to finish the exercise. I asked the client to contact me the following Monday after she had given her talk. She did and said it was a resounding success. She pointed out there were still a few nerves, but there was no shaking and she felt great. She did not need any follow-up sessions despite having three very important speaking engagements over the next two weeks.

In this session, as in many NLP coaching sessions, there are many parts of the NLP toolkit in use simultaneously – anchoring, sub-modality change, utilization of natural trance, ecology check, future pacing, etc. – and as you continue to read this book you will pick up on these. Suffice to say in this exercise the use of Meta Model questions was useful to maintain a light trance state and allow the coachee to notice specifically how her limiting representation was constructed. When this had been done fully the coachee could clearly see that she was making vast generalizations in the present from an incident that had happened many years ago and this was totally inappropriate. Without the use of the Meta Model, her limiting beliefs (generalizations) would have remained in place and the coachee would have continued to distort and delete information from both outside and inside of herself to confirm that she did not have the capability to stand up and talk about a subject she was passionate about to other people.

BRAIN TEASER

1 'Books are a good way to communicate, however if you don't actually put into practice what is communicated you stay the same and learn nothing. Better to go to a party!' … Using Table 6.1 go through this sentence and spot each Meta Model violation. What questions would you ask to get a fuller representation of this sentence? I will start you off: 'Which books?'

The Milton Model

7

Anyone purporting to be a coach who fails to develop precise tools for the explicit participation of unconscious processes is not a coach but a clown.
(John Grinder, 2012)

The quote from John Grinder helps us recognize the incredible importance the role of the unconscious mind has within the coaching process. When your coachee walks through the door and as a coach you have ticked all of the professional protocols, it is time to go to work. If the problem your coachee has was resolvable by the conscious mind, they would just sit down, plan what needs to be done and then conscientiously work their plan. They have probably done that many times and are stuck and that is why they need a coach. If as a coach you do not have a set of tools in your coaching tool box to deal with this 'unconscious', you will find yourself being led a merry dance and will go around and around in circles.

Theory

The Milton Model is provided by the originators in book form: *Patterns of the hypnotic techniques of Milton H. Erickson, M.D.* Volume 1 (Bandler & Grinder, 1975a) and Volume 2 (Grinder, DeLozier & Bandler, 1977). As in the first model of NLP, the Milton Model starts by pointing out that one 'theory' behind NLP is that of transformational grammar (TG) and Noam Chomsky is referred to. Chomsky points out that the search for rigorous formulation in linguistics has a much more serious motivation than mere concerns for logical niceties or the desire to purify well-established methods of linguistic analysis. Precisely constructed models for linguistic structure can play an important role, both negative and positive, in the process of discovery itself. By pushing a precise but inadequate formulation to an unacceptable conclusion, we can often expose the exact source of this inadequacy and, consequently, gain a deeper understanding of the linguistic data (Bandler & Grinder, 1975a: 1–2).

Chomsky's perspective is a key to understanding why NLP is regarded as atheoretical. It is not that NLP does not acknowledge the minds which have developed 'logical niceties' previously, but rather is centred on a belief that the best way to learn and change is to build models of unconscious models. This is why the Meta Model is called the Meta Model – it is a model which is meta (Greek meaning above) to another model, and that model is one we all know unconsciously, that of language. The transformational mappings between deep structure and surface structure are an unconscious process. These derivations are believed to have a structure and that has been explicated in the work of TG.

As in TG then, building a 'precisely constructed model' is the theory behind the Milton Model. It is the building of a model through observation, testing of that model through replication in the same context and finally coding of that model for the purpose of conscious understanding and training. The exemplar for this model was Milton H. Erickson who was a psychiatrist who used hypnosis and practiced in Phoenix, Arizona.

What is Hypnosis?

A brief section will not answer a question that has been raging ever since Mesmer took on Johann Gassner and the Catholic Church to demonstrate that the symptoms of someone possessed could be explained through hypnosis. This purported to demonstrate on behalf of the Enlightenment in 1775 that demon possession was a psychological phenomenon and not a spiritual one. What this section can do though is provide some pointers concerning modern hypnosis research and how the Milton Model fits into the ongoing discussion.

One distinguishing characteristic we can immediately clarify is that the Milton Model uses utilization within the hypnotic relationship rather than an authoritarian or standardized approach. The Milton Model stresses the interactional nature of the hypnotic relationship. The authoritarian approach emphasizes the control and power of the hypnotist over the client and the standardized approach suggests hypnotizability is a function of the coachee's trait, and is measured by psychometrics. The hypnotist is not important, neither is the client – the person either is or is not hypnotizable. Often inductions are standardized to fit in with this concept.

For Stephen Gilligan, who also modelled Erickson, trance is a special learning state that occurs whenever identity is threatened, disrupted or needs to reorganize. Hypnosis is the social tradition that can provide a ritual space and process to receive and positively guide the trance in helpful ways (Gilligan, 2011). By accepting what the coachee brings to the coaching space and utilizing that, Erickson used to move his clients forward. Erickson resisted building a theory for what he did as he believed to do that would mean you would need to work with your client so as to fit your theory, and individuals are much more complex than any theory. The often quoted observation of Erickson regarding this is about the kidnapper Procrustes who would cut his tall victims or stretch his short victims to fit an iron bed upon which he kept them.

As with NLP, Erickson taught by modelling and writing about what he did (Battino & South, 1999: 59–60).

Psychologists have not yet agreed what hypnotism is and even if it exists. Kroger (1963: 26) writes about 13 separate theories of hypnosis. From a psychological perspective the one which seems highly reasonable to me, and one that seeks to integrate the many diverse perspectives, is that of Graham Wagstaff (1998: 155). He suggests hypnosis can be best understood as a category error. He gives an example of someone suggesting, 'I can see a lecture theatre, I can see a library, I can see an administration building, but where is the university?' This person is making a category error because the university does not exist independently of its components. In a similar way there is a danger in talking about 'hypnosis' independently of the psychological variables which constitute it. He lists the variables as: motivation, relaxation, imagination, absorption, expectancies, attitudes, belief, concentration, suggestibility, placebo effects, selective attention, stress reactions, role enactment and compliance.

Are there any other components to hypnosis? Maybe there are. If we go back to Kurt Lewin's T groups in 1945 (Chapter 1), we understand NLP started in a similar way by discovery through interactions and experiences in group situations. Charles Tart conducted an interesting experiment to test the hypothesis that these types of group situations increase hypnotic susceptibility. The date was 1970 and participants were from the Esalen Institute, the crucible and time frame out of which NLP sprang. Statistically significant results suggested these situations did increase hypnotizability and Tart suggested that personal growth groups encouraged participants 'to overcome many of the inhibitions about experiencing, reporting and acting on other states of consciousness' (Tart, 1970: 264). An interesting replication of this research which compared *inter*personal interactions with *intra*personal interactions found that there were only significant increases for hypnotizability in the personal growth group which emphasized *inter*personal interactions. The researchers suggested on the basis of this that a further component which increases hypnotizability is interpersonal trust (Shapiro & Diamond, 1972). Bowers suggests that it is this interpersonal trust within encounter groups that allows individuals to experience unusual trance-like states without being threatened or regarded as suspiciously strange. However, he suggests unfortunately as we age we lose this trust in others (Bowers, 1976: 72).

Research using sensory deprivation chambers has shown that when participants begin to experience cognitive and perceptual deterioration (hallucination, sensory shifts, an inability to think logically), their susceptibility to hypnosis increases if they are then subjected to a hypnotic induction. Results showed that participants who were specifically selected on account of low hypnotizability dramatically increased susceptibility to hypnosis as measured through standard scales, and at one week post-experiment this hypnotizability increased even further. The control group of low hypnotizable participants who were put in chambers, but had access to radios, magazines, etc., did not demonstrate an increase in hypnotizability (Sanders & Reyher, 1969). Two further variables therefore could tentatively be added to Wagstaff's list: interpersonal trust and cognitive disorientation.

Kurt Lewin suggested a cognitive model of change which involved three stages: un-freezing, moving, re-freezing (French & Bell, 1995: 81). It could well be that in order to 'un-freeze' our limiting unconscious maps of the world, our orientation does need to be disrupted somewhat. It is possible that interpersonal trust is a key factor for a coachee to allow this disruption to occur. Phenomenologically it seems entirely consistent that if someone should start to change the sensory sub-modalities of an unconscious map which has been a reference point for many a year, this would be experienced as an altered state of consciousness. Providing these high levels of trust remain during the 'moving' stage, the coachee is free to experiment and understand which map of the world is most ecologically sound for them and those they care about. When coming back to a more familiar state of full consciousness, if the appropriate alterations co-created in trance to the unconscious maps remain, it is also consistent that new outcomes are achieved with the minimal amount of effort. This does indeed precisely accord with the experiences of those who have been on the receiving end of the Milton Model within a coaching session. For the Milton Model the disruption to the left hemisphere in order to gain access to the unconscious is through the use of Meta Model violations which overload and confuse the conscious mind.

> For the Milton Model the disruption to the left hemisphere in order to gain access to the unconscious is through the use of Meta Model violations which overload and confuse the conscious mind.

Hemispheric Difference

Through pacing and then tying up the left hemisphere of the brain with language, this leaves the coach employing the Milton Model free to engage the right hemisphere. As can be appreciated from above, the coach acts as a bio-feedback mechanism whereby they feed back to their coachee what they see and what they do not see, and as this is verified by the coachee for themselves they find themselves focusing more and more internally on their own continuing experience and the maps which create that experience. Acceptance of what is provided by the coachee and utilization of it in order to pace their map of the world means that there is no need for the coachee to 'defend' their map and resistance to suggestions fades. The research above, indicating that trust has the effect of increasing hypnotizability, emphasizes the importance of rapport in coaching and indeed 'the rapport' was the name given to describe the first stage of Mesmer's magnetization. It was described as a kind of 'tuning in' process (Ellenberger, 1970: 69).

Natural language is often associated with left hemispherical activity. For example, damage to a region of the inferior left frontal lobe disrupts the ability to speak and causes Broca's aphasia. Damage to a region in the auditory association cortex called the superior temporal gyrus of the left hemisphere disrupts word recognition and language comprehension, causing Wernicke's aphasia. Just behind the Wernicke area is the posterior language area. Damage to this area means people can recognize words and repeat them, even correcting grammar, however they cannot understand language or create meaningful sentences of their own. This area seems to be responsible for interchanging information from the auditory representation of the words and the meaning of these words stored as memories in the rest of the sensory association cortex (Carlson, 1994: 514–16). The Milton Model is predicated on the understanding that, very generally speaking, while we tie up the more conscious, logical, linear, linguistic and factual left hemisphere, we can creatively engage with the more unconscious, holistic, pattern-oriented right hemisphere. When discussing self-awareness Carlson (1994: 11) suggests that the parts of the brain associated with language play a critical role in the experience of consciousness. The work of Sperry and Gazzaniga (1967) support this belief. They showed we can act intelligently on information received in the right hemisphere with limbs on the left half of our body (which are controlled by that hemisphere) without even consciously understanding why or how, when the fibres which connect the two hemispheres together are severed. For example, a participant sits in front of a screen and has access to a pile of objects obscured from sight behind the screen. The word 'car' is flashed for one tenth of a second to the left side of the screen to ensure only the right hemisphere visually processes this. The participant will then pick up the car with their left hand from behind the screen; however, they do not know why it is they have picked up this particular object and do not know what word was flashed on the screen. This research obviously demonstrates that the right hemisphere does possess rudimentary linguistic capabilities; however, in order for these to become conscious they appear to need processing through the left hemisphere. Carlson talks of similar research for the sense of smell when only the right hemisphere receives the smell as one nostril is blocked and the participant denies smelling anything at all, yet will always pick the appropriate object from behind a partition, such as a plastic flower, fish, tree, etc., with the left hand. When trying to do the same with the right hand the participant fails in the test.

Vance Packard (1991) in his classic study of the American advertising machine shows how marketers consistently and successfully alter our perceptions of products through bypassing our conscious mind, as does experimental research. See Boxes 7.1 and 7.2 below.

BOX 7.1 MANIPULATION OF PERCEPTION OF HUMOUR (BEM, 1965)

Participants firstly answered questions about themselves into a tape recorder. They were asked to answer truthfully if the amber light was lit, but to tell a lie if the green light was lit. For 50 per cent, light colour was reversed to control for that variable.

Participants were then shown a series of cartoons, all of which had previously been rated neutral by them. They were told to either say into a tape recorder 'this cartoon is very funny' or 'this cartoon is very unfunny', depending on the researcher's instructions. While they were speaking, either the green light or the amber light would be lit in the background.

Finally, the cartoons were all rated again by the participants.

What Bem found was as expected. The participants had 'learned to believe themselves' in the presence of the truth light and vice versa. As a result, attitude change was significant for the cartoons which were rated in the presence of the 'truth light', but not so in the presence of the 'lie light'. All participants were interviewed afterwards and none said they were aware of the presence of the green or amber lights in the background in the second part of the research when they re-rated the cartoons according to the researcher's instructions.

BOX 7.2 COGNITIVE DISSONANCE (FESTINGER & CARLSMITH, 1959)

Participants were asked to come into a room and for 30 minutes to work a repetitive and boring task (stacking spools and turning pegs).

Later they were offered either $1 or $20 to enter another room and convince the next subject that actually the task was really interesting and enjoyable.

It was found that the $1 group did the better job of convincing the next subject, which supported Cognitive Dissonance Theory.

Because participants could not justify the use of their valuable time financially (only $1), they reduced the internal dissonance (doing a boring job for 30 minutes *but saying* it was interesting and enjoyable), by unconsciously reframing their experience of the task from boring to interesting and enjoyable. Because of the unconscious reframing, their communication was much more authentic and believable.

Generally speaking, just as the Meta Model is the linguistic tool to activate the more analytical left hemisphere of the brain, the Milton Model is the linguistic tool to activate the more holistic right hemisphere. The two pieces of research above show how feasibly in everyday life we move from our initial sensory awareness (*average* funny cartoons and *boring* task) to somebody else's position created through the clever juxtaposition of contextual markers: *funny* cartoons and *interesting and enjoyable* tasks. In the Bem research it was through

> Generally speaking, just as the Meta Model activates the more analytical left hemisphere, the Milton Model activates the more holistic right hemisphere.

simple association (anchoring in NLP), and in Festinger and Carlsmith it was through the manipulation of social variables. What is interesting about these two pieces of research is that in both cases all participants did not attribute their change in perception or behaviour correctly. They had effectively been 'manipulated' without even being aware of it. In other words, as in the research with the split-brain patients mentioned above, the right brain had picked up on a pattern and consequently discharged this patterning through different thinking and behaviour and the conscious mind had absolutely no awareness of it at all.

The reason coachees come into coaching is that their unconscious mind is not supporting their conscious mind. Consciously they want to achieve something; however, unconsciously their personal map of the world is working against them. The more they change the more they stay the same, and this is because the meta messages sent out unconsciously through their map of the world undermine all the conscious messages they send to themselves and others through language and behaviour.

Application of the Milton Model

1. Pacing and Leading

Your use of the Milton Model will start as soon as you meet your coachee. The key in NLP coaching is working with the coachee's model of the world, and the key to that is pacing it effectively. The two aspects of verbal pacing are:

1 Descriptions of the coachee's ongoing observable behaviour. For example, 'As you talk about your team your jaw tenses …'.
2 Descriptions of the coachee's ongoing non-observable experience. For example, '… and that tension means certain things for you'.

Verbally what the NLP coach is doing here is noticing that when the coachee is talking about their team at work they clench their jaw. The coach then, at an appropriate time, and while the coachee is in the same emotional state, feeds back the sentence, 'As you talk about your team your jaw tenses', and waits until they get the verification from their coachee which is observable, and as the coachee tenses their jaw in recognition of the accurate mapping of their map of the world, the coach says, 'and that tension means something to you'.

As you can appreciate, in order to 'describe' something which is non-observable, the coach has to be sufficiently vague in order to ensure the coachee can interpret the words according to their map of the world. So according to the

NLP presupposition, 'The mind and body are part of one system', whenever a coach sees a piece of involuntary behaviour from the body, they 'know' that is connected to the mind in some particular way and has 'meaning'. However, they do not know the precise nature of that meaning, thus the vague language in describing the ongoing unobservable meaning-making process.

In NLP coaching, when structured correctly this process can take a person into trance quite quickly without them even being aware of it. Usually the experience of hypnosis is very enjoyable so when the coachee finds themselves in the state they rarely come out, but enjoy the various sensations as the coach guides them, through the use of artfully vague language. What happens when in this state is that the coachee begins to lose awareness of the boundaries between their behaviour and behaviour which has been guided by the coach. So if when in trance the coachee hears, 'And as you sit in the chair and continue to hear my voice, you find yourself relaxing even more and begin to wonder what it would be like to have this ability even when you talk to your team', the boundaries between their behaviour and behaviour responding automatically to the coach's suggestion become very blurred. Of course such a suggestion would only be ethical if, when fully alert during the goal-setting stage of coaching, the coachee had explicitly stated one of their goals is to be very relaxed when they talk to their team at work.

> Usually the experience of hypnosis is very enjoyable.

As you learned in the previous chapter, ideally when we speak to each other, and if time allowed, we would derive the full deep structure from our surface structure. However, we do not do that and what the NLP coach would be listening for specifically is, 'What are the modelling principles in use by their coachee?' Do they often use generalizations, for instance: 'My team *never* listen to what I say, they *always* go out of their way to disrupt any plan I propose and it is as though they are *consistently* out to sabotage my career'. If the modelling principle they like using is that of generalization then in hypnosis it is useful to make use of exactly the same modelling principle, 'As you continue to sit in that chair, you *always* feel relaxed at some time in your life, *consistently* enjoying those times that you enjoy such enjoyment, understanding you *never* say no to a good thing, *always* making the most of the situation'. By not only pacing the content of your coachee, but also pacing their modelling process, you create a much more powerful rapport and are in a much stronger position to begin to lead according to the well-formed outcomes already agreed upon.

As the coachee continues to become oriented to their internal world, pacing can soon turn to leading. Just as through natural language sales people, politicians, marketers, parents and children all make use of the Milton Model naturally, so too the NLP coach will make use of natural language in an artfully vague way in order to lead. So, for example, they could say, 'And as you are enjoying that calm relaxed state, you might begin to see yourself talking to your team and you are surprised to see yourself beautifully relaxed, talking to them in measured tones'. Here there is a presupposition: 'You are beautifully relaxed, talking to them in measured tones'. In order for this clause to make sense there has to be a 'them' – this just so happens to be the coachee's team. If they accept the clause, they accept the whole sentence, and therefore the possibility that they have the requisite variety to talk to their team in a relaxed way. If this suggestion is accepted then the coach can begin to build on this new representation and map of the world in such a way that it is ecological and then test it through future pacing.

Hopefully our very brief discussion on hypnosis in 'What is hypnosis?' makes clear why it is that a suggestion offered within the Milton Model is accepted and consolidated in the unconscious map, leading to an effortless achievement of outcome, yet resisted when also offered when the coachee is in a fully conscious state of mind.

2. Communication with the Right Hemisphere

There are many ways through which Milton Erickson used to communicate with the unconscious maps of his clients. Below are just three methods, and the would-be NLP coach would be well advised to work with a reputable NLP trainer to gain experience with this fascinating NLP model which can be used very effectively in coaching.

2a. Interspersal method

One coaching technique which influences the pattern detector in the right hemisphere is the interspersal technique. During the coaching session key words or phrases are given in such a way that they are repeated within the ongoing dialogue to create a coaching theme, but not one really obvious to the conscious mind.

For example: 'I am glad that *success* is something you are striving for. *Successful people* enjoy their *success* and I can see how you are easily going to achieve your *successes* given the *successful* attitude which you have'.

Even though these interspersals are a little close together to save space, you will be surprised how when they are delivered congruently by the coach consciously the coachee does not really pick up on the theme of success, as they are too busy concentrating on the content. However, the unconscious mind picks up on the theme very readily and it drives the coachee's emotional state through changing internal representations and the patterning of those representations. Remember that according to the APET model what drives an emotional state is not thinking, it is patterning.

2b. Metaphors

Coaching metaphors bypass the conscious mind because the content (surface structure) is about something other than the coachee's experience. However, what is similar to the coachee's experience are the relationships (deep structure). You can see how a metaphor was created in Coaching Session 3 below. Here a manager was not responding to organizational change. In developing rapport with him it was established he loved sport, and in particular football. A metaphor was created around this to develop some of the psychological states Wagstaff above talks of. The theme was how people who had different values and criteria came in and changed the game completely and this nearly destroyed the key figure as he resisted these changes and was marginalized as a result. The coaching aspect of the metaphor is that the body of the metaphor matches the problem situation but the end of the metaphor matches the coachee's outcome. As the coachee listens to the content generally through the left hemisphere, the patterning of the story and the relationships, which resonates with the problem situation, matches and paces those relationships precisely. Because a well-constructed metaphor will match and pace relationships perfectly, by the time the new solution arrives the coachee is in an appropriate emotional state to be led to a solution. However, this is occurring as a result of awareness of patterning in the right hemisphere, and not of content in the left hemisphere. Consequently there is usually no conscious recognition of the metaphor as being the source of this change.

COACHING SESSION 3

The client was a senior manager in the public sector. He had come to see me because he was really angry at changes in his organization. Such was his anger that he actually shook and literally turned red when he spoke about the people and processes responsible. Whenever reframes were offered in the initial sessions they were not accepted because he was determined to explain why he was justified in being so angry, providing many colourful metaphors of his own, which always led to unproductive ends. When options were discussed along with the probable consequences of each of those options, it always seemed that the only option which met his financial and career criteria was to accept the changes and return from his holiday as a team player and with a modified map of the situation which did not see his directors as Satan and accompanying angels personified. Often the coachee would spontaneously go into trance throughout the coaching sessions in response to a Meta Model question, for example, 'So what precisely *are* you going to do?' These situations were seized upon to use Milton Model language in order to pace and lead. At the very beginning of one coaching session, after establishing rapport I asked the question, 'So how do you see your future?' The coachee went into a light trance state as he spoke of options and consistently came up with dead ends. As I was matching and pacing him, just as he came to a natural finish I said, 'And those are indeed interesting and useful options to consider and as you continue to think about them I would like you to relax, and when you are ready just close your eyes'. With some more pacing and leading the coachee was soon sitting in a very relaxed state

(Continued)

(Continued)

with his eyes closed. I read out my metaphor which had been prepared during the week to ensure the deep structure matched what was happening in the organization. John was the captain of a football team and much loved by his colleagues and the local community. However, a change in ownership meant that they were going to change the game into rugby – this would provide added value to the local community as they could learn about other sports. The first phase was to learn to kick the ball over the posts, then they had to learn to handle the ball, then they had to learn to pass the ball backwards while going forwards, etc. There were five pages of A4 to read out and the crunch period came when John lost his captaincy because of his refusal to change to the new game. He lost his house and his relationships in the family began to disintegrate but then he saw a television programme about the dinosaurs and how they went extinct despite their strength and long-time domination of other species. They became extinct because they could not change. From then on the story changes and John manages to get his captaincy back, and despite learning how to play rugby very well still played amateur football in his spare time as well as acting as a coach.

The consequence of this session was the client, although still angry, began to accept some changes as inevitable, and gradually began to relax more in the face of change. Although he delighted in throwing the occasional spanner in the works, he became a more relaxed and productive member of the senior management team. Eventually he decided to leave the company on terms that were acceptable to him.

2c. Double binds

We will be visiting double binds as well as the Milton Model again in Chapter 13 when we look at systems theory. A double bind is simply a suggestion which gives the *illusion* of choice. For example, 'You may want to make this change straight away or wait for a few days'. The suggestion and assumption is that change is going to happen. It is more easily accepted by the other person as there is the illusion of choice.

I have just discussed three Milton patterns very briefly. In one chapter which seeks to provide a taste of Milton Erickson's work it would be unwise to cram too much in. In Chapter 17 you will find many resources where you can discover more thoroughly how to develop your competence in this fascinating area of coaching.

We all use the Milton Model unconsciously in our everyday language, and consequently we 'hypnotize' ourselves and others into behaviours and thinking which are both productive and unproductive. The difference is that when you use the Milton Model within a coaching context you are using it for a specific purpose and you are using it consciously to assist a coachee in accessing and transforming outdated maps.

When an NLP coach obtains a good understanding of and through experience is familiar and competent in the use of Milton Model patterns, it is difficult to recognize any coaching context which would not benefit from the use of such patterns.

We will talk more about the ethical argument in Chapter 15 and there are a couple of brain teasers to follow which will stretch your thinking about the questions we should, as coaches, be asking ourselves.

In order to use the Milton Model within a coaching context I would strongly recommend attending a course which specifically teaches the Milton Model.

BRAIN TEASERS

1 The Milton Model is the opposite of the Meta Model and rather than clarifying communications seeks to mystify so as to access the unconscious and to influence through patterning that the conscious mind does not register. Is this ethical?
2 What would *your* definition of hypnosis be?

Reframing: The Cognitive Element

8

An ounce of framing
is worth a pound
of reframing
(attributed to Judy DeLozier)

Reframing is taking something your coachee says and putting it into a different frame. This changes the meaning of what has been said, usually in a positive way if the frame is accepted. For example, 'I am hopeless at doing this job'.

A context reframe could suggest, 'Being hopeless at doing a job is really useful in those situations when you want to get out of doing something'. The coach asks himself, 'Where would this behaviour be useful?' and then verbalizes what he comes up with. Such a reframe cognitively might be considered a bit trite; however, what it probably would do is change the emotional state of the coachee quite quickly, and when considering the APET model every NLP coach understands the primacy of emotional state in driving and *framing* our thinking process. The importance of the quote attributed to Judy DeLozier is that the larger frame will always influence the smaller frame. If within your coaching relationship you frame your language and behaviour in such a way your coachee does not believe you think he can change it does not matter how eloquent your reframes are within the coaching context, they will not work as the larger frame will win out. This means getting your own frame as a coach right in the first place will make the reframing during the coaching session much easier and more importantly much more effective too.

Another type of reframe could be a content reframe: 'Recognizing you are hopeless at your job means you really care and want to get better'. What the coach asks himself here is, 'What else could this statement mean?'

What these verbal statements do is linguistically frame what is happening in the sensory-based representations (the **Pattern** of APET) so they are interpreted in such a way that the coachee is empowered rather than restricted.

Theory

The reason this chapter is called the cognitive element is that along with Socratic questioning, cognitive reframing is a key tool in the toolbox of the cognitive behavioural coach. This flows from the presupposition they work from: 'The way you think about events profoundly influences the way you feel about them' (Neenan & Dryden, 2002: ix).

Beck (1995) explains there are three levels of cognitions – automatic thoughts, intermediate beliefs and core beliefs – the latter two of which develop in early childhood and lead to automatic thoughts in adulthood.

Where NLP differs from cognitive behavioural coaching (CBC) is in the texturing of importance concerning the cognitive element. Even though Albert Ellis recognizes the interaction between emotion and cognition, he also points out: 'it is true, however that RET (Rational Emotive Therapy) is most noted for the special place it has accorded cognition in human psychological processes, particularly the role that evaluative thought plays in psychological health and disturbance' (Dryden, 1990: 5). We will see later that experts in the neurophysiology of emotion see this texturing as an oversight (LeDoux, 1996: 52).

> It is a given that any form of emotional arousal makes us more single minded – and hence more simple minded.

The centrality of cognition can be appreciated when we understand Ellis even believed humans had a *biological* tendency to think irrationally (Dryden, 1990: 6). These irrational thoughts, he believed, lead to emotional arousal which then exacerbates the irrationality of thinking leading to a double-bind situation.

Griffin and Tyrell point out modern neurophysiology does not support the time line concerning the creation of cognition and that it is not biology that creates irrational thinking but aroused emotion. Griffin has developed from his NLP training days in the 1990s towards a social psychological approach which he calls the 'Human Givens'. When talking about why the cognitive approach takes so long, he and Ivan Tyrrell say:

> By focusing on the idea that irrational thinking causes emotional disturbances cognitive therapists are less likely to be as effective as those who look at their clients from the perspective of the Human Givens, which fully takes into account current knowledge about the way the brain works. It is a given that any form of emotional arousal makes us more single minded – and hence more simple minded. (Griffin & Tyrrell, 2000: 21)

I talk about the integration of this relationship between emotion and cognition into a coaching model which is built upon the principles of NLP and outlined in Chapter 14. A flavour of the coaching model can be understood from the following quote:

> It takes half a second for exposure to an external situation to become fully conscious in our minds (McCrone, 1999). Of that half second the first 1/10th second of information processing is via the unconscious maps of our world. These maps distort, delete and generalise the sense data we are exposed to. They are highly personalised and are built as a result of experience and the use of language. These individual maps act as frames which determine the parameters of our existence. (Grimley, 2005: 3)

From a coaching point of view, what an NLP coach appreciates is that linguistic reframing needs to be conducted within the frame of the underlying unconscious sensory map of the coachee's world. If there is not this appreciation, the majority of your reframes will be met with a polite acceptance, but will have no leverage in terms of transformation, because even though they resonate at a verbal left-brain level, they do not resonate at a sensory, holistic right-brain level.

The Meta Frame, Emotional State: Neuropsychology

So what is this 'current knowledge' which Griffin and Tyrrell talk about? Much of it has supported the increase in popularity of emotional intelligence and centres around the neurophysiology of emotional hijacking, where we unexpectedly find ourselves at the mercy of our emotions rather than being in control of them.

A good place to start is when things go wrong. A couple of conditions which throw light on the relationships between cognition and emotion are Alexithymia and Capgras syndrome.

Daniel Goleman talks about Alexithymia as a condition where people have no emotional life and a very restricted emotional vocabulary (Goleman, 1996: 50). These people can cry, but they don't know why they are crying. They can have palpitations, sweat, feel butterflies in their tummy and experience dizziness, but they have no idea they are anxious. He goes on to talk about a man who he calls Elliot who had this emotional flatness – he could talk about tragic events with complete dispassion; in fact, the consulting neurologist became more upset when listening to Elliot's story than he did. Cognitively, tests showed Elliot functioned as well as ever; however, he could no longer hold down a job as a successful corporate lawyer.

The neurologist concluded this condition must have been caused by the removal of part of Elliot's prefrontal lobes when a tumour was taken out. Effectively the circuitry between the Amygdala and the neocortex had been removed. The neurologist concluded it was this severance between the emotional and cognitive brain which created faulty reasoning. Elliot could quote a whole list of reasons as to what and why he was doing tasks on days of the following weeks; however, he was in a total muddle when it came to making the next appointment because despite the excellent logic, he had no idea of how he felt, and thus what was of value to him. The suggestion that this emotional flatness is caused by a disruption to the connections between the limbic and cortical areas is supported by Dr Sifneos (Goleman, 1996), who notes that other patients who have these areas removed also develop the same symptoms.

Capgras syndrome is a similarly interesting condition. Ramachandran (2005: 161) explains how the Freudian explanation, which of course is all about repressed sexuality and denial, was blown away for him personally when a patient developed this syndrome in relation to his pet Poodle, though he admits there might be some latent bestiality in all of us. With Capgras a close relative is not recognized as such because the sufferer does not have the appropriate emotions of love and closeness, even though they recognize the face is identical to their relative. The sufferer then reasons the relative must be an imposter. The temporal lobes allow us to recognize faces and objects and to make distinctions which help us see that two people or objects are different. These lobes then relay this information to the emotional limbic structures so we automatically experience the appropriate emotion for each object or person. When the Capgras sufferer does not experience the warm glow, normally associated with the people they love, they automatically assume the person is an imposter, an alien or in one case a robot. In the latter case the patient chopped off his step-father's head to look for microchips so as to provide evidence for his faulty reasoning. Ramachandran successfully tested the hypothesis that it was damage to the relays from the temporal lobes to the emotional limbic areas which caused this faulty reasoning.

> Even in the most rigidly cognitive of us access to our emotional centres is essential to make decisions and act appropriately.

These two interesting conditions show us that there is a very definite emotional role in our everyday thinking. Even in the most rigidly cognitive of us, Alexthymia and Capgras syndrome demonstrate we must have access to our emotional centres in order to make decisions and act appropriately.

As Griffin and Tyrell say, this is why the cognitive behavioural approach works, as it recognizes the link between emotion and behaviour and also focuses on keeping the intervention related to the present and desired outcomes.

Joseph LeDoux has done more than anyone to help us understand that we initially process information emotionally and this provides the frame within which our cognitions operate. He tells us his philosophy is simple – in order to experience emotion we must be conscious of an emotional system of the brain, like the defence system or the attraction system (LeDoux, 1996: 268). He tells us one aspect of consciousness is the ability to conceptualize the self as the experiencer. Most other animals do not have this reflexive ability owing to smaller cortical areas. What makes the human experience of emotion even further removed from other animals is language. With language we literally can make ourselves crazy, and DSM–IV-TR (2000) testifies to the fact we do.

LeDoux shows us in his excellent book how the peripheral theory of emotion was succeeded by the central theory of emotion, and the understanding concerning the primacy of the emotional brain in information processing unravelled.

The peripheral theory started with William James in 1884 with the article, 'What is an emotion?' He argued that it is this conscious awareness of our physiological response which causes our emotion. So we do not run away from the scary bear because we are afraid, rather we are afraid because we run away from the scary bear. Unfortunately James ignored the question as to what causes the behavioural response of running in the first place.

It was not until 1920 that Walter Cannon suggested that James was wrong for two different reasons. The automatic responses by the internal organs for different emotions are often the same and are regulated by the sympathetic branch of the autonomic nervous system (ANS). For instance, when we are scared *and* when we are angry, our heart beats more quickly and blood is redistributed to skeletal muscles in an instant, so how do we differentiate between fear and anger? This is the weaker of the arguments, as James did actually point out it was the *whole* body response that determines the character of an emotion and not just the ANS response. The stronger criticism was that ANS responses, though quick, are in fact too slow to account for the subjective experience of an emotion. We are already scared before the heart gets pumping; we are already smitten before we begin to move towards an attractive person. Cognitive psychology got into the act with Stanley Schachter and Jerome Singer (1962). They agreed with everyone. Yes physiological feedback was essential to the experience of an emotion and yes physiological feedback on its own lacked specificity, the missing variable was cognition. For them what it was that gave the emotion we experience its specific character was how we label it, and we label it according to the social context we find ourselves in.

> Automatic responses, though quick, are in fact too slow to account for the subjective experience of an emotion.

However, despite there being some experimental support for Schachter and Singer's two-factor theory, it still did not explain why some people felt sad in a happy social context.

Stuart Valins (1966) conducted a similar piece of research to that of Daryl Bem, mentioned in the previous chapter, in that he manipulated participants' attributions of attractiveness to partially nude women. By feeding back to participants exaggeratedly quick heart beats which were false, participants believed they were more attracted to the women who were associated to the times when they were hearing the false bio-feedback. He consequently argued it is not the arousal of emotion but the *cognitive representation* of the arousal which interacts with the context so as to produce the experience of emotion.

In a cognitive era the word unconscious was finally uttered by Magna Arnold (1960). She suggested that when we see the scary bear that William James spoke of, we appraise it *unconsciously* – this then produces a feeling and an action tendency, rather than the actual action of running away. Her reasoning, as was the reasoning of other cognitive psychologists, was that once we have registered this action tendency, we can then examine the internal processes which gave rise to the emotion. However, the research of Bem, Festinger and Valins, as well as many others, suggests that the processes which create our emotions are in fact not available for introspection. This research suggests we are not rational animals but rationalizing animals, after the event. From an NLP perspective Stuart Valins is absolutely right – it is the cognitive *representation* which interacts with the context to create the emotion; however, so is Magna Arnold, in that this *representation* is unconscious. From an NLP perspective and from the APET model, this representation, this *patterning*, is a sensory map, and we also discovered in the last chapter that even the right hemisphere of our brain has rudimentary linguistic capabilities, so attached to these maps are rudimentary unconscious limiting beliefs in the form of unconscious internal dialogue. For the NLP coach this is the point of leverage. When the cognitive psychologist thinks he is engaging in Socratic questioning and obtaining leveraged reframes at the level of belief, in fact often he is simply reframing the rationalization … thus the more things change, the more they stay the same, and Griffin and Tyrrell's comments about the cognitive approach taking so much longer hold true.

From a coaching perspective what this means is your coachee will have a story to tell as to why they cannot do something they want to do. This story is their best rationalization which allows them to look upon themselves in a favourable light. Meta Model questions often provide sympathetic nods and a recognition that it is all a bit odd. Surely with their education, their status in the organization and their drive they should be able to do this, and around and around the coaching session goes. However much the coachee wishes to don more empowering beliefs, unless they change the underlying unconscious representations which are at a different logical level and coded in emotional language, they will simply be a poor actor and others will recognize this.

Application

What the APET model means is that for the NLP coach the unconscious patterning is at the root of the solution and is *the ultimate frame*. Unless this patterning changes the thinking may change in form, but it will not change in meaning. Very often a coach working from a cognitive perspective provides an excellent reframe, however, despite its excellence, it is not accepted fully by the coachee. The reason is that consciously and in relation to the well-formed outcome, the reframe makes total sense, however it does not resonate with the underlying unconscious pattern which is triggered by the context in which the coachee wishes to perform. That the NLP coach works at the process level of pattern is echoed by the co-founder of NLP, John Grinder, who suggests the leverage point for intervention in the application of NLP patterning is sensory representations, whether addressed directly through language (the Meta Model, the Milton Model) or through non-verbal techniques (anchoring formats, for example) (Bostic St Clair & Grinder, 2001: 208). Grinder puts it more forcefully at another point, suggesting that if the professional fails to recognize that they are in the business of manipulating representations, which is the domain over which the application patterning of NLP (or any system of change) is defined, the task is literally impossible, undoable (Bostic St Clair & Grinder, 2001: 42).

Everything we do as a coach *will be a frame* for the coachee, especially as transference develops throughout the coaching session. Transference is an unconscious relationship between the coachee and the coach. The coachee unconsciously projects feelings from former relationships on to the coach. If the coach does not pick up on this transference and consequently responds according to the former relationship as a result of their feelings, coaching cannot occur. For example, I had a client once and our relationship moved towards that of manager and managerial association representative. The coachee perceived me as someone who needed to be sympathetic with his map of the world and support it from an organizational and legal perspective. I needed to point out I was neither a member of the board of directors, nor a managerial association representative; I was an executive coach, and while I understood his representation of the situation, it was this very representation which had got the coachee into the situation where he had been recommended for coaching. In common parlance, 'What had got him here, was not going to get him there'. If I had not picked up on the transference and had allowed my feelings of empathy to turn into feelings of sympathy, I would have unwittingly ended up reinforcing a map of the world which was not useful for this coachee in the specific context of his work. Further, this hypothetical communication would have been totally congruent, as I would have been *unconsciously* influenced by my coachee. Because I picked up the transference, we were able to have a coaching conversation which allowed the coachee to take responsibility for the behaviour and language which had brought him to the point where he needed a coaching intervention to address performance issues and make the desired changes. Because everything we do and say is a frame for the coachee, it is important we are congruent in our communications. For example, if the coachee suspects we do not think they can achieve what they wish, they will have developed this belief through some piece of our own behaviour within the coaching dyad. We ourselves as coaches can also say one thing, such as, 'That was an excellent piece of work' and mean something else. Our own coaching frame needs to be excellent, because if we let our coachee down in terms of *our* unconscious beliefs, reframing at a later time will be a bit like swimming against the tide.

Linguistic Reframes

What the coach needs to understand is that when using a linguistic reframe it needs to be delivered congruently. For example, consider the context reframe provided at the beginning of the chapter: 'Being hopeless at doing a job is really useful in those situations when you want to get out of doing something'. If the coach actually did not believe in this reframe, or could not effectively act 'as if' he believed it, the communication could come over as an inauthentic attempt to manipulate the coachee's beliefs. I remember once, quite by accident in a coaching session, when a coachee said, 'I just need a holiday'. I somewhat spontaneously said, 'Oh, that is so sad that you need a holiday from your life – why don't you just improve your life?' She responded very positively to this and it led into a coaching conversation about developing the capacity to enjoy one's work, while holding on to the notion that even if you enjoy your work you still deserve a holiday once in a while. There are many types of linguistic frames and the 7 C's coaching model (Chapter 14) makes a point specifically of eliciting the specific frame within which a solution is sought. Below are some frames and reframes within coaching which you might like to experiment with in order to ensure the coachee is using language in the way that can most effectively support movement towards their outcome.

1 **Content reframe.** Coach to ask, 'What else could that mean?' If coachee cannot answer, coach can provide their own reframe, keeping in mind the desired outcome of the coachee.

2 **Context reframe.** Coach to ask, 'When has that behaviour/language been useful to you?' If coachee cannot answer, coach can provide their own reframe, keeping in mind the desired outcome of the coachee.

3 **Outcome frame.** Coach to ask, 'What is it precisely you wish to achieve?'

4 **Ecology frame.** Coach to ask, 'As you consider this outcome is there any part of you that objects to it?' If there is a part, a conversation needs to be had with that 'part' and its considerations need to be incorporated into a revised outcome.

5 **Time frame.** Coach to ask, 'When do you wish to achieve this by?' This can usefully be followed by, 'And how will you know you are on track to achieve your outcome by then?' This turns 'achievement' into a process rather than a static noun.

6 **Specificity frame.** Coach to ask, 'And how specifically will you know you have achieved your outcome?'

7 **Achievement frame.** Coach to ask, 'And do you believe you can really achieve this?' Like the ecology frame, the coach needs to check for congruence. If there is incongruence, the coach then needs to anchor the coachee's emotional state, and ask, 'As you just stay there tell me what else is it you need?' Perceptual positions can be used to good effect using this frame.

8 **Orientation frame.** Coach to spot an 'away from' Meta Program operating (see Chapter 11). Coach paces it and leads to, 'So I understand what it is you *do not* want; what is it that you *do* want?'

9 **Preservation frame.** Coach to ask, 'By achieving this outcome is there anything you will lose which you have in the present?' If there is – for example, promotion might mean less security – the coach needs to work with the coachee to incorporate the benefits of the present into the gains of the future outcome.

10 **Ownership frame.** Coach to ask, 'Do you have complete ownership of this outcome?' An example might be, 'I want a pay rise'. The coachee does not have ownership over this outcome as it is not up to them to provide themselves with a pay rise if they work for an employer. However, what they do have ownership over

is their behaviour. So the outcome needs to be reframed to something like, 'I will follow the sales process more thoroughly over the next month'. The belief is that this will lead to improved performance and the pay rise they have been promised. Often in coaching interventions, people want to change the behaviour of other people and they focus on what they have no control over ... the other person's behaviour. When they focus on their own behaviour and what *they can do* to change, the other person in the systemic relationship has no option but to change their behaviour.

11 **Motivation frame.** Coach to ask, 'Is this something you really want?' Coach checks the response of the coachee and if there is incongruence asks the question again in a different form, for example 'Are you sure about that?'

12 **Backtrack frame.** The NLP coach will always recognize that because language is an imperfect representation of a deeper more sensory-based representation, they may not be fully understanding the meaning of what is being said. Effectively when using the backtrack frame, the coach will say something like, 'So if I understand you correctly there are no circumstances in which you will accept a salary of less than £50K per annum?' If there is hesitation or a lack of congruence, this can then be usefully followed by the motivation frame: 'Are you absolutely sure?' and – if incongruence persists – the ecology frame: 'What part of you is not sure?'

13 **'As if' frame.** As the NLP coaching intervention proceeds, the coachee will become familiar with the understanding that *they* are not their map of the world. *They* are something at a different logical level that has the capacity to manipulate maps so as to provide *them* with a different set of experiences. The 'as if' frame invites the coachee to suspend their personal map of the world in the particular context of their desired outcome and act 'as if' they are someone who has achieved their outcome and to learn from that experience. If the person is running an 'away from' Meta Program (Chapter 11), a part of the pacing process can be to act 'as if' their worst fears had actually occurred and, in sensory terms, they experience their world 'falling apart', 'blacking out' or 'sounding the death Knell'. Theoretically an 'away from' person will become highly motivated after becoming so acquainted with that which they wish to avoid.

14 **The difference frame.** In NLP the smallest unit of information is a unit of difference. Bateson suggested that a difference which makes a difference is an idea; it is a 'bit', a unit of information (Bateson, 1972: 272). With modelling at the centre of its methodology in coaching, it is useful for the coach to invite the coachee to think of an excellent exemplar. Once the coachee has a full appreciation of this exemplar a simple question is, 'What are they doing differently from you?' or even more elegantly, if the coachee has high levels of self-awareness, 'What is the difference?' If the exemplar is truly excellent at what they do, this frame can be expanded to, 'How are they different from *everybody* else?'

15 **The negotiation frame.** The coach simply asks, 'What *can* we agree on?' This is to be contrasted with what is absent, in disagreement, negative or cannot be acted on. A polarity response[1] to the question would be 'Nothing', in which case agreeing

---

[1]A polarity response is one that goes in the opposite direction. 'You would benefit from X' ... 'No I wouldn't, I want Y'. This form of responding for some people is a general pattern within and sometimes across contexts.

that you can agree on nothing invites a conversation about ending the coaching assignment. The polarity response to this logical solution is for the coachee to obtain high levels of motivation to continue coaching.

The Breakthrough Model: The Six-Step Reframe

If the Meta Model was how a coach communicates with the left hemisphere of the brain, and the Milton Model was about how to communicate with the right hemisphere of the brain, the six-step reframe is how to integrate both parts of the brain concerning whatever the coachee brings into the coaching space.

The genesis of the six-step reframe is interesting. John Grinder had provided a four-day seminar to staff at St Paul's Psychiatric Hospital in Vancouver, British Columbia. After several months of the staff integrating the patterns which they had learned, Grinder had agreed to return to provide one day of demonstrations working with schizophrenics followed by two days of training.

John Grinder explains that when he woke up running a fever of 104°F he made a deal with his unconscious. He effectively said, get us through the demonstration day and I will down a couple of shots of brandy and sweat it out in bed tonight.

The day went very quickly and John worked with five different schizophrenics with high quality results according to the participants. The difficulty was the next day he had no conscious memory of what he had done after 13 hours of sleep and a good sweat-out. He started the two-day follow-up training by using Meta Model questions to elicit what it was he had actually done which was so effective. John talks about the 'tug of his unconscious' which concentrated his eyes on the blackboard towards the front of the room. On it, he noted he had written:

REFRAMING

1 Identify the behaviour to be changed.
2 Establish a reliable involuntary signal system with the unconscious.
3 Confirm that there is a positive intention(s) behind the behaviour(s) to be changed.
4 Generate a set of alternatives as good or better than the original behaviour(s) in satisfying the positive intention(s).
5 Get the unconscious to accept responsibility for implementation.
6 Ecology check.
   (Bostic St Clair & Grinder, 2001: 209)

What is interesting about this pattern is that John Grinder insists it was 100 per cent the product of his unconscious mind; he had no recollection of writing it up on the board, nor of working with the five schizophrenics the previous day. It is only when that same unconscious mind communicated with his conscious mind through that 'tug' did he notice what he had done, and begin to develop a conscious understanding of the patterning which had provided the template for his demonstrations.

Obviously, in order to learn the six-step reframe, a coach will need training from a competent NLP trainer. However, in breaking it down, it goes like this:

1 **Identify the behaviour.** Often it is something you want to do but something is stopping you, or it is something you want to stop, but somehow can't.

2 **Establish a signal system.** A good way of starting this is by using Milton Model skills and identifying the 'part' which is responsible for the unwanted behaviour. This part will always be unconscious. Once you have established communication, you will know you have established communication as there will always be some involuntary expression which is associated with such a communication. The coach will need to keep their senses open to notice what this involuntary signal is. Once something is spotted then the coach needs to establish a digital yes/no system. To do this you can ask the unconscious part to increase the communication for yes and to decrease it for no.

3 **Confirm the positive intention.** This is simply asking the part if it will communicate to the conscious mind what its positive intention is. If you get a yes, then you will get the intention. If you get a no, the coach will need to continue with the yes/no signalling system to ascertain under what conditions the unconscious part would communicate with the conscious mind what its intentions are.

4 **Generate a set of alternatives.** At this stage set up a communication system with the creative part within your coachee and ask the part responsible for the unwanted behaviour to communicate with that part. The task of the coach is to facilitate this communication so the creative part can generate many alternative behaviours, which will accomplish the positive intention in a way that is acceptable to both parts.

5 **Obtain responsibility for implementation.** This is quite simply asking and, if necessary, arranging for the part responsible for the unwanted behaviour to agree to try on the new behaviour generated by the creative part for the next few weeks. The more the coach can create agreement at stage 4, the easier it is to obtain agreement at stage 5. Some NLP coaches do step 4 with no involvement of the part responsible for the unwanted behaviour.

6 **Ecology check.** Here the coach asks the coachee whether or not there are any parts which object to these new changes. If there are not, the coach future paces and exits the pattern. If there are, the coach can take the coachee back to stage 2 and reframe the objections. An alternative is to ask the objector to communicate with the creative part and the original part that created the unwanted behaviour and generate a set of behaviours which is acceptable to all.

COACHING SESSION 4

A coachee we will call David came for coaching because he wanted to get rid of anxiety which had been plaguing him for 14 years. Sometimes it was so severe he had panic attacks and at the last moment could not attend meetings.

(Continued)

(Continued)

I thought a six-step reframe would be useful. The behaviour he wished to stop was the sweating and shaking associated with his anxiety and the general tenseness he consistently felt. When I asked to communicate with the part responsible and to establish communication externally, very little seemed to happen. Breathing seemed to increase and seemed to be higher up in the chest. As I did not seem to have sufficient acuity to notice an involuntary signal I asked David what was going on for him internally. He told me he had tightness in his chest and felt 'swimmy in his head'. I asked the part responsible for those physiological responses to increase if they were willing to communicate with me. They did increase and when I asked them to subside, if this was the part responsible for David's symptoms, they did subside.

I asked this part what its positive intention was and 'it' told me 'to doubt'. I was treated to an internal visual metaphor where a goblin had a rope and it was tied to a door which was called doubt. The positive intention of 'doubt' was to exist. The purpose of existing was to make sure everything was done correctly.

On accessing the creative part of David, several alternative ways of ensuring everything was done 'correctly' were discussed. Finally, the option that was accepted was to plan everything within the available time frame, and then congruently deliver according to the plan. A part of this plan was to accept that you cannot please all of the people all of the time, and if something has been missed out then David can learn from that in reflection.

All parts seemed to agree with this; however, the goblin was concerned that he would no longer be needed. We did an exercise where the goblin went through the door of doubt to see what was on the other side; all he could see was 'nothing', it was just 'white'. I asked the goblin if there was anything to doubt and he said no. David told me each time the goblin went through the door and accepted there was nothing to doubt he would then magically reappear. I asked the goblin to do this as many times as was necessary and used Milton Model language to thank the goblin for being so useful in the past in bringing to David's conscious mind everything that needed to be attended to. Finally, the goblin went through the door and did not reappear. It was made clear that the goblin was a part of David and even though he was not needed at this time of David's life, he was still a resource to be used if necessary and again he was thanked for his positive contribution.

The ecology check went well and after six months David pointed out he was much more relaxed now and did not have any panic attacks. Sometimes he felt a bit anxious and the goblin came back. However, he had built up a nice relationship with him and each time the door of doubt was opened to show a blank wall of white, the goblin was quite happy to disappear again and allow David to get on with his executive function within the company.

Framing and reframing is something humans do naturally all of the time. It is very important when reframing and indeed framing that the coach does so according to the stated outcomes of the coachee. It is important that after developing rapport, the quality of the framing and reframing does not reduce to a casual 'well, the way I see it' type of approach which we hear in everyday conversation. Also, just as we have the placebo effect which increases wellbeing, we also have the nocebo effect which reduces wellbeing. Unless effectively trained, well-meaning coaches can be sloppy with their language skills and set up a negative self-fulfilling prophesy unintentionally.

BRAIN TEASERS

1 NLP is about developing choice and flexibility. If you have a red vase it may look great in a room with magnolia paint and a pink trim on the walls, however if you take the same vase and put it in a room with sky blue paint on the walls it would probably not look right. What behaviours, language patterns, thoughts or emotions do you hold on to even though they are not appropriate? How is this holding you back? What do you need to do?

2 A frame is a bit like a blueprint. The builders build the house according to the instructions on the blueprint, and they know if they follow those instructions they will end up with a lovely house. What is the blueprint of your life? Do you really know what you stand for? Do you really know where you are going? Is your blueprint dictated to you by your circumstances or do you decide what your blueprint is?

9

Anchoring: The Behavioural Connection

For the NLP coach the DNA of mental life is the anchoring together of sensory representations

Anchoring is the process whereby an environmental or mental trigger becomes associated with an internal response. The famous example in experimental psychology is that of Pavlov, where dogs automatically associated food and increasing salivation with the sound of a bell. Another is Watson, where 'Little Albert' learned to exhibit a fear response when exposed to a rat. Previously neither a bell nor a rat was associated with salivation or fear, and so change was created through the process of associating (anchoring) a conditioned stimulus (CS), which was the bell and the rat, with an unconditioned stimulus (UCS), which was food and banging a steel pole behind little Albert. Addiction works in a similar way when the high of a dopamine rush (UCS) is associated with addiction paraphernalia (CS). For the NLP coach the DNA of mental life is the anchoring together of sensory representations in a similar way. The idea behind synesthesia is useful. Dilts gives some examples: 'Hearing a harsh tone of voice and feeling uncomfortable is an example of auditory-kinesthetic synesthesia. Seeing blood and feeling nauseous would be a visual-kinesthetic synesthesia' (Dilts, Grinder, Bandler & DeLozier, 1980: 23). In Chapter 7 we understood how perception of humour can be changed through simple anchoring in the research of Daryl Bem (1965). After dipping our toes into what psychology has to say about this fascinating phenomenon, we will look at the NLP coaching applications.

Theory

Each and every one of us does NLP naturally. To date we have learned how to frame and reframe, how to ask good questions, and how to influence people through using vague language. We do all of that naturally, and we also naturally anchor. Do you ever get a particular feeling when someone walks into the room, when you go to a particular place, or when you hear a particular tone of voice? Then you are experiencing an anchor. Any external stimulus which significantly changes our emotional state is evidence of anchoring at work.

In the behaviourist paradigm however, the stimulus was always an environ-mental cue – linking food and a bell together, and the response was always a measurable behavioural response – the amount of saliva secreted. The reason food is termed a UCS in this paradigm is because when a dog is hungry, if it is presented with food, it will *always* salivate. When this is associated with a CS such as a bell for a long enough period, the salivation response will automati-cally be triggered simply by sounding the bell alone. Figure 9.1 below shows visually how a juicy steak (UCS) can be associated with a bell ringing (CS), so over time a hungry individual will automatically salivate and their tummy will rumble every time they hear a bell ring. Such a response is termed a condi-tioned response (CR). The law of contiguity states: 'Events (or Stimuli) which occur close together in time and space are likely to become associated with each other' (Gross, 1987: 63).

Hebb's law (Figure 9.1) is the neurophysiological basis for the law of contiguity and convolutedly states if a synapse repeatedly becomes active at about the same time that the postsynaptic neuron fires, changes will take place in the structure or chemistry of the synapse that will strengthen it (Carlson, 1994: 434).

NLP has not only borrowed the concept of classical conditioning, but it has taken it inside the 'black box'[1] and applied it to thinking and emotional states.

NLP has also associated choice with anchoring, so an NLP coach will believe any emotional state of a coachee is not a function of inevitability given the indi-vidual's personal history, but *choice*. We can choose how we feel and this is crucial

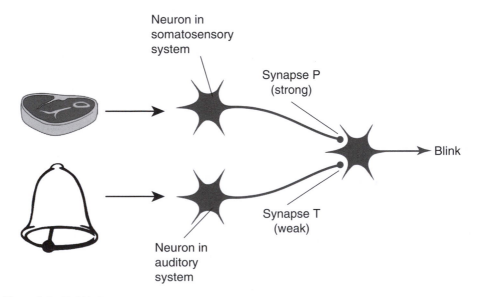

Figure 9.1   Hebb's Law

---

[1]The black box was a metaphor used in the days of behaviourist psychology. It stood for the belief that internal events, such as thoughts and beliefs, were irrelevant in psychology as they were not observable and therefore could not be directly measured.

to quality of life, as Mihaly Csikszentmihalyi (1990) tells us: people who learn to control inner experience will be able to determine the quality of their lives, which is as close as any of us get to happiness (*The Therapist*, 1998). Anchoring as a coaching technique evolved in NLP from the Milton Model. While Bandler and Grinder were working with Milton Erickson they noticed how he suggested particular cues as posthypnotic triggers to help a person change their internal state at a future time in a particular context. Yapko tells of the generic structure: later, when you are in situation A, you'll be able to do X (Yapko, 2003: 256).

The term anchor is highly relevant as it demonstrates that anchoring is not designed to cause a response in a somewhat linear and mechanical way, like Pavlov's dogs, but rather is designed to keep the boat of feeling and consciousness in a particular positive and useful area on top of the vast sea of unconsciousness as a coachee enters a particular context or meets a particular person. Pyotr Anokhin, who was a student of Pavlov, provided a nice mathematical metaphor for the complexity of this process. He suggested in a paper that he published in 1968 that the minimum number of possible thought patterns in the average brain is represented by 1 followed by 10.5 million kilometres of typewritten zeros! (Ritter, 2002: 99). Anchoring therefore is not associated with a specific behavioural response, but a highly complex unconscious systemic response which then leads to the appropriate behaviour and language.

People as Systems

People are individual systems, self-organizing entities, and they organize around attractors. Attractors are stable states, so a coachee could be on the brink of a peak which is a very unstable place to be, and the attractors each side would be seeking to pull the coachee into a stable configuration (see Figure 9.2). These attractors can be regarded as akin to Rowan's sub-personalities. Rowan describes these as 'a semi-permanent and semi-autonomous region of the personality acting as a person' (Rowan, 1990: 8). Most of us have a sense of what we are like when we 'fire on all cylinders', or 'when we are down in the dumps', when we are in 'proactive mode', or when we are being highly 'reactive'. For each of us these will be stable emotional states, and often they will be triggered, sometimes unconsciously, by environmental events or an internal thought. However, these emotional states are not simple – they are highly complex and are a unique configuration of Anokhin's 10.5 million kilometres of typewritten zeros.

The key to successful anchoring is not, as is often thought, just the intensity of the state, or we could say the depth of the trough in Figure 9.2, but rather the appropriateness of the state. A coachee may come to coaching wishing for more confidence at work, however this begs the question if we use the Meta Model: 'What do you mean by confidence?' 'Confidence in what?' The Meta Model can continue to work its coaching magic until the coachee finally recognizes that what they actually need is not confidence at all, but capability

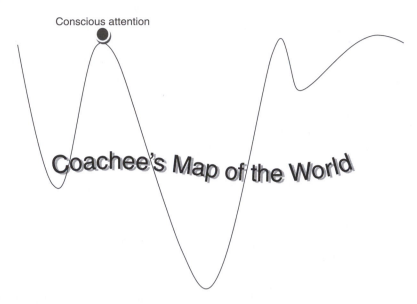

Figure 9.2   How attractor states trap conscious attention

and they need to access their best learning state to develop that. A learning state is probably very different from a general confidence state. However good the coach is technically, if they attempt to anchor an inappropriate emotional state they will probably not be successful. In this example if the coach directs the coachee to access a confident learning state, then the anchoring format will probably work very well as the exercise will accord with the ecology frame (Chapter 7).

Steve and Connirae Andreas (2000) make the above point very well:

> A resource state for concentration on mathematics will be very internal and utilize very little proprioceptive kinesthetics, while a resource state for skiing will be very external and will utilize exquisite distinctions and feedback in the kinesthetic system. While neither of these resource states is particularly 'intense,' each is a powerful resource for the appropriate skill. On the other hand, each of these states will not be resources at all for the other task; they will be hindrances. A skier who attempts to do mathematics in his skiing resource state will do as poorly at that as a mathematician who tries to ski using his mathematics resource state, and each may become intensely frustrated as a consequence.

When we get into an emotional state of any kind, you may remember that according to the APET model this has to be a function of the underlying sensory representations, the pattern. The fact that cognitive functions are affected in this way too is demonstrated by research into memory.

Internal and external sensory cues present during the encoding of material are represented in the resulting memory traces. If such cues are present during retrieval then retrieval will be enhanced. Evidence for this is demonstrated by research which shows a reduction in retrieval when the encoding context is removed, compared with retrieval when the encoding context remains intact. Tulving and Thompson call this the encoding specificity principle (Tulving & Thompson, in Smith et al., 1998: 95).

From an anchoring point of view what this means is not only must the NLP coach first of all ascertain what the appropriate emotional state is, but it is then useful to work with the coachee to recollect from their memory the encoding context, in other words the sensory representations which give rise to the emotion. Indeed mind–body psychology will point to certain bodily changes too during this process. Rossi and Cheek quote Jung who talks about feeling toned complexes: 'The phenomenology of complexes cannot get around the impressive fact of their autonomy, and the deeper ones penetrate into their nature – I might almost say their Biology' (Jung, 1960: 98). This reciprocal interaction between emotional state, encoding context and biology is demonstrated through the phenomenon of state-dependent memory. Rossi tells us research has shown the hormone Oxytocin, which is released during labour and after childbirth, has a fundamental role in the creation of amnesia experienced by women concerning events of that time (Rossi & Cheek, 1988: 274).

What we need in anchoring then is the appropriate state, and also that appropriate state *fully* experienced. If the coachee only experiences a pale cognitive and verbal representation of a state, the process of anchoring will not work; it is the intensity of the emotional state which is a precondition of learning through association. Just like when someone 'learns' to develop a phobia after only one exposure to a spider because of the emotional arousal, so too the coachee must literally at the cellular level of DNA experience this appropriate emotion in order to 'learn' to access that new and appropriate emotional state when entering a context of their choice, for example sitting in an exam room, standing behind a lectern or jumping out of a plane. One trial learning can work for positive as well as negative events.

> One trial learning can work for positive as well as negative events.

There are interesting examples in the NLP literature of how we literally hold these different emotional states and associated capabilities in certain parts of our body. For example, in the wake of the popular film (*The King's Speech*) about King George VI who had a stutter, Michael Hall talks about the work of Dr Wendell Johnson (Hall, 2011b). Wendell Johnson stuttered himself; however, by applying the principles of general semantics he cured himself. What Dr Johnson did was challenge the very fundamental frames which supported stuttering. These frames of course are the fundamental and rudimentary dialogues which emanate from sensory patterns in less than one tenth of a second and are at an unconscious level. Michael Hall talks about the meaning frame: 'stuttering is terrible'; the self-frame: 'stuttering means I am inadequate'; the other frame: 'stuttering means no one will like me'; the intention frame: 'I must stop myself'; the power frame: 'I can't stop myself', and so forth. Hall points out that loading initial sensory representations with these rudimentary linguistic frames can create a phobia of mis-speaking represented kinaesthetically in the throat. When we talk of any emotional state which we wish to use as a resource state to replace an undesired state, it is very important to recognize that such states are represented at many different levels, and the coach needs to check at each one of these levels that the experience is authentically represented and has the quality of purity.

As an aside Michael Hall points out that part of the cure for King George VI was demonstrated quite nicely not at the level of meaning but at the level of representation. When King George VI read in such a way that he could *not* hear his own voice (he had headphones on playing loud music to him), he read fluently. All King George VI had to do was *delete* (one of the key modelling principles) the sound of his own voice and he no longer stuttered. Why? Because he no longer heard his unconscious condemnation and negative judgement of himself as he semantically loaded the auditory trigger of hearing his own stuttering voice.

The Garcia Effect

The Garcia effect helps us understand that there are some environmental triggers which are naturally associated with certain psychological states. The research of Garcia and Koelling (1966) also suggests conditioning does not need many, many associations before learning takes place, nor does the CS and the UCS need to be presented in temporal proximity as the law of contiguity suggests. Their research suggests that nervous systems have a bias towards forming certain associations. Box 9.2 shows the research which provided evidence for these suggestions.

BOX 9.2

1 Rats taste a solution of saccharin. Contact with drinking spout automatically triggers two other conditioned stimuli: a bell and a flashing light.
2 Six hours later rats are given an injection of Apomorphine which creates severe intestinal illness.
3 Rats are presented with plain water with a bell ringing and with a light flashing. They drink the water with no hesitation. Conclusion: no association between sound/light and severe intestinal illness.
4 Rats are presented with a solution of saccharin. They refuse to drink it. Conclusion: an association has been formed between taste and severe intestinal illness, even though the UCS (Apomorphine) was presented six hours *after* the tasting of saccharin.

The above experiment may seem 'common sense'; of course we will more readily associate taste with intestinal illness compared with a trigger in any other sensory modality; however, it is something the NLP coach will need to appreciate. Another example of how anchoring can give us an insight into how the human mind is wired comes from the work of Ramachandran and Hubbard (2001: 19) based on Köhler (1929). If you look at the two shapes in Figure 9.3, which one would you say is Bouba and which one is Kiki? Irrespective of language, 95–98 per cent of people will respond as you have done and as labelled in Figure 9.3. There is a natural anchor between visual shape and auditory sound. There is a roundness to the sound Bouba which is anchored to the curves of the shape, and a sharpness to Kiki which is anchored to the acute angles of a very different shape.

It is not surprising the words synapse and synaesthesia both start with the prefix 'syn', meaning with or together. The heart of human creativity, according to Fauconnier and Turner (2002), lies in the ability to take two different scenarios and combine them to creatively develop a third. Essentially in anchoring this is what we are doing. We are taking an unresourceful state, combining it with a resourceful state and developing another resourceful state for use in a particular context. Fauconnier and Turner call it double-scope blending, and the experts in anchoring, the marketing profession, use it all the time in adverts. They take two scenarios which are not necessarily compatible and blend them in such a way that a particular product all of a sudden is associated in the public unconsciousness with a certain positive spin, which results in increased sales.

In my NLP practitioner training back in the 1990s Stephen Brooks told me he believed that when people have been severely hurt in the past, they store that representation of hurt primarily in a particular representational system – for the sake of argument, let us say visual. Stephen believed this would set up an internal strategy to make *less use* of visual sensory representations and *develop* other representations more fully, such as auditory and kinaesthetic. What this could mean is if you worked with such a coachee it is possible that a visual anchor would not work very well; however, an auditory or kinaesthetic

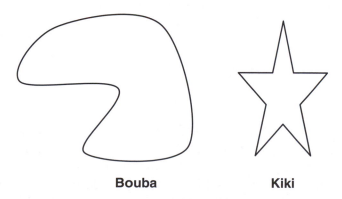

Bouba   **Kiki**

Figure 9.3   Cross-activation between visual and auditory sensory maps

one would. It is possible that those who already have very negative associations anchored in one representational system will not respond well when an NLP coach attempts to bring that system into play. I believe this is a typical example of a great NLP idea which has not been experimentally tested yet holds much promise. We will turn to the interesting debate on untested ideas in Chapter 16.

Application

When done well anchoring, like every other NLP pattern, is invisible. Dilts (1990) tells us the kinaesthetic anchor came from Virginia Satir. When she performed it, one would think that her touch was just a natural expression which seamlessly supported the ongoing interaction. There would not be a sense that 'some technique' was being applied. When anchoring is applied in NLP coaching, it is applied in concert with many of the other NLP coaching skills.

COACHING SESSION 5

I had one client who often referred to the phrase 'back in the day'. Whenever he used this phrase he accessed a very high energy and positive emotional state, as though anything was possible. I picked up on this and put it into my mental library. Later on during the coaching session when he began to struggle in maintaining a positive orientation when considering certain tasks, I would intermittently ask him to remember when he was 'back in the day' and I patted him on the left shoulder as I would say this. He would then access the positive emotional state, and just before he was at his most intense I would say, 'So how would you look at this problem now?' and as I said 'now' I would give him another pat on the left shoulder. Even though the coachee still struggled with the task, it was a positive struggle textured with a determination that he would find his way through and an answer did await him, rather than the defeatist state which he often experienced previously. I got into the habit of always saying goodbye to this coachee at the end of the session by patting him on the left shoulder rather than shaking hands with him and he always broke out into that positive state with a wide grin on his face. After three sessions he went from not being able to perform at work because of anxiety and self-doubt to working enthusiastically.

As mentioned above, in order to assist the coachee in Coaching Session 5, anchoring was just one part of NLP that allowed me to help him access his resources and then apply them to his functioning in the context of work. Even though the NLP coach will use other techniques, anchoring is one that is fundamental to an NLP coaching intervention. Here are some anchoring tips:

1 95 per cent of NLP coaching is listening and observing. There will be a natural pattern to your conversation; sometimes the coachee will focus internally, sometimes externally. Sometimes they will be enthusiastic, sometimes they will be defeatist. Make a note of recognizing what your coachee's natural anchors are. When they go into an emotional state which is similar to the resource state needed in order to perform whatever they have come to you for, notice what is associated with that state. If you are not sure (because it may be internal), just touch your coachee on the shoulder, or mark out the state in another way by waving your hands, or saying something like 'great', and tell them, 'I want you to hold that state just there and tell me what is happening'. Ask for what they see, and explore the sub-modalities of those visual representations. Are they big or small, in colour or black and white, in focus or fuzzy, close or far away, etc. Ask for what they hear and again the sub-modalities. Is it loud or soft, high or low, faint or near, if a voice a man or woman. All the time you are doing this, you can present an auditory, kinaesthetic or visual anchor. If you have ascertained which is the favoured representation of your client, it may be a good idea to use that representation. If it is auditory keep saying the word 'great', if it is kinaesthetic keep tapping them on the shoulder, if it is visual you can wave your hands in front of them. If you remember the encoding specificity principle, what you are doing here is assisting the coachee in accessing the state fully by detailing the representations and sub-modalities which are associated with this state. If this is done effectively then by the end of one coaching session your coachee will have an excellent anchor which they can use to access their resourceful state at any time they deem appropriate.

2 Sometimes an anchoring format may not go as planned. (Remember my six-step reframe and the goblin in Chapter 8). A very important thing the NLP coach needs to remember is their own emotional state and ensure they have sufficient resource anchors themselves to be able to continue to coach according to the professional standards of their professional body. It is important not to try to force an anchor. Remember learning through association is a natural process, and if an association is not being formed there is usually a very good reason. Rather than attempt to create an anchor for a resourceful state which does not work, it is important to find out what else you have in your NLP toolkit that will work.

3 One reason an anchor may not work is that intermediary states are needed to get from a problem state to a resource state. In this case the NLP coach can chain anchors. This again is a natural process. For instance, the transtheoretical model of change goes through five specific stages which can equally be regarded as specific emotional states: pre-contemplation, contemplation, preparation, action and finally maintenance (Prochaska & DiClemente, 1984). One key in making this process work is to ensure there is an element of overlap between adjacent emotional states. So if a coachee is contemplating change, rather than access a powerful emotional state of action, it may be appropriate to access a powerful planning then preparation emotional state. The coachee can then set off the planning anchor, and then, when appropriate, chain this to a preparation anchor, then an action anchor. Finally, such action can be further chained to a maintenance anchor.

4 Stacking anchors is a bit like being a good comedian. Their first joke makes you laugh a little bit. While you are still giggling internally, another joke then makes you laugh even more as you are primed in a certain emotional state. A third joke makes you laugh so much the audience turn around and look at you. And finally, a fourth joke has you crying you are laughing so much.

5 Anchoring is a natural process so often it is a useful coaching technique to simply allow the anchor to work naturally as you develop the appropriate emotional state. Your coachee already knows the context in which they would like to access this emotional state. I have found it is often useful to find something in that context to which the desired state can be anchored. This would be contrasted with the way anchoring is often taught, where the appropriate emotional state is anchored to a conditioned stimulus like pinching your fingers together, saying something to yourself, or seeing a picture. After this has been successful the NLP coach is then taught to associate this conditioned stimulus with another stimulus so as to access the appropriate emotional state. I have found it useful sometimes to just miss out the middle step, so to speak. So, for instance, if someone wants to be calm when their boss shouts at them, I work with them so they can anchor the sound of their boss's voice to a state of serene and robust calmness. I then future pace this and when the future pacing is congruent that is a good indication and predictor of success in real life. An example of this can be seen in Coaching Session 6.

6 Words are anchors. Any good hypnotist will know how to use words to anchor another person into a particular emotional state. Just as a coach can make use of the placebo effect through the use of words, so too can they inadvertently make use of the nocebo effect through the use of their words. If you notice as a coach you use a certain word and obtain an unexpected negative response, recognize too that that particular word in that context is an anchor. The words we use in coaching need almost to be like a painter's brush and palette. As we speak we need to consistently calibrate what we say to the emotional state of our coachee and ask whether these words are taking them closer to their outcome or further away from it.

COACHING SESSION 6

A client was referred to me by an organization because they believed she was depressed. I asked the client how she knew she was depressed and also how she continually managed to maintain that particular emotional state throughout the day. I noticed that the more she talked to me, the more she began to curl up into a ball and though eye accessing[2] noticed she was representing depression kinaesthetically. I complimented her on being able to do something so exquisitely and then asked her to stand up, put her hands up in the air, raise her eyes upwards and smile. Once I had managed to ensure she was congruently in this physiological state, I then asked her to repeat the strategy for depression which she had just told me about a few minutes previously. She burst out laughing and said she couldn't. The more I 'ribbed' her, reminding her she had told me in detail just a few minutes ago, the more she laughed. I concluded that simply by changing her physiology she had become amnesic to how to be depressed. I began to anchor this new physiology to contexts where she had previously been depressed and within six sessions she no longer was 'depressed'.

---

[2]We talk about eye accessing cues in Chapter 10. NLP believes that eye movement is associated with internal representation. Generally if a person looks down and to their right this means they are processing information through their kinaesthetic representation.

BRAIN TEASERS

1 Think of times when you have been well and truly anchored, and this has been a negative experience. After reading this chapter, how are you now going to change your emotional state within those contexts?

2 The Garcia effect has been shown to demonstrate that certain sensory associations are easier to make than others. Do you personally find that you get more irritated in one sensory channel than another? If you think you do, see if you can explore the sub-modalities of that representation and experiment with how your feelings change if you alter those sub-modalities. Find out also what happens when you represent what irritates you in another sensory representation. What effect does changing the sub-modalities have in that other sensory representation?

Eye Accessing Cues

10

The scales fall away and the eyes have it

The discovery of eye accessing cues followed NLP's second model: representational systems[1]. Bandler and Grinder were both very enthusiastic as they had simultaneously yet separately noticed the same eye accessing patterns during the week following their discovery of representational systems. This pattern is now synonymous with NLP and can be summarized in Figure 10.1.

It is quite possible 'the scales had fallen from their eyes' (Bostic St Clair & Grinder, 2001: 171) because Grinder recalls that both he and Bandler had their auditory filter for representational predicates very cleanly in place after the testing and analysis of representational systems. Because eye accessing cues are so closely linked to the experiment Bandler and Grinder performed in Santa Cruz, they will be discussed alongside what is referred to as NLP's second model by Bostic St Clair and Grinder (Bostic St Clair & Grinder, 2001: 164).

Discovering exactly what happened in the early days of NLP is a bit like a hermeneutist trying to piece together the synoptic gospels ... each tells the story a slightly different way ... as one would expect from different maps of the world. In Robert Dilts's account (1990) Robert himself was instrumental in bringing the eye accessing cues into NLP. You can get a brief look at his research below in Box 10.1. He was attending a second lecture at Santa Cruz on linguistics. It was at this time that Bandler and Grinder were visiting Milton Erickson. Grinder was talking about the phenomenon of 'naming' and how it shapes our perception as we discovered in the research of Carmichael (Carmichael, Hogan & Walter, 1932) in Chapter 6. The group of 20 students were tasked with finding something they had never noticed before and 'naming' it. As Dilts sought clarification from Grinder, Grinder said 'What about that?' Dilts understandably said 'What?' Grinder pointed out that just before Dilts

---

[1]Representational systems refers to the neurological mechanisms behind the five senses. NLP believes individuals have a preference for a particular sense system, which is used to receive, process and store information. This can be noted by listening to the words people use, their tonality and pitch, and observing their posture and physiology as well as eye accessing cues.

Imagine this picture superimposed over the eyes of the person you are looking at.

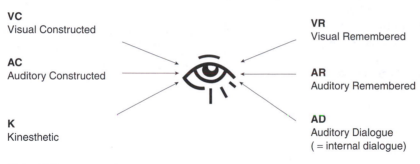

VC
Visual Constructed

AC
Auditory Constructed

K
Kinesthetic

VR
Visual Remembered

AR
Auditory Remembered

AD
Auditory Dialogue
(= internal dialogue)

Figure 10.1   NLP eye accessing cues

asked a question his eyes darted to one side. Dilts recognized on immediate reflection he had 'gone inside' into a trance-like state and produced what he called a minimal cue to John. It is interesting that Dilts uses exactly the same phrase as Bostic St Clair and John Grinder when he explains 'the scales falling from his eyes' in his account of his memories. Such a phrase seems to exemplify the collective excitement around discoveries made during the formative days of NLP. Once he had 'named' minimal cues he could not stop noticing that when people talked their eyes would be going all over the place as they searched internally through different sensory modalities to find the experiences to express their thoughts. As the visual chatter forced itself upon Dilts subsequent to 'naming', he made observations and these were pooled with the observations of Bandler and Grinder to eventually emerge as 'eye accessing cues'.

Theory

NLP's second model, according to Bostic St Clair and Grinder (2001), was representational systems. Bandler and Grinder had noticed that people say things like, '*I feel* you are *telling* me something', '*I see* what you are *saying*' or '*I hear* the picture you are *painting*' – it is as though people are receiving sensory information through one channel and then representing it in another.

Following the above conversation Bandler and Grinder drove to Santa Cruz for a group meeting, and John Grinder brought with him sheaves of green, red and yellow paper. When their group meeting started, as each participant introduced themselves they were allocated a colour depending upon the words they used. So mainly kinaesthetic words would get a yellow sheaf, visual would get red and auditory would get green. After this two sets of discussion took place. Firstly participants were only allowed to talk with others who shared the same colour of paper for ten minutes. After that they were then told to only talk with people who had a *different* colour of paper for ten minutes. Bandler and Grinder were astonished at the difference between the two sets of ten minutes. The first set was resonant of good rapport and matching with laughter and excited talking, the second set was characterized by mismatching, extended silences, lower volume and

> What is certain is that a synaesthete who sees the letter O as red is no more at liberty to experience it as not red as they are to experience it as not circular.

little physical movement. Grinder identified this pattern as 'synaesthesia' (Bostic St Clair & Grinder, 2001: 167).

When Jamie Ward asks such questions as, 'What colour is the letter A?' or 'What does the number 1 taste of?' he finds as many as 1 per cent of his intake of psychology undergraduates at University College London (UCL) are certain they experience something like this (Ward, 2003: 196). Synaesthesia is not understood, for example colour is the most common synaesthetic experience but we do not know why. What is certain is that a synaesthete who sees the letter O as red is no more at liberty to experience it as not red as they are to experience it as not circular. For synaesthetes there is no choice. Of course NLP is about choice and Grinder takes this pattern into the realm of choice and uses the term more generally to denote such experiences as a natural part of being human. He says he has had clients who are in the clinical sense synaesthetes and has had success in assisting them to regulate their experiences (Bostic St Clair & Grinder, 2001: 192). It is this type of claim which fascinates me as a psychologist. For instance, Nunn et al. (2002) have conducted functional imaging studies which show that synaesthetes who see colours when they hear words do actually have neural activity registered in the V4 area of the left hemisphere. However, despite training in word-colour association this area was not activated for non-synaesthetes when they heard words. When these non-synaesthetes then looked directly at the colour patterns the V4 area did light up. This tends to support the belief that synaesthesia is associated with perception rather than memory. If NLP practitioners could write up their work so claims such as John Grinder makes above can be understood and replicated, and therefore tested, I think NLP would be in a stronger position than it is now.

For the NLP coach the benefit of being aware of these linguistic representations of 'synaesthesia' – 'I *see* what you are *saying*' – is that the coachee is not aware of them. They are providing the coach with unconscious information as to how they model the particular experience they are talking about. Because the coachee is unconscious of it their coach can use this information for many useful coaching activities. For instance, simply matching the pattern of the unconscious process will generate rapport very quickly. A response to the above, for example, could be, 'So if I *show* you this you will *understand* what I mean?' The answer almost definitely has to be 'yes'.

It could well be that synaesthesia is simply an extension of the cross-modal perception and integration that all of us naturally engage in. Jamie Ward talks of the research of Marks (1982) which shows that when non-synaesthetes make cross-modal matches between pitch and colour, the higher the pitch the lighter the colour. The research of Marks (1975) shows that this actually is the direction of relationship in synaesthetes who really do have developmental synaesthesia between the pitch of sounds and colour. So just as with Bouba and Kiki in Chapter 9, maybe synaesthesia is telling us something about the natural cross-connections between the sensory maps within our brain.

Eye Accessing Cues

The importance of representational systems as the second model of NLP is underlined when we go back to the APET model. For the NLP coach the main leverage in working with the coachee is these patterns of anchored representations. If a coachee says, 'I feel depressed every time I walk into work', linguistically this coachee is telling us they have an unconscious map of the world which goes $K^e \rightarrow K^{i-}$. So they walk into work which is a physical external kinaesthetic activity (K^e) and this is associated with an internal negative kinaesthetic activity of feeling depressed (K^{i-}). As the coach looks at the coachee, even though eye accessing cues could suggest the accessing of many sensory modalities, the NLP model would suggest there will be proportionately more movements down and to the right as they talk of how they manage exquisitely to do depression as they walk into work. NLP suggests we need to work with

> The coachee is providing the coach with unconscious information as to how they model the particular experience.

these representations and *not* the client's theory as to what these representations mean, which is usually after the fact rationalization in the form of limiting beliefs and 'understandings'. When these representations can be changed then all of a sudden the so-called 'depression' is emotionally expressed very differently, almost as though it is no longer 'depression'. This is because it is the patterning of representations which create the emotion. For example, when the coachee says 'walk into work', if the coach then anchors those words by making a visual, kinaesthetic or auditory anchor, and then in a Frank Farrelly[2] way purposely misunderstands the word depressed and repeats back to the coachee, 'So you are deep dressed every time you walk into work?', that could well shift the internal negative kinaesthetic to an internal positive kinaesthetic. When the coachee repeats, 'No, I said depressed', again the coach could anchor another ludicrous statement, 'So you are de-dressed when you walk into work?' and then de-stressed, and then de-meshed. The point of such a coaching strategy is simply to associate a positive internal feeling (K^+) or a positive internal visual (V^+) with the act of walking into work, rather than a negative representation.

All of NLP coaching is about changing these underlying patterns of representation in order to develop a choice of experiences rather than be at the mercy of only one experience. Bostic St Clair and Grinder sum up the whole gamut of every NLP coaching strategy as a function of five strategies (2001: 198–9).

---

[2]Frank Farrelly developed his own elicitation model. In a nutshell he would take the verb or noun which seemed to be most important and then deliberately interpret it within a hallucinated context which was unlikely and ridiculous. He then would listen to the correction from the coachee. If the coachee did not correct, he would continue with the ridiculous fiction until they did. For 'provocative therapy' humour and having the coachee laugh is indicative the model is being delivered correctly.

Each of these strategies has nothing more than the manipulation of these unconscious representations as their core objective:

1 The Meta Model, designed to verbally challenge the mapping between first access to the outside world through our senses (F^1), and our linguistically mediated mental maps (F^2).

2 Operations defined over representational systems and their sub-modalities, for example the Swish technique.

3 Reframing patterns, where representations are placed in a different cognitive structure.

4 Anchoring, where undifferentiated groupings of representations are brought together for purposes of integration.

5 The Milton Model, where representations at F^1 (first access through our senses to the world) are shifted by using F^2 (linguistically mediated maps) patterning without the need to map those representations onto the client's conscious understanding.

By using eye accessing cues as per Figure 10.1, as the coachee tells the coach their story, the coach can understand through the non-verbal cues how the individual content is represented. With this extra information the coach can work with the coachee to 'manipulate' those representations, which will create a very different emotional state, meaning the coachee will begin to think differently and therefore also act and talk differently. By making use of eye accessing cues the coach can work at a content-free level if necessary, without the coachee even knowing it.

You will notice that the central eye positions are not represented in Figure 10.1. Generally if the eye is above the horizontal the coachee is believed to be accessing visual representations; it is believed too that straight ahead also usually means visual, though not necessarily. When the eye movement goes below the horizontal and is in the centre, the coachee could be accessing kinaesthetic or internal dialogue and one will need to use further calibration[3] skills in order to ascertain which representation is being accessed.

Generally speaking NLP has noted physiological and auditory associations with specific sensory representations. Visual representation is associated with a much higher and quicker tone of voice, with the breathing being higher in the chest. Auditory representation is associated with a more even tone of voice and with the breathing being from the middle of the chest. Often highly auditory people will put their fingers to their chin and take on the classical 'thinker' pose, or sometimes tilt their head to one side almost as though they are listening to someone on a telephone. The kinaesthetic representation is associated with a much lower and slower tone of voice. Often the breathing comes more from the diaphragm. You will notice in Dilts's research, in Figure 10.3, there is a space for body description in the researcher's

> NLP has noted physiological and auditory associations with specific sensory representations.

---

[3]Calibration is the ability to know a person's internal cognitive and emotional state through noticing associated external cues. Eye accessing cues are one of these external cues.

notes. Often it is the case that visual people are more of the ectomorph type, auditory people are more of the mesomorph type and kinaesthetic people are characterized by endomorphic features. These, like many of the NLP generalizations however, need to be calibrated to each individual coachee.

Eye accessing cues is one of the most controversial 'discoveries' of NLP. Overall research which has tested the phenomenon has not come up with any conclusive results. An early pioneer of NLP, Robert Dilts did test eye accessing cues himself in 1977 and his research is summarized in Box 10.1.

BOX 10.1

In 1977 Robert Dilts conducted a study at the Langley Porter Neuropsychiatric Institute in San Fransisco (Dilts, 1983: 1–29). Participants (N = 25) were asked a series of questions in four groupings using two processes:

Memory
Visual, auditory, kinaesthetic, feelings.
Construction
Visual, auditory, kinaesthetic, feelings.

Electrodes were used to track eye movements and brainwave characteristics as the series of questions were asked. Baseline measurements were taken from the electrode readouts, and then each subject was asked a series of questions. They were instructed not to respond verbally, but only to raise a finger to indicate they had secured an answer – 16 seconds was allowed for participants to access an answer. Typical questions for each condition were:

Visual Remembered: Think of the colour of your car.
Visual Constructed: Can you imagine the top half of a toy dog on the bottom half of a green hippopotamus?
Auditory Remembered: Can you think of one of your favourite songs?
Auditory Constructed: Imagine the sound of a train's whistle turning into the sound of pages turning.
Kinaesthetic Remembered: What does a pine cone feel like?
Kinaesthetic Constructed: Imagine the feeling of dog's fur turning into the feeling of soft butter.
Visceral/Emotional Remembered: When was the last time you felt impatient?
Visceral/Emotional Constructed: Imagine the feeling of being bored turning into feeling good about feeling bored.

Conclusions: Dilts concluded that eye movement was associated with sensory-specific cognitive activity. Dilts found an association between specific cognitive activity and eye accessing cue/verbal representation of internal experience (Figure 10.2).

He found visceral/emotional language was associated with high amplitude alpha waves with eyes open and shut. Visual access was associated with low amplitude beta waves with eyes open and spindles of alpha waves when eyes were shut. Kinaesthetic accessing was associated with low amplitude beta waves with eyes open and shut, and, finally, auditory accessing was associated with higher amplitude beta waves with intermittent alpha waves with eyes open and shut.

(Continued)

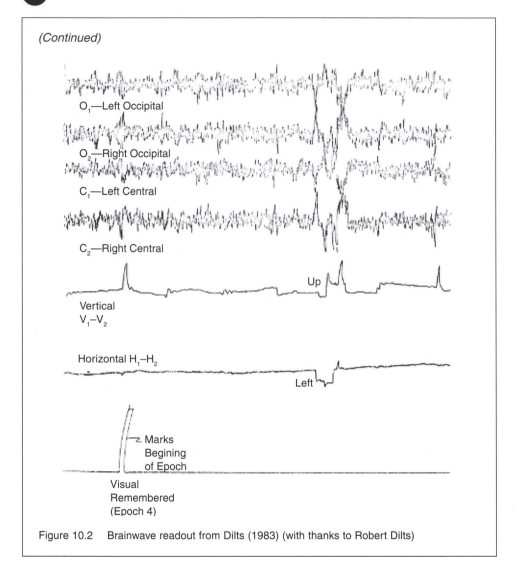

(Continued)

O_1—Left Occipital

O_2—Right Occipital

C_1—Left Central

C_2—Right Central

Vertical
V_1–V_2

Up

Horizontal H_1–H_2

Left

Marks
Begining
of Epoch

Visual
Remembered
(Epoch 4)

Figure 10.2   Brainwave readout from Dilts (1983) (with thanks to Robert Dilts)

Dilts thought his methodology was not ideal and believed that using the researcher's recording template (Figure 10.3), where the researcher made direct observations of eye position and qualitative notes using that template, and could then check them against a video recording later, was a better way to check for eye movement than to rely on electrical measurements taken from electrodes around the eye sockets. His replication of this research, which used direct observation, confirmed his initial findings. He discovered though that people have specific strategies for accessing sensory cognitions. For instance, in order to hear the engine of a car a participant may first experience the feeling of being in their car, then see themselves operate the ignition key before they could *hear* the sound of the engine of the car, which is what the question required of them. It is this subjective differentiation of accessing the required sensory mode which makes this type of research very difficult.

It is also important that raters and researchers know the NLP model well enough in order to understand precisely what it is they are researching. Heap (1988) conducted a meta analytical study of eye accessing cues and his interim conclusion was that there is no evidence for the phenomenon. In his excellent paper Michael Heap, in my opinion, tries to sum up NLP too succinctly. He does so by referring to only one of the NLP presuppositions, 'The map is not the territory'. Chapter 5 of this book shows that NLP has many more presuppositions, which do not just come from general semantics, but also systems theory/cybernetics, modelling and transformational grammar. This appreciation of NLP is much richer and calls for an experimental paradigm in which statistical analysis certainly may play a part, but so also does trained observation and interpretation. Heap also seems to wish to categorize the concept of primary representational systems too readily as a trait. Many NLP coaches tend to take a more situational or state view, which puts the individual much more in control of how they are and who they wish to be in a particular context. Finally it is possible Michael Heap is not aware of all of the NLP research conducted. He does not include Dilts's research in his meta analytical study, and if he had he would have recognized that Dilts (1983) was aware of the

REPRESENTATIONAL SYSTEM SCORING SHEET

Question	Eye Movements	Predicates
1) Tell me something about your present living accommodations or conditions.	Right ☐ ☐ ☒ Left / ☐ ☒ ☐ / ☐ ☐ ☐	YELLOW CURTAINS / A LOT OF LIGHT
1A) Tell me something important about these accommodations or conditions.	☐ ☐ ☒③ / ☐ ☐ ☐ / ☒ ☐ ☐	A GOOD VIEW
2) Tell me about some event in your life that was particularly meaningful for you.	☐ ☐ ☒⑤ / ☐ ☐ ☒ / ④☒ ☐ ☐	TRAVELING IN EUROPE / SAW A LOT OF DIFFERENT CULTURES
3) Tell me about something that you are particularly interested in. What is interesting about it?	☐ ☐ ☒③ / ☐ ☒ ☐ / ☐ ☐ ☐	DRAWING & MOVIES
4) What is something that has always been easy for you to learn?	☒ ☒ ☐③ / ☐ ☐ ☐ / ☐ ☐ ☒	SCIENCE
5) What is something that you consider to be really true?	☐ ☐ ☒④ / ☐ ☐ ☐ / ☒ ☐ ☒	PEOPLE GET BACK OUT OF LIFE WHAT THEY PUT IN TO IT
5A) How do you know it's true?	☐ ☐ ☒ / ☐ ☐ ☐ / ☐ ☐ ☐	SEEN IT HAPPEN OVER AND OVER AGAIN.
6) Describe some time that you were in an altered state of consciousness, or some state of consciousness other than your normal state.	☐ ☐ ☐ / ☐ ☐ ☒ / ③☒ ☐	RUSHES OF FEELING / A BODY "TRIP"

Body Description: (weight, tenseness, posture, etc.):
THIN - TIGHT SHOULDERS

Tonality (pitch & tempo): HIGH PITCH, NASAL

Handedness: RIGHT _____ Wear glasses or contacts: YES

Figure 10.3 Researcher's recording template (with thanks to Robert Dilts)

existing experimental literature on eye movement and cognitive mode, quoting Kinsbourne (1972) among many others in his bibliography.

We will talk more about the research into eye accessing cues in Chapter 16.

Application

As mentioned above our coachee will not be aware of the eye movements they make as they tell us their story and how they strive to achieve their objective. By looking at the coachee the NLP coach can calibrate what the coachee is saying to what the eyes and physiology are telling them. Almost invariably an NLP coach will be coaching someone who has come to see them because their unconscious maps of the world are not supporting their conscious endeavours. The difficulty for the coachee is that they are not fully aware of this conflict, neither are they aware of the nature of the conflict. They just know something is stopping them and they do not know what.

During the rapport-building phase of coaching the NLP coach may elicit and test certain patterns within the coachee. So the coachee may talk about being disgusted and display many relevant minimal cues and a certain pattern of eye accessing cues. Then at a later time they may be talking in very glowing terms about their boss, however the same pattern of minimal cues and eye accessing cues momentarily flit across their face and body. This information provides the NLP coach with an understanding of how their client is stepping into a double bind[4] from which they cannot escape. They not only cannot comment upon it, they are not even aware of it. They are simultaneously telling us their boss is a saint and a sinner, and their unconscious map of the world will always win out, leaving their conscious mind non-plussed and desperately seeking a coach.

> This information provides the NLP coach with an understanding of how their client is stepping into a double bind.

As the coach is now aware of the double message it is possible for him to comment upon it and invite their coachee to meta comment, that is make comments about his comments. Using the Meta Model and the Milton Model in conjunction is very powerful in these instances, as when the coachee begins to experience the nature of their double communication they will often go into a light trance. At this time, while observing the eye accessing cues, the coach can use Milton Model language to assist the coachee in exploring the nature of the unconscious map of their boss, which is clearly at odds with their linguistic and conscious map of their boss.

---

[4]A double bind is a situation where a victim is at the mercy of two contradictory messages from different sources. The second source is often more abstract in nature and very difficult to comment upon accurately.

COACHING SESSION 7

A client called Barbara came to see me because she kept bursting into tears unexplainably at work. She said in the coaching that among other things she wished to 'find herself'. At the third session I decided to formally make use of eye accessing cues. I put the exercise into a cognitive frame and suggested that whenever we do anything well we actually make use of *all* of our sensory equipment. Even if we primarily make use of one sensory representational system more than any other, we will still make use of the others at some time during execution of the particular skill. I had noticed that when Barbara thought very deeply she looked down and to her right (kinaesthetic for a right-handed person). However, she never moved from that eye accessing point. I invited her to put her eyes in any other position other than down and to the right and *see* if she could tell me more about herself. Her eyes went up and to the right, however as she spoke her tonality changed and her body seemed to become more tense.

I had discovered that Barbara, after she had her episodes of crying at work, was very good at putting her executive hat back on and performing extremely well in the workplace, which she needed to do as she worked at director level. However, when she did this she often spoke in very visual and auditory predicates and her eye accessing was almost always above the horizontal.

I made my observation available to Barbara and asked her if when she was talking about what she saw in the coaching session she was really commenting upon herself, or doing something else.

This session ended up with a bit of a breakthrough as Barbara believed what she did was to literally make up a visual and auditory story about who was acceptable as a person to her and others. However, this had no relation to the person she was describing when she was representing herself to herself kinaesthetically. She began to realize that what she was doing at work was keeping out of kinaesthetic mode as much as possible, in order to act out a persona who was very vibrant and very efficient, but just was not her.

During later coaching sessions we engaged in sensory overlap, always starting off with Barbara talking about herself using feeling predicates and getting in touch with that person through the use of eye accessing cues, and from that point we would congruently discuss what she saw and what she heard. Barbara said this process was key for her in beginning to really discover who the 'real' her was. She developed the ability to represent herself to herself in all sensory modalities and her crying episodes stopped.

As with many of the NLP variables, making use of any one in isolation without bringing others into play is not possible. As the NLP coach is noticing eye accessing cues they are also attending to so many other aspects of the client's ongoing behaviour. As mentioned above, using Meta Model and Milton Model language is very useful to assist coachees in changing the sub-modalities of their various representations. For example, to a very visual person, 'I can understand you describe your boss as a very big person, however, if you get on a plane and look at him as you take off he gets smaller and smaller until he is almost insignificant; when you land how you represent him to yourself *now* is up to you'. If the coachee is able to represent their boss as smaller and is able to transfer that representation to the context of work, then this can be anchored, and more Milton Model language can effectively future pace it so such a representation can be even more firmly anchored in the context of the work environment. All of our map making is a function of the three universal modelling principles: deletion, distortion and generalization. The key to assisting your coachee get the best out of their life is assisting them represent themselves in the various contexts of their life in such a way that they can elicit confidence in who they are and what they can do. If that means distorting their visual representation of their boss so they are smaller than before, then this is a useful thing to do. The realist will say 'but this distorts reality'; the NLP practitioner will say 'precisely'.

As with so many of the NLP patterns, experimentation and practice are at the heart of success. As this chapter has suggested, eye accessing cues is still highly controversial, and a bit like a good psychometric should not be used as the sole arbiter of information about a coachee. Rather eye accessing cues should be used as an extra tool in the NLP coaching toolkit, to assist in calibration and from there in development of choice for the coachee.

BRAIN TEASERS

1 Having read this chapter what kind of experiment would you have to conduct to provide compelling evidence that the NLP representational model and eye accessing cues are valid? What objections can you imagine sceptics talking to you about after the research? How would you demonstrate that your research had controlled for what they mention?

2 See if you can find out which representation you prefer the most. One way is to think of your favourite sayings; what types of predicates are used in those sayings? Another way is to have a friend time you for 30 seconds at a time while you put your eyes into each of the nine eye accessing positions (see the grid in Figure 10.4). How did you feel in each of those nine positions?

    Write down words to describe your experience after each 30-second encounter. The positions that you found most comfortable and easy to

(Continued)

(Continued)

maintain are possibly representative of your favourite way of representing the world to yourself.

Figure 10.4   Eye accessing grid

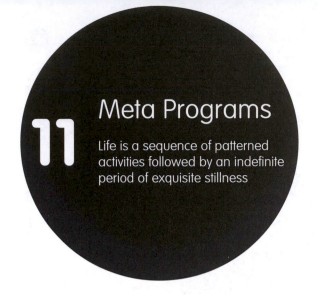

Meta Programs

11

Life is a sequence of patterned activities followed by an indefinite period of exquisite stillness

Meta Programs are the nearest thing NLP has to personality, according to Rodger Bailey, who was the first person to seriously research the idea in the late 1970s and early 1980s and create a system for eliciting which Meta Program is being used by someone in a specific context.

Bailey wanted to develop what he had learned from Leslie Cameron-Bandler and make it into an understandable, learnable and teachable system. Cameron-Bandler taught both Bailey and Ross Stewart to use a questioning grid, so if you use enough slightly varying questions and listen to the responses, you start to recognize what NLP calls Meta Program patterns. Much of 1978–80 was spent by Bailey searching for specific questions which would elicit specific Meta Program patterns. For Bailey the key criteria were whether the skills were learnable and teachable; also whether the eliciting questions and Meta Programs discovered related predictably to specific thinking patterns which led to specific behaviours or not. For instance, he tried out the Meta Model's modal operator of possibility or necessity and discovered they did not seem to be reliably or significantly related to any thinking or behavioural pattern at all. On the other hand asking, 'Why did you choose …?' reliably led to two types of answers: those who would answer the question and give you their criterion (these people use the Meta Program of 'options' in the context of the question) and those who distorted the question into a 'how' question and answered with a story of what happened (these people used the Meta Program of 'procedures' in the context of the question).[1] He developed

> What struck both Bailey and Stewart at the time was the lack of a clear elicitation process to identify the rather vague and diffuse language patterns which Cameron-Bandler and Bandler had named 'Meta Programs'.

---

[1]Options is a Meta Program which means an individual is open to experience. This is to be contrasted with Procedures where individuals enjoy a more planned and organized approach to life. This Meta Program is similar to the perceiving and judging dimensions on the MBTI. As Isabel Briggs Myers says, judging people order their lives and perceptive people just live them (Briggs Myers & Myers, 1980: 8).

the Bio-Data Profile consequently in 1980 followed by the Language and Behaviour Profile (LAB profile) in 1984 (www.labprofile.com).

Tad James and Wyatt Woodsmall (1988: 95), who introduced Anthony Robbins to the idea of Meta Programs, say that the simple Meta Programs of NLP are based largely on Carl Jung's work, as outlined in his book *Psychological types* (1923). This is possibly another one of those areas where there are different stories within NLP. Bailey's work was not based upon type theory, but rather on behaviourally anchored elicitations to specific questions in very specific contexts. What struck both Bailey and Stewart at the time was the lack of a clear elicitation process to identify the rather vague and diffuse language patterns which Cameron-Bandler and Bandler had named 'Meta Programs', possibly after their first usage by John C. Lilly (1967). They found that Meta Programs at that time had not yet been tagged to enough observations to make realistic descriptions of behaviour or thinking patterns. An example of the lengths to which Bailey would go to establish a context can be appreciated as a result of research into shoe shoppers by Bill Huckabee.[2] The researchers know that shoe shoppers are 80 per cent Options about the shoes they shop for and only 20 per cent Options about the store where they buy them. So, these two apparently similar contexts generate very different responses in shoe shoppers depending on what the question is.

Cameron-Bandler first presented Meta Programs at a seminar in Chicago in the context of therapy. As mentioned above Bailey and Stewart then took these 'diffuse set of linguistic observations' and applied them to a business context. In 1987 *PNL-REPERE* was co-founded by Brian van der Horst and granted the first rights to train the LAB profile. Wyatt Woodsmall later (James & Woodsmall, 1988) integrated the Myers Brigg Type Indicator with what he calls the complex Meta Programs noticed by Cameron-Bandler and Bandler and developed a Meta Program questionnaire called the MPVI. In 1991 Edward Reese and Dan Bagley applied Meta Programs to selling and later still Shelle Rose Charvet (1997), who was a student at *PNL-REPERE*, applied Meta Programs to the idea of influencing language.

It was as a result of the work by Bailey and Stewart that the concept of Meta Programs began to become current in NLP literature. In 1986 Anthony Robbins, the NLP popularizer, devoted a chapter to Meta Programs in his bestseller *Unlimited power*, and apart from Bailey's work this seems to be the first mention of the concept of Meta Programs within NLP in published form.

Since those early days in the 1970s and 1980s Meta Programs have become synonymous with NLP. Modern development of Meta Program questionnaires such as Iwam, Thinking styles and Cdaq, are interesting developments. However, the question as to whether they represent the original concept of Meta Programs through their administration protocols is a moot point. The only one of these questionnaires which has been reviewed by a scientific body (British Psychological Society) received a good evaluation of the test materials but

---

[2]Personal communication (email) from Rodger Bailey (22 April 2011).

The forced choice design and scaling in some cases, it could be argued, set up a false dichotomy.

significantly the reviewers made a crucial and salient point. They said that even though the questionnaire derives its rationale from NLP and is based upon the concept of a Meta Program, the user would need a deeper understanding of NLP than the introduction provides to use the instrument effectively within the NLP paradigm. They go on to suggest it could be argued the forced choice design and scaling in some cases set up a false dichotomy. It is exactly this and many other interesting questions that we will raise later in the chapter as we look at how Meta Programs fit into the NLP model of personality.

Theory

Personality will mean something different depending upon who you listen to. Take the definitions of the following psychologists compiled by expert-in-the-field Roy Childs of Team Focus Ltd (TFL, 1997):

BOX 11.1

Carl Rogers: Behaviour is energized by the single, unitary motive of actualization (i.e. enhancing the person).

Sigmund Freud: Behaviour is the dynamic interplay of our biological needs (the id) and our socialization, which creates our values, ethics, norms and attitudes (the super-ego).

Edwin Guthrie: Those habits and habit systems of social importance that are stable and resistant to change.

Gordon Allport: The dynamic organization within the individual of those psychosocial systems that determine their unique adjustments to the environment.

George Kelly: Our unique way of making sense of the world.

Ray Cattell: That which permits prediction of what one will do in a given situation.

Block, Weiss and Thorne: More or less stable internal factors that make one person's behaviour consistent from one time to another and different from the behaviour other people would manifest in comparable situations.

Will Schutz: The person I choose to be at this point in my life to fulfil my needs, both conscious and unconscious.

As you can see from the above, 'personality' definitions range from those of Cattell and Guthrie suggesting a greater degree of stability and therefore also predictability concerning people, to those of such as Schutz who put the individual in charge of their own personality. Here people consistently have *choice* over who they choose to be and how they operate.

NLP most definitely will fall into this 'choice' camp and would agree with the definitions particularly of George Kelly and Will Schutz. However, as a discipline NLP would start off with the language and point out the word 'personality' is a nominalization which, according to the Meta Model, means a lot of information is deleted and distorted as a series of highly complex and dynamic processes are linguistically represented, as though they were a static object or thing which remains constant. For example, 'Oh she has a great *personality*', 'What kind of *personality* do you think he has?', 'Take this questionnaire and it will tell you what your *personality* is', etc.

This is the approach Hall, Bodenhamer, Bolstad and Hamblett (2001: 7) take as they set about de-nominalizing the word personality. They suggest that rather than *having* a personality we *do* personality. Personality is a function of how we sequence our micro and macro behaviours. And how we do that is a function of *choice*. Hall, Bodenhamer, Bolstad and Hamblett (2001: 17) point out we have five basic functions – thinking, emoting, behaving, languaging and relating – and the components of these processes provide us with a starting point to understand personality. As we grow within a social context we learn how to use these basic functions to meet our basic needs.

> 'The person I choose to be at this point in my life to fulfil my needs, both conscious and unconscious.'

The key question is, to what extent during that explosion of learning during the first seven years of our life are our preferences for a particular usage developed irrevocably? Briggs Myers makes it quite clear that type theory, upon which MBTI is based, assumes preference for the 'Meta Programs' is inborn. When she talks about the individual's road to excellence she tells us pressure to convert a child to operate in a way contrary to their natural preference can be a serious hindrance to the development of a person's rightful gifts (Briggs Myers & Myers, 1980: 193). Linder-Pelz (2011: 79) suggests that turning our attention to personality structure (trait) and personality process (cognitive strategy) might help us here. In particular it will help psychologists understand how even within the dimensions of stable traits like the big five,[3] such tremendous cognitive and behavioural diversity manifests itself. However, she recognizes in her research project that at present no systematic study has shown which Meta Programs are malleable, and if they are malleable how that malleability works. It is probably wise to say at the moment that we do not know the answer to these questions. The NLP position is having choice in any situation is better than having no choice, and it is a more useful belief to think that you own your 'personality', compared with the belief that your 'personality' owns you.

---

[3]Five high-order factors are believed to explain all other lower-order factors of personality by some psychologists. These factors are: Openness, Conscientiousness, Extraversion, Agreeableness and Neuroticism (OCEAN).

The NLP Model of Meta Program and Personality

Leslie Cameron-Bandler and Richard Bandler were very interested in the question of how it can be that an individual could have exactly the same sequence of sensory experience and yet have widely varying experiences and display widely differing behaviours as a consequence. What they were finding out was that NLP did not work, in its current form. Meta Programs came out of the realization that if people are using the same sensory strategy and getting different experiences then there must be something at a higher (or Meta) level acting upon the sensory strategy to explain the differences in behavioural output. Just as all the books ever written in the English language are a function of the same 26 letters and basic application of lexical meaning, syntax, semantics and pragmatics, so too at the heart of NLP are our basic sensory representations, but there must also be the 'rules' of how these are put together and applied to manufacture experience, and these rules are 'Meta' to the sensory experience itself. Initially experience was regarded as the systematic ordering of sensory representations. Typical of NLP is to have its cake and eat it; not only are these sensory representations anchored together (behaviourist psychology), but the content of behaviours is also compiled using the TOTE paradigm of Miller, Galanter and Pribram (1960) (cognitive psychology). So in Figure 11.1 you can see typical early NLP notations for correctly spelling a word. The decision point within the sequencing of sensory representations is essential because different values (sub-modalities) of the representation which is the decision point will determine what happens next. For example, in terms of influencing, if you knew the strategy for spelling below was the one an individual used, the decision point is K. If you emphasize the good feelings (K^+) and encouraged deletion of any negative feelings (K^-), there is a greater chance that speller will accept that visual representation as correct, irrespective of what they are actually seeing. Early NLPers found the TOTE representation (Figure 11.1b) a bit cumbersome so the shorter one (Figure 11.1a) eventually became common practice. This is known as the four tuple and represents the belief that any experience must be composed of a combination of these primary representations: V – visual, A – auditory, K – kinaesthetic, O – olfactory/gustatory.

> The decision point within the sequencing of sensory representations is essential because different values of the representation which is the decision point will determine what happens next.

NLP Notation for Sequences of Representations and the TOTE Model

At this time in NLP it was recognized that consciousness is an emergent property of our unconscious systemic ordering. Because of the famous 7 plus or minus 2

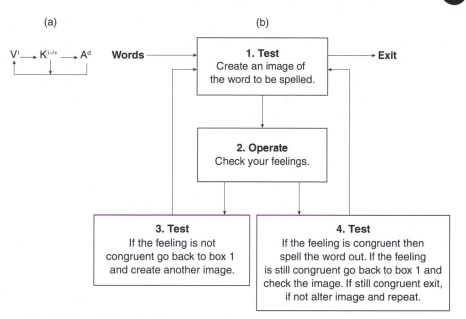

(a)

(b)

$$V^i \rightarrow K^{i-/+} \rightarrow A^d$$

Words ⟶ **1. Test** Create an image of the word to be spelled. ⟶ **Exit**

2. Operate Check your feelings.

3. Test If the feeling is not congruent go back to box 1 and create another image.

4. Test If the feeling is congruent then spell the word out. If the feeling is still congruent go back to box 1 and check the image. If still congruent exit, if not alter image and repeat.

Figure 11.1a & 11.1b   NLP notation for sequences of representations (11.1a) and the TOTE model (11.b)

of George Miller[4] who helped create the TOTE model, it was recognized NLP needed an R operator. An R operator refers to the part of the four tuple at any point in time which has a greater signal level and consequently breaks through into consciousness. Difficulty in communication – and therefore life – occurs when the recipient picks up on only one part of the communication (four tuple), and takes this to represent the *whole* communication. If my wife says to me that was a great meal darling, as she gives half of it to the dog, I might delete the auditory message and focus on the visual message, and get upset. The answer in the early NLP days was to inculcate the C operator. This means that every part of a four tuple in communication at any point in time represents exactly the same message. In this case it does not matter which signal is picked up by the R operator of the recipient as all representations are communicating the same message. The same principle applies to the communicator. Often they may be aware of only *one part* of the message they are communicating (R operator) and the recipient picks up on the other parts of the communication of which they have no consciousness at all. Their belief then is something like, 'He has no clue as to what I am trying to say'. Thus the NLP presupposition: the meaning of your communication is the response you receive.

In talking about NLP in the first textbook (Dilts, Grinder, Bandler & DeLozier, 1980: 7) the authors unwittingly stumbled upon the first Meta Program without mention of the concept 'Meta Program' anywhere in the volume. They talk about all outcomes being a function of environmental

---

[4]George Miller published a paper in 1955 providing evidence of why the human working memory only has the capacity to hold and work with 5–9 bits of information.

variables (outside of your control) and decision variables (in your control). One of the ways in which people consistently misuse their internal sensory representations is to represent them as an environmental variable. NLP coaching is about helping people along this well-known variable of locus of control[5] to understand that they in fact have great control over their personal sensory representations and therefore also their experience and thinking.

We can imagine the way such a Meta Program, in conjunction with others, could affect the thinking and behaviour of two people with the following strategy for completing a jigsaw: $V^{i+} - K^{e+} - A^{i+} - K^{i+} - K^{e+}$.

Both clients build an internal positive visual representation: V^{i+}. They then start putting the jigsaw together and enjoy the experience: K^{e+}. They then say something to themselves which is perceived as positive: A^{i+}. And they both finish feeling good: K^{i+}. The only difference is that one has completed the jigsaw and the other has not: K^{e+}.

One of our clients has a Meta Program of 'external locus of control', in which they approach the task of visualizing a holiday. They do this because they 'know' they can't do jigsaws. They have tried so many times and failed, so they just 'play' at putting it together and quite enjoy the experience. They then start talking to themselves and planning their holiday in their head which helps them pass the time and is very enjoyable. They finally finish their task with a happy smile on their face because they are now closer to going on their holiday and the jigsaw pieces have been arranged in the shape of Tenerife.

> One of the ways in which people consistently misuse their internal sensory representations is to represent them as an environmental variable.

The other client visualizes the completed jigsaw and feels confident. They then start putting it together and because they know they can do this they enjoy developing an internal auditory strategy to motivate them when they find a piece that fits but also when they find a piece that does not fit. They finally finish and feel good because they have completed the jigsaw.

Now clearly there are points along these two sensory strategies where Meta operations are occurring. We have already discussed decision points where individuals make a decision on the basis of the value and signal strength of a sensory representation. In this case there are no decision points but we can see generalizations are being made right at the beginning of the four tuple. These are in the form of a belief: 'I cannot do this jigsaw' compared with 'I can do this jigsaw'. This immediately determines the content of the internal visual and the strategy of each individual. Let us suppose these different beliefs are a function of the Meta Program, 'locus of control'. In other words, in the context

---

[5]Locus of control is a well-known psychological variable developed by Rotter (1954). Generally people who have an internal locus of control believe they can influence events, and their own actions determine the rewards they get. People with an external locus of control do not have these beliefs and think what they do does not matter much and any rewards are generally outside of their control. Lefcourt (1976) relates the concept to learned helplessness.

of any novel task the first client could genuinely have a belief they cannot use their powers of thinking, emoting, behaving, speaking and relating, to develop a strategy to succeed or even partially succeed, and they consistently use these internal and external powers to divert their attention away from the task in hand. If this becomes a habit then this person may become the type of person who hates change and always wants things to stay the same (Sameness versus Difference NLP Meta Program). Another Meta Program that could be operating is that of criteria. For one client it is possible they hate jigsaws whereas the other person loves them. One can also imagine that for one person the David McClelland[6] Meta Program of achievement and affiliation could be operating too. Our client who completes the jigsaw could be high on the achievement scale but low on affiliation; the client who is looking forward to their holiday could be very high on affiliation and very low on achievement. What is really important in the traditional NLP notation is not just what representation there is, but what is going on in the move from one representation to another and how the representation is created in the first place.

> In NLP we *do* personality, we do not *have* a personality. Just as we do not *have* values, we *do* values.

In NLP we *do* personality, we do not *have* a personality. Similarly we do not *have* values, we *do* values. There is a simple formula for you to follow to make this work:

1 Get a very clear representation of your outcome. Is this representation **S**pecific? **M**easurable? **A**chievable? Appropriate **C**hunk size? Has a **T**ime frame? **E**cological? **P**ositive? **P**reserves all that you currently value? Do you have **O**wnership of the outcome? Are you **M**otivated to achieve it? Can you congruently **F**uture pace it? (SMACTEPPOMF) (Grimley, 2008).

2 Ask yourself this question: 'Can I achieve all I want to as represented in my outcome with my present personality?'

3 If the answer is yes, take your first steps and enjoy successful completion of your outcome within your time frame.

4 If the answer is no, find out what has to change, make the alteration and then recycle the strategy.

The better you get at setting clear objectives for yourself as in stage 1 above, and the better you get at NLP, the more you will realize you own your personality and your personality does not own you. My inelegant SMACTEPPOMF acronym was presented to the First European Coaching Psychology conference in 2008 by myself and Dr Ho Law. I often find when coaching clients the 'hard' work is in obtaining the well-formed outcome by putting a tick after each of the question marks at stage 1. When that stage is congruently achieved

---

[6]David McClelland (1961) developed a motivational theory where some are motivated by seeking out realistic goals to achieve ($N^{achievement}$), others by friendly relations ($N^{affiliation}$), and others by being influential, making an impact and having their ideas prevail (N^{power}).

minimal coaching is required afterwards, as a self-fulfilling prophecy has been set up and the coachee is systemically and phenomenologically primed to achieve what they wish.

From a psychology perspective the key difficulty is, 'Where is the science behind this?' What characterized Rodger Bailey's approach to Meta Programs was two years of painstaking work to find which questions would elicit Meta Programs in specific contexts. After thousands of elicitations Bailey is confident that the structure and the context identified in the question are absolutely crucial. Even though his data during the late 1970s was not gathered in appropriate ways for academic publication, Rose Charvet (1997) has published two MSc research abstracts which have provided evidence of good inter-rater reliability and significant differences along eight LAB profile categories between students who could make career decisions they were comfortable with (N = 41) and those who could not (N = 20).

Getting Back to Basics

In the introduction to this book I suggested NLP as a paradigm sat squarely on the anti-positivist spectrum of epistemology. Personality questionnaires that suggest you can *predict* an individual's behaviour on the basis of a score along dimensions on a questionnaire clearly fall on the positivist side of this dichotomy.

Both Robert Dilts (Dilts, 1990: 137) and Rodger Bailey see Meta Programs not so much as programs but rather as a set of dimensions which creates a contextual space that gives people the resourcefulness *to use* their primary sensory experience in such a way that they develop both choice and flexibility of behaviour. Figure 11.2 shows such a space created by Dilts (1990: 138) and often used in NLP workshops under the name of 'jungle gym'. Even though logical levels, time orientation and perceptual position are not regarded as Meta Programs in NLP, from a process perspective they are exactly that. One could create such a contextual space with the 51 Meta Programs identified by Hall, Bodenhamer and Min (2003). As I have suggested, psychologists could lay claim to a host of other Meta Programs from the psychology literature as James and Woodsmall (1988) have done. One could then apply such a Gestalt to many different contexts and find that the phenomenological representation for each person will change. This awareness puts the coachee in control of their 'personality'. Hall (2011c) sees such static representations, however, as somewhat problematical, in that they are too rigid. His preference is to use the metaphor of such energy forms as tornados which spiral dynamically up and down, creating energy wells, never staying the same. In fact the two co-founders of NLP do not make use of Meta Programs in their NLP work, which raises the question of their legitimacy within NLP in the first place. We will discuss this further in Chapter 13 when we talk about systems theory and cybernetics.

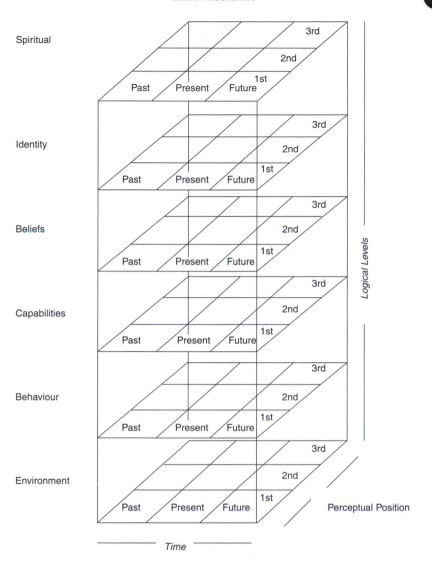

Figure 11.2 Jungle gym

What is key about this NLP model is that it helps us realize why the British Psychological Society reviewers suggested, in a modern Meta Program questionnaire, that the forced choice design and scaling in some cases set up a false dichotomy. When faced with a question about our thinking, feeling, behaving, languaging and relating the usual response is, 'It depends'. What it depends upon of course is the context. In different contexts there are different triggers which are associated with different patterns of sensory representation housed somewhere within a Gestalt of Meta Programs, which in turn lead to different emotional states. These emotional states lead to the habituated cognitive patterns which of course cognitive psychologists work with. Do you remember Bill Huckabee's shoe shoppers? Deciding what shoe you are going to purchase activates a totally different set of meaning-making processes compared to deciding where you are going to buy them.

> The NLP model attempts to describe the full range of personality traits, including the emotional response.

The NLP model attempts to describe the full range of personality traits, including the emotional response which is generated through an interaction of sensory representations, the Gestalt of Meta Programs, as well as habitual adjustments. For the NLP model emotional state is at the heart of personality, for the cognitions you habitually run and become conscious of are dependent upon the emotional state you instantaneously access in any given context. In NLP coaching to try to change dysfunctional thinking without previously addressing dysfunctional feeling is truly to put the cart before the horse. If context is king then emotional state is certainly queen. The feeling we have at any point in time and in any context is a function of the patterning of sensory representation and the unconscious cognitive Gestalt that sensory ordering finds itself in. It is almost a primitive kind of Thalamic self-speak, however we cannot hear ourselves as it is all over in 1/10th of a second and we are experiencing a feeling … and we don't know why. The art of NLP coaching is about learning how to calibrate and elicit what goes on in that gap of 1/10th second. Knowing what constellations of Meta Programs are operating is a part of that process. This is where the leverage is; after that, it is all over and dusted, and after that all we have is consolidation and rationalization. Some people spend their whole lives justifying why they are right, and, while they are right of course, no change will occur … why should it? As the cognitive dissonance paradigm of Festinger (1957) suggests, humans are more rationalizing than rational and it is for this reason 'personality' has the illusion of being permanent. It is, but it need not be (Grimley, 2005).

When we ask intelligent questions about our emotional state we can begin to get inside that 1/10th of a second gap. When we are in that gap we can then model our emotional state and understand how we have created a map of the world that is no longer useful. Clean Language, a coaching model we will look at in Chapter 14, has this type of questioning at its heart as it explores the metaphorical landscapes painted by the coachee. In the very first NLP textbook (Dilts, Grinder, Bandler & DeLozier, 1980: 63) there is a coaching example of how a map of the world was created at three years old. At eight years old and at 15 years old and in the ongoing experience the K^i (internal feelings) were exactly the same, however the other sensory representations at the different time points were different (Figure 11.3). The verbal label for this K^i was jealousy. As the linguistic representation for 'jealousy' was explored and experienced at different times, this triggered ('anchored up') the other representations and thus the map was textured differently. This process stopped when the coachee recalled screaming because he did not want his mother and father to leave him with a babysitter. With access to this initial model at three years old, state-dependent memory made it quite straightforward to model the strategy

$$< A_n, V_n, K_1, O_n > \qquad \text{Ongoing experience } (K_1 = \text{Jealousy})$$

$$< A_3, V_3, K_1, O_3 > \text{ Age 15}$$

$$< A_2, V_2, K_1, O_2 > \text{ Age 8}$$

$$< A_1, V_1, K_1, O_1 > \text{ Age 3 – Original experience } (K_1 = \text{Jealousy})$$

Figure 11.3   The affect bridge

for being 'jealous' and then modify it so it was no longer a problem. Many psychotherapists will recognize this strategy as the 'affect bridge'.

One of the great utilities of Meta Programs is the appreciation that we are always communicating in any one instance from *our own Meta Program*. We cannot at any point in time do both Meta Programs together. It is because people do not realize this that they develop blind spots and cannot appreciate the key moments when they lose sight of what they are trying to achieve and drop the ball, so to speak. (Remember the R operator?) In terms of using the TOTE model in NLP coaching, it is key that your coachee develops an awareness of when this happens, so they can change their *Operation* in order to ensure the next *Test* takes them closer to their outcome. Too often coachees only change the language or behaviour, and do not change the Meta Program they are operating from. They then get frustrated because they attract the same negative response from their environment. They do not understand that the changes they are making are at too superficial a level; they need to move to the deeper and more abstract level that encompasses and frames their behaviour and language, as this is the level of Meta Program.

Think of the following scenarios:

1   A person who is normally 'options' and is open to the experience of not being treated at all well in the workplace, all of a sudden finds she has had enough and, charged with high emotion, switches to 'procedures' and becomes incredibly rigid and intolerant of other people's views, and alienates everybody.

2   A 'small chunk' person who is passionate about her product pitches to a consortium full of 'large chunk' investors. They ask her from a large chunk perspective about the market place, her vision for the product, competitive advantage and price points. She feels totally lost and does not get the investment.

3   An 'away from' person who complains that she has no motivation in her life, feels too comfortable and that there are no challenges left for her. She refuses to engage in goal-setting exercises because she regards them as superficial and contrived, but still insists on complaining about having no motivation in life.

If each of these three people could step back and look at the 'space' or 'Gestalt' from which they are relating, they would see their results occur because of operating from an inappropriate Meta Program. This is because at a higher logical level the communication is working against the individual's outcome. If number 1 could assert herself more in the first place and 'put some rules' in place she would not get to explosion point. If number 2 could see that she is signed off at small chunk level whereas what the investors want is an appreciation of the future and large chunk possibilities, rapport would then be established and investment would be forthcoming. If number 3 could appreciate that the reason she has no motivation is that she is working perfectly. This is because she is far removed from any danger; there is no need to be motivated, as she is operating from an 'away from' Meta Program. In this context elicitation of times in her personal history of when she used a 'towards' Meta Program would be useful. Once elicited the 'towards' map could be modelled and then used to help her generate a motivating goal in the present. This would help her become excited by moving towards something and solve her problem.

If we could appreciate the power of recognizing at any point in time the Meta Programs we are operating from and ascertain whether or not they are fit for the purpose of achieving our outcomes, life for all of us would be delightful, as it should be (modal operator of necessity!)[7]

COACHING SESSION 8

Bill referred himself to me because he was having difficulties in relationships which were effecting his performance at work considerably. He could not make up his mind whether to commit or not to one or the other of two partners. As a framework for the coaching session I suggested first of all the coachee establish in his mind what his outcome was concerning a relationship and a partner. Having established this I asked him to fill in a Meta Program questionnaire which looked at 9 Meta Programs with 14 items for each of them (126 items in total). Armed with this information and an education concerning the concept of Meta Programs we set about 'typing' the two partners in the context of a relationship. This exercise uncovered many blind spots for Bill. Firstly, he discovered he was operating from an 'away from' and externally referenced Meta Program in this context. What this meant practically was he was not sure what he really … really wanted in a relationship and being externally referenced he was being run ragged by both partners, complying with as many of their requests as possible. He also found that the nature of attraction for him was very different. For one partner he discovered it was a case of opposites attract, and in the other it was a case of birds of a feather flock together. He was very high on the feelings Meta Program and while operating from this he recognized he found it very difficult to make

(Continued)

---

[7]If you do not know the relevance of the words in brackets re-read Chapter 6 on the Meta Model.

(Continued)

any decisions which could be perceived as 'rocking the boat'. This paralyzed him to a great extent. He never took any decisive action in the context of 'relationship' because he did not wish to 'hurt feelings'. Interestingly when looking at the procedures/option Meta Program results Bill was more or less in the middle. I asked him about this and he said that at work he was very procedural, however he recognized in the context of these relationships he was very options-led. Another Meta Program where this dynamic was demonstrated was proactive/reactive. At work Bill was proactive, however in personal relationships he was reactive. We used this information to model someone who Bill felt would be useful to him in this context. Such a person was someone who was towards being internally referenced, proactive and procedural. He felt that to become thinking would be to alienate the partner who he would finally decide to settle with. He also felt he would need to texture the procedural and the proactive with some options and reactivity in order to allow for flexibility in the relationship. Over three coaching sessions Bill started behaving and talking 'as if' he was this person. He found it much easier to make his decision and settle down. The five coaching sessions did not act as a magic bullet. However, what they did was allow Bill to make a decision, be happy with that decision and concentrate on his work so as to return to his previous good levels of performance.

As the theme of this book suggests, NLP is about techniques, but it is more about the attitude and skill of the practitioner as they make use of those techniques. NLP is anti-positivist in nature and therefore each coachee who comes to see us is regarded as a unique coachee with a personal history. This means we need to use our NLP skills to listen and observe before we start applying. The coach will also need to be aware of the Meta Program they operate from within a coaching context and consistently monitor this to ensure it is appropriate. Noticing the Meta Programs the coachee operates from and matching them will expedite rapport and effective communication. The NLP coach will also need to appreciate that the Meta Program the coachee runs is not consistent across contexts. In those contexts where the coachee appears to be stuck because they identify too strongly with their Meta Program, the NLP coach can work so the coachee begins to experience the flexibility possible at the deeper levels of their neurology. This means that change within a context which was thought not possible due to the 'barrier' of personality, now becomes possible.

The originators of NLP do not use Meta Programs in their work to any great extent. They are regarded as *content* models, whereas NLP is a *process* model. However, this is not the case to my way of thinking. Meta Programs are created as a consequence of an interaction between biology and experience. Einstein tells us that the only way *process* can get its meaning (i.e. *content*), is by association with sense experience (Schilpp, 1979). Our sensory experiences in those first seven years of life help create and consolidate our Meta Programs which are unconscious processes. It is only when we allow these processes to become rigid that they act as environmental variables. It is only when we buy into this cult of the personality that we find ourselves not being able to make the simple changes needed in any context to move quickly towards our outcomes.

BRAIN TEASERS

1 Look at the list of Meta Programs in Appendix 1 (Rose Charvet, 1997). Make a list of which Meta Program you run at home and which Meta Program you run when you are at work. Think of a specific activity in those contexts if that makes the exercise easier. Do you run different Meta Programs? Why do you think that is?

2 Some Meta Programs seem to be more resistant to change than others (remember the Garcia effect?). Again using Appendix 1, which, if any, of the Meta Programs do you think you tend to use irrespective of the context? Conversely, with which Meta Program do you think you feel quite confident and comfortable, at either end of the continuum depending upon the context? Why do you think you have flexibility for one Meta Program, but not the other?

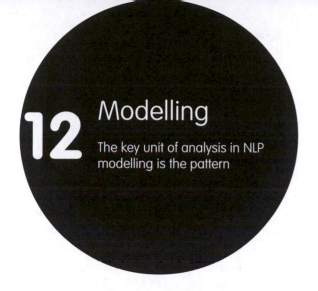

12 Modelling

The key unit of analysis in NLP modelling is the pattern

Over and over you will hear *modelling* is the core discipline in NLP. Yet there is not much modelling being done. From what has been done in the 40 years that NLP has existed, only anecdotal evidence is available. This would apply also to work that has been written up. There is no published work to my knowledge which has robustly defined excellence, modelled it, coded the model in a format that means such excellence can be transferred to others in a training environment, and then tested the efficacy of that code by developing a valid instrument or protocol to take a base measure, an experimental measure and a longitudinal measure to test for reliability of transfer. Gordon and Dawes (2005) and Dilts (1998) have written up their modelling projects in book form, however the writing up is a far cry from the above, and certainly does not provide the robust evidence which would be needed to validate a model. As mentioned in the Introduction, Tosey and Mathison (2009: 143) tell us there is no substantive support for NLP, and they tell us again that the evidence for modelling is largely anecdotal (Tosey & Mathison, 2009: 17).

Modelling is the way we acquire our maps of the world during the first seven years of our life. Jean Piaget described the stages of child development and suggested, as a result of experimental research, that it is not until age 7 that a child can de-centre and critique their model of the world, or fully appreciate another person's perspective. Until that time ego-centrism is the norm and the child is fully associated (1st perceptual position) into their model of the world. Gradually, as the child grows and develops cognitively, they can represent what they have learned at a sensory level at a cognitive level. Children can now manipulate their models *independently* of the sensory referents in the world from which they were derived. Internal logic, as well as external sensory experimentation, is now an extra tool. From 12 years onwards, the child can now act in the world on the basis of a formal set of mental operations, or maps of the world. It is the consolidation of these maps through rationalization which represents the problem. At the sensory stage of development, if something did not work, the child had no option but to either burst into tears until help came or

As soon as we develop the ability to represent our sensory experience through language we develop the ability to defend substandard behaviour through private logic.

find another way of solving the problem. Whichever option the child took, the behavioural consequence was they moved closer to their goal. After the stage when abstract maps of the world are consolidated and used as the basis for our behaviour, rather than change our maps of the world when we do not move towards our outcome, we use language and reason to defend our abstract models of the world. As mentioned in Chapter 7, rather than change our behaviour when we do not get what we want, in order to reduce the dissonance created by 'failure', we change our attitude and language. We create reasons pre-consciously and consciously to support the unconscious sensory maps and associated Meta Programs to help us feel 'right' and 'good'. In terms of the APET model we change our thinking, but we do not change the sensory patterning and associated beliefs that create the behaviour and emotional response. Eventually we develop cognitive strategies for feeling good about underachievement and successfully acquire excellence in being mediocre at the very best. Excuses and blaming others often become the norm in such a culture as people see true learning cultures exponentially storm ahead in the race for continual development and innovation so as to raise the bar.

As soon as we develop the ability to represent our sensory experience through language, we develop the ability to defend substandard behaviour through private logic. The cigarette smoker, rather than give up, will recount endlessly the story of their aunt who lived until 108 and smoked 40 a day. They will cite research which shows how cigarette smoking improves concentration. This ritual helps them justify and keep in place a model of the world which is probably not very healthy. Of course, the appropriate model is one that generates smoking-free behaviour. However, a lack of behavioural choice in this context means that something else has to change and, as discussed previously, what changes is not the unconscious sensory pattern but the attitude and thinking. Our personal and collective models are so important that we go to war when other people disagree with them, while some are prepared to commit murder over them, and some of us literally change colour with rage when our model of the world is criticized as inadequate. In professional circles, colleagues who work from a different model of the world are chastened and 'cut off'. However, this same obsession which can create so much misery has also developed models which have taken us from caveman to twenty-first-century masters of the known universe. This ability to notice similarities and differences, causes and effects, has allowed us to make models, meaning we can now predict, travel, build, communicate, paint, draw, compose and create in a way no other animal can. Not only can we do this, but we can pass on our discoveries and models to future generations so they can build upon what we have done. However, these models have been tested in a scientific way and this is something we will discover in Chapter 16 is sadly lacking with the NLP models.

In the coaching environment the reason we find a coachee at our door is always the same. At a conscious level (1), they know what they want. They try to improve by developing area (2), which is the area where they know they need to develop and lack skill or

These models have been tested in a scientific way …

information. However, everything at these conscious (cognitive) levels is held in place by an unconscious (emotional/cognitive) map of the world which operates at a different level of consciousness and according to different rules (3). The more the coachee operates at levels 1 and 2, the more 3 is reinforced, thus the more change occurs the more things stay the same.

1. What we know we know.
2. What we know we don't know.
3. What we don't know we don't know.

Some CBC models of coaching assume that if we make better strategic use of what we know (**1**) we will improve. This is a type of single loop learning. Other cognitive models suggest changing our thinking at level (**2**) and developing in areas where we are ignorant leads to more profound change. This is double loop learning. However, learning in these areas is sometimes limited, and often not sufficient to provide the coachee with what they want. At level (**3**), which is by far the greatest area, we see that change here leads to transformation of the whole system.

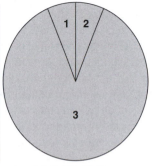

Coaching Session 9 shows how a coachee was so associated into their unconscious (**3**) model for 'failure' the only conscious option for improvement was to do more of the same. In this way they made themselves even worse.

Figure 12.1   Differing levels of consciousness

COACHING SESSION 9

John wanted to feel relaxed during a panel interview. He complained that in every interview he had done previously he tensed up, forgot his 'best' lines and generally felt terrible. During the initial sessions I discovered he was operating from a small chunk and away from Meta Program. I also discovered beliefs which supported such cognitive and behavioural operations originated from his father and secondary school education where he was continually told not to make mistakes and pay attention to detail. The coachee also discovered that any thought of the coming panel interview was anchored to this 'model' which had high anxiety attached to it and insisted on attention to detail and avoidance of mistakes. John could not appreciate the only model of the world he had in the context of presenting his work and himself was governed by a small chunk, away from orientation, which generated anxiety. He spent a lot of time talking about the merits of paying attention to detail and not

(Continued)

(Continued)

making mistakes. Consequently he would rigorously spend many hours planning everything out. Because John attempted to improve by paying even more attention to detail, and generating as many possible mistakes so as to develop strategies to avoid them, he developed a blind spot. He could not appreciate a change at a different level would be more appropriate. He literally did not know what he did not know. What John had been doing was making himself even more anxious by using a model generated in the past which had not been very useful. By finding within John's personal history where he was highly successful and modelling that, we both discovered a naturally occurring secondary model where John presented himself at a process level operating from a large chunk and towards Meta Program. John found this model was generated when he used to play with his grandparents. He recollected in those contexts he was always encouraged to follow his dreams and think big thoughts. He was told over and over again he could do anything he set his mind to and as he recollected the model developed in that context he remembered he was relaxed, outgoing, confident and happy. Milton Model language was used to assist John to appreciate that presenting his ideas professionally and presenting his ideas to his grandparents in play was a similar process. During the coaching session the old model which generated anxiety and the other model which generated vision and excitement were considered and spatially situated in each hand out in front of John. John considered the pros and cons of each model and was also aware of the different emotional state each model generated. Using more Milton Model language John was encouraged to trust in his unconscious ability to take the best from both models to develop just the right model for presenting himself and his work to the panel during the following week. Milton Model language suggested that the more he moved towards a model that would work perfectly for him the more his hands would come together. John was very surprised at how this process seemed to work automatically and his 'hands were moving by themselves'. Afterwards John felt very relaxed and very excited. John imagined himself using this new model to listen and talk to the panel interviewers and he said he felt confident, grounded and excited. John phoned me the next week to say thank you and that the panel interview had gone even better than he had hoped for.

We can see from the above coaching session that when we discover the appropriate model from which to operate and consequently generate a powerful positive emotional state, the language and behaviour generated are seamless and authentic. However, if that natural language and behaviour are used within the context of a different unconscious model they appear contrived and artificial. If 'John' had managed to develop the language and behaviour he did, but only at a conscious level (1 and 2), then used such language and behaviour in the context of a small chunk and away from Meta Program (3) he would have communicated an internal inconsistency which would have concerned both 'John' and the panel interviewers. Because 'John' generated

> We all have the cognitive, affective and behavioural resources to succeed and within our personal history we can often generate examples of such excellence.

his own new model from his personal history and could authentically operate from a totally different set of Meta Programs (3) he communicated in an authentic way. NLP believes we all have the cognitive, affective and behavioural resources to succeed and within our personal history we can often generate examples of such excellence.

Theory and Practice

I have put theory and practice together in this chapter because a part of the theory is that in your life you must practice – NLP modelling is not an academic or intellectual discipline, it is a practical one based on utility. Timothy Gallwey (1986) of Inner Game fame made the point that if you can just shut off your internal dialogue and pay attention to your performance, compare this with your outcome, and then calmly allow your unconscious to make the appropriate adjustment, you do not need to read any further in his book (1975: 24).

The four pillars of NLP are:

1 Having a well-formed outcome.
2 Having the acuity to notice what your present model of the world is providing for you.
3 Having the flexibility to change your behaviour when you notice what you are getting is not taking you to your well-formed outcome.
4 Retaining a positive and energetic emotional state.

If you can access a state where you can suspend all judgement and habitually recycle the above, don't bother reading the rest of this book. You have all you need to achieve anything you wish. A lot of NLP is about learning to forget so much of what we have learned. This is because it is interference. It interferes with what the unconscious mind *knows* it can do with the utmost ease. The Nike strap line, Just Do It, harnesses this intuition. The unconscious mind knows it can perform, however, as soon as we begin to take that first behavioural step to change our life for the better, a piece of internal dialogue pops up and provides a reason why we should not, or why we can't. Milton Erickson knew this and this is why distracting the conscious mind is a key component to using the Milton Model.

The discovery of mirror neurons by Rizzolatti, Fogassi and Gallese in the early 1990s showed there is a distinct set of neurons which fire both when an action is performed and when it is only observed (Mathison, 2007). The neurological mechanisms whereby we understand the complexities and skills of people through non-cognitive/rational pathways and just through observation are only just beginning to be uncovered. However, the obvious question to those who realize life is not a rehearsal is why wait until we can consciously understand before making use of the principles which are readily available to us now? Rizzolatti and his colleagues suggest that this discovery implies that whenever a human generates an action they also produce a sensory copy of the action. This supports the simple four-step model above whereby we compare the sensory components of our well-formed outcome with our present behaviour and notice the difference and make the adjustment.

As mentioned in Chapter 4, modelling as a discipline for learning came from Alfred Bandura (Gross, 1987: 70) and social learning theory. The five essential components were:

- The learner must attend to the pertinent clues in the stimulus situation and ignore incidentals which do not affect the performance of the behaviour which they seek to learn.
- They must record in memory a sensory-based or semantic code for the modelled behaviour for storage purposes.
- Rehearsal of this stored memory is important.
- The learner has to reproduce the motor activities accurately. This will involve as many trials as needed in order to get the 'muscular feel' of the behaviour through feedback.
- The learner must value the consequences related to that behaviour in order to learn through modelling.

When we look at John Grinder's formulation of NLP modelling we can see striking similarities:

- Identify an appropriate model/exemplar.
- Adopt a 'know nothing' state and suspend all of your cognitive filters. Attend only to sensory patterns. This is known as unconscious uptake.
- Carry out a rehearsal of the assimilated pattern until one can match the performance of the exemplar within the same time frame and context and produce the same results. Until this can be done behaviourally one continues with stage 2 and loops back to stage 3 until this can be achieved.
- Code the assimilated pattern and the pattern within the exemplar. Within NLP this is still regarded as an art. According to John Grinder there is no known useful and explicit strategy for digitalizing analogue processes (Bostic St Clair & Grinder, 2001: 146).
- Test the coded pattern by training interested learners in it. Do they achieve the same mastery as measured by behavioural outcomes within the same time frame and context as the exemplar?

It is understandable that many NLP practitioners develop skills for their personal use within a particular context through modelling, then stop at that stage. However, the challenge for NLP is to determine how to code and then transfer these patterns to other people who have not had exposure to the original exemplar. Also, how do you assess that improvement has taken place in the modeller, let alone those they train in the model? It is these activities which could transform NLP from a pop psychology to a unique scientific activity. This is because it differentiates NLP from other activities in the sense that it explicitly puts modelling at the centre of its methodology, and because it is then open for such models to be scientifically tested and differentiated from other competing psychological models.

The key unit of analysis in NLP modelling is the 'pattern'.

What is a Model?

The key unit of analysis in NLP modelling is the 'pattern'. When you notice a pattern you can predict perfectly what will happen given just one portion of the pattern. For example, you may notice that whenever your son or daughter pays attention to what you say and demonstrates this through appropriate language and behaviour, within 10 minutes of first demonstrating this behaviour they will always ask you for some money.

The NLP coach will describe ordering of the pattern using *sensory*-based language. They will describe what will happen as a consequence of the congruent application of such ordering, again using sensory-based language, and they will finally describe the context in which the pattern operates. In the example above, it may well be that paying attention to parents is only followed by a request for money in the context of the son or daughter having less than £50 readily available or in the wonderful context when the son or daughter are genuinely interested in what their parents have to say.

A model is usually a collection of patterns and needs to be differentiated from a replica in that a model of something is always a *reduced* representation of more complex behaviours at the source. The purpose of such reduction is to increase elegance and ease of learning for the person wishing to learn the model. This is very similar to Malcom Gladwell's concept of thin slicing (2005: 23). He describes this as the ability of our unconscious to find patterns in complex situations based on very narrow slices of information. For example, Gladwell talks of marriage and how John Gottman can predict with 95 per cent accuracy whether a couple will be married 15 years later on the basis of looking at a 15-minute tape; this is compared with experts who do little better than chance at 58 per cent. Gottman is successful because he has an effective model and has learned to focus on what is relevant. For example, if there is a ratio of positive to negative emotion which is less than 5:1 there will be difficulty in a relationship. The four Horsemen (of the apocalypse) within intimate relationships are defensiveness, stonewalling, criticism and contempt, and within this group contempt is the one which has the most leverage in undoing a relationship. When listening to a couple, professionals will have all types of implicit models and consequently will focus on and attend to a vast array of material. John Gottman, however, looks and listens for just five process variables and consequently outperforms all the professionals – which is very much a case of less is more.

A model is also different from a theory in that the only criterion for a good NLP model is: does the learner display within the same time frame the same quality of results as the exemplar? John Gottman, for instance, has produced a Paul Ekman[1]

[1]Paul Ekman modelled Silvan Tompkins who had the amazing ability to read faces. Ekman developed a taxonomy of facial expressions. He identified 43 action units (distinct facial movements). Over seven years he then studied combinations of these action units. For example, using combinations of just five facial muscles he identified over 10,000 visible facial configurations. This taxonomy was called FACS (facial action coding system).

> NLP is a very practical psychology and, simply put, it is about helping a client find and install the appropriate models so they can effortlessly achieve their outcomes.

like coding system so learners can transcribe a 15-minute encounter between husband and wife into digital information and thus make predictions. These learners are as good as Gottman in outperforming professionals in this task subsequent to training.

A final differentiation is that between a model and a design. A design is a pattern or model which has been created from the variables elicited from a modelling project. So, for example, one could create a design around assertiveness and use the Meta Model distinctions in order to do this. The assertiveness 'model' may be very effective and, when used, will allow the learner to retain a state of confidence and relaxation and the ability to communicate excellently. However, such a model would more properly be called a design as it is created from the Meta Model distinctions developed through the modelling of Perls and Satir. 'Models' that are created from other NLP variables such as representational systems, Milton Model patterns, eye accessing cues and anchoring formats would all be examples of design rather than models.

NLP is a very practical psychology and, simply put, it is about helping a client find and install the appropriate models so they can effortlessly achieve their outcomes. I say effortlessly because that is the internal experience of people who are in the flow and when all of their internal resources are working together. The appropriate model of the world in a particular context is installed when, through the unconscious processes of generalization, distortion and deletion, the necessary behaviours and language needed to take the coachee to their outcome are automatically generated.

Top-Down and Bottom-Up Modelling

This differentiation is identical to the design/model distinction above. Top-down modelling is when we take an NLP pattern, for example the Meta Model, and make use of it to model the experience of our coachee. Bottom-up modelling is when we suspend all of our linguistic (F^2) transforms and only make use of senses (F^1) in order to imitate our exemplar. This is sometimes referred to as the difference between analytical modelling and NLP modelling.

The essential difference between NLP modelling and analytical modelling is the relative contributions of the model and modeller to the final model. It is assumed by some that NLP modelling is superior as the relative contribution of the exemplar is much greater. This is because the final model to that relative extent does not contain the generalizations, deletions and distortions of the modeller. However, Steve Andreas makes the point that this is irrelevant. If the model is good and coded in such a way that transfer can be demonstrated and tested, how the model is arrived at is irrelevant (Andreas, 2006). My difficulty with this is that if we do take this sensible perspective, how is NLP really any different from psychology as a general discipline which has been doing just this since William James in the USA and Wilhelm Wundt in Europe? The answer to such a rhetorical question is that it is not different.

Let us put this into a coaching context for demonstration purposes. Your coachee says to you, 'I feel a failure'. As a *non*-NLP coach who, let us pretend, happens to possess towards, proactive, procedural and internally referenced Meta Programs, your map of the world, distorted by your Meta Programs, literally deletes this information as it does not fit in with the way *you* operate. As a coach who generally works using these Meta Programs you would say to yourself something like, 'She doesn't really mean that, how could she?' and you proceed to use reframing formats or Socratic questioning in an attempt to shift such private logic. An NLP coach who has modelling at the centre of their methodology, however, has suspended all of these Meta Programs and may ask, 'Wow! How do you do that?' As the coachee explains, the coach will inevitably access the coachee's strategy for 'feeling a failure'. This will be generated by the generalizations, distortions and deletions generated by the coachee's unconscious map of the world as it is. As they do that the NLP coach might notice certain body postures, eye accessing cues, metaphors, complex equivalences, tones of voice, shifts in micro muscle movement, or causes and effects. By second positioning such behaviour the NLP coach is literally imitating a model for failure. They may notice as they go through this process they find cognitively they are operating from an 'away from', reactive, options and externally referenced Meta Program process; this information is put to one side for possible use later, as the modelling process continues. Once one has noticed certain NLP design variables in use, it is useful for the coach to mentally put these to one side (visually, kinaesthetically or auditorily), and continue to model. By doing this the coach builds a much more robust model of the coachee and a more comprehensive model of how they consistently manage to undermine their own performance. With this extra information it is but a small step to inviting the coachee to make a key alteration in the structure of their subjective experience, and thus enter a totally different world where they achieve what they wish with ease.

In order for this to work effectively it is *essential* the coach has an unconscious strategy to assist them to ensure they do not assimilate the coachee's limiting model of the world themselves. Grinder needed six months before he was congruent in order to go and model Milton Erickson. Even great people have Achilles heels which we do not wish to adopt, nor incorporate into our model of excellence. Despite being an excellent clinical hypnotist Erickson had succumbed to polio twice in his life, he was tone deaf, he had dyslexia and was colour blind. Grinder was concerned that in the modelling process he may learn how to develop some of these limitations. The last thing a coach wishes to do is to begin to model the limitations of their coachee and not even be aware of it.

As the model for the coachee's failure is developed it becomes easier and easier to ask questions which have a high amount of leverage in terms of challenging the model. For example, the coach may notice that in modelling their coachee they feel much worse when they move from visual representation to kinaesthetic representation because they tend to get stuck in a negative emotional state and can no longer access positive images or positive dialogue. As the coachee is talking, what the coach could do in this instance is anchor a positive visual representation, and then stack another anchor on top of that anchor, so accessing a strong visual representation for the coachee becomes very easy. Whenever the coachee moves from visual to kinaesthetic predicate as they speak, or access eye positions which tell the coach such a transition is under-way, the coach can fire the anchor and pull them back into a visual represen-tation. As they do this they can support such a new strategy by using Milton Model language and say something like, 'It is really interesting that you talk about your bright future and all the prospects you see for you there in that future, and as you get a sense of that fully I would like you to look up even more and see how bright you can really make that future for yourself. What car can you see yourself driving? What kind of suit will you be wearing? And as you smell the leather in your car and wool against your skin you can say to yourself this is the life for me and see your brand new office fully fitted and waiting for you to move in. How do you now feel as you see this success and hear such positive words?' Providing these are the 'success' criteria elic-ited at the beginning of the coaching session, such a coaching strategy will drive a new map of the world in the context of career which is characterized by kinaesthetic representations only being accessed subsequent to the elicita-tion of robust positive visual and auditory representations. So again here we can see in coaching we start off by modelling, but then make use of NLP design variables to suggest changes in subjective structure which accord with the well-formed outcomes elicited through dialogue at the beginning of coaching. In the example above, the design variables being made use of are those of representational systems, anchoring and Milton Model language patterns.

Top-down modelling is a very much more conscious process. It is especially good for self-modelling as it provides a ready-made set of variables to under-stand at many levels how you operate. This prevents the self-modeller literally getting lost in themselves and simply going round and round in circles because they cannot see the wood for the trees. These other design variables are the closest thing NLP has to the missing algorithms for non-verbal behaviour which Grinder speaks of.

The top-down modelling of Fiat's key leaders in the 1970s by Robert Dilts almost reads like a piece of psychology research. Words such as needs analysis, in-depth discussions, interviews, surveys of current literature on leadership theories and methods clearly does not fall into the NLP modelling category (Dilts, 1998: 134). Similarly the work of Gordon and Dawes (2005) in model-ling passion uses a template with distinct elements called the experiential array. Gordon and Dawes work on the assumption that the primary distinc-tions for modelling are beliefs, strategies, emotions and external behaviours. In this sense both modellers are imposing a cognitive model upon what they model. NLP modellers would say it is this top-down imposition that ensures what is unique and excellent about the model is lost, as that data is deleted and distorted to fit in line with the cognitive imposition. Excellence by its very nature is different from the norm, so how can one possibly capture it by using a standardized template? This would be the rhetorical question from the NLP modeller. The rhetorical repost from the top-down modeller is that the unconscious as well as the conscious mind does have perceptual and analytical categories, and to suggest a Zen-like state where even these unconscious categories are suspended is not feasible.

The key difficulty within the NLP literature though is that how one actually manages to access this state of being when one suspends one's personal filters in order to model others has not been comprehensively coded or tested as an NLP model should, so those who are keen to be able to acquire this skill are left high and dry. In *Whispering in the wind*, Bostic St Clair and Grinder (2001) talk about how the verbal patterning of early models overlapped and the overlap was explicated by reference to the already current code of the transformational syntactician. However, the non-verbal patterning modelled in the early days had no comparable code to make use of. They had to come up inductively with their own design variables, which are listed as rapport, multiple perceptual positions and framing. These design variables were useful in transferring the original NLP patterns to other people in workshops. Bandler and Grinder even found that by changing the original patterning it would then become easier for the workshop delegates to learn. It is at this stage that Bandler and Grinder separated. Bandler took the design variables to develop Design Human Engineering® and Grinder took them to develop New Code. Effectively what happened in the early days of NLP was the 'know nothing' state was used to model. However, in early workshops what was taught was not how to access the 'know nothing' state, but the design variables, developed as a result of the NLP modelling undertaken. This natural emphasis on design variables takes the focus of attention away from what is key to NLP – the use of the unconscious mind to assimilate patterns of excellence. It takes the focus towards a more cognitive type of psychology where the left brain attempts to understand the techniques, steps and procedures for being excellent. This leads to a hardening of the categories and development of foveal vision rather than a softening of the skills and development of peripheral vision. It is interesting that this is the time when Bandler and Grinder parted; it is almost as though once they had consciously explicated what they had learned unconsciously they thought they had no need of each other. Maybe, just as in the Garden of Eden when man and woman had a desire to develop a conscious knowledge of what God knew and this resulted in expulsion, so too in our modern world, a conscious understanding of the unconscious provides a sense of security and omnipotence ... for a while.

> A conscious understanding of the unconscious provides a sense of security and omnipotence ... for a while.

John Grinder makes it clear in *Whispering in the wind* that he accepts responsibility for allowing this current state of affairs, and his development of New Code 'games' is an attempt to ensure that those who presently learn and then practice NLP also apply it to their own lives. The New Code format does make use of the 'know nothing' state in order to transfer 'NLP' to practitioners and thus provide them with the flexibility to make much more use of the unconscious in generating change. This has to be closer to the spirit and presuppositions of NLP compared to the more left-brain and technical pedagogy often produced in practitioner courses, where participants eagerly seek to understand the specific steps of a technique and then what they must do in order to congruently deliver those steps in an ecological way. Time indeed will tell.

BRAIN TEASERS

1   If you go to the website of Steve and Connirea Andreas (www.steveandreas. com/articles.html), who were two of the earliest developers of NLP alongside John Grinder and Richard Bandler, you can see they share some NLP models they have developed. These range from resolving grief to responding to criticism. Have a read of them. After reading them ask yourself the question: 'Do I really need to test these in the way a psychologist would ask for?' After experiencing the simplicity and elegance of many NLP models and also experiencing profound, sustainable change as a result of that experience, many NLP practitioners feel they have enough evidence, and they will in evangelical terms talk about the 'power' of NLP. Do you think such subjective evaluations are sufficient to validate such models?

2   Gregory Bateson talks about the importance of code congruence. When modelling, the benefit of using the unconscious mind is that when we code the information this way it is more likely to match the relationships between elements within the exemplar. This is contrasted with putting those same elements into a pre-designed modelling format as in top-down modelling. The consequence of having a code-congruent model is that it is much simpler and more elegant. For example, in order to explain the orbits of planets when the earth is the centre of the universe the orbits do strange twirls and somersaults which don't really seem right. However, when you put the Sun at the centre of the solar system as Copernicus did, all of a sudden the orbits are simple and elegant ellipses. Take a bit of time, and consider where in your life you are going around in strange twirls and doing somersaults. Could you make use of a different model in that context?

Systems Thinking

13

Open systems offset decay by interacting with the environment and altering throughput so as to ensure relevance in the wider environment

The key NLP presupposition which relates to systems thinking is 'the mind and body are part of the same system'. The Cartesian dualism which suggests that mind in some way is not embodied is rejected within NLP. NLP insists that our mind and body are constantly influencing each other and, at the individual level, one main reason coachees cannot move forward in their life is that they are only attending to one part of the systemic relationship – the part of the mind that is conscious. They are not aware of how the unconscious part is creating the problem. Thus famously they attempt to solve the problem with the same thinking which created it in the first place; this is a single loop recipe for going around in circles, and experiencing consistent frustration. What of course is not recognized is that consciousness is merely an emergent property of a highly complex interaction of neurological activity and physiological feedback and not the cause of those systemic relationships. Single loop learning merely feeds back into the system information that reinforces the whole system, thus the more things change, the more things stay the same.

Gregory Bateson (1972), who wrote the forward for the first NLP model, *The structure of magic*, describes the tangle we can get into when we ignore the unconscious messages within this systemic relationship. He points out that to be infinitely intelligent implies to be infinitely flexible. However, unlike Von Neumann robots, humans have an emotional commitment to the solutions they discover. It is this psychological commitment which creates our blind spots. Bateson talks about us being hurt if we discover we are wrong when we thought all along we have been right. It is this desire for internal consistency, which we discussed in Chapter 7, that distorts information to accord with what we think and want to know and prevents us from obtaining feedback more objectively and then acting upon it by changing. The more enduring the commitment to this initial adaption, the closer it becomes a habit and experienced as difficult to change. As a Buddhist saying goes, it is a terrible thing to be attached to anything; this would certainly apply to a mind–body system that continually frustrates the owner and is not capable of flexibility so as to behave in a *different* manner and then produce language and behaviour which allows elegant fulfilment of well-formed outcomes.

Bateson's use of logical types explains how we get into this fix. Conscious communication and unconscious communication are of a different logical type. Unconscious communication is of a sensory nature and, for instance, does not have grammatical complications like negation in it. Conscious communication makes use of language and has within it all the syntactical rules associated with language. Literally these different parts of the human which define who we are use different languages and when we do not recognize this we end up in what Bateson called a double bind.

He gives as an example a mother who becomes anxious when her child responds to her in a loving way. This sets up a double bind for the child who consistently receives two different sets of messages:

1 The message from the unconscious: hostile, withdrawing behaviour by the mother when approached in a loving manner by the child.

2 The message from the conscious, which is loving language when the child responds to the hostile withdrawing behaviour.

The reason this sets up a double bind for the child is that the loving linguistic message of the mother is 'Meta' to the unconscious hostile behavioural message, and is thus a comment on that behaviour. However, this linguistic message also contradicts the behavioural message. The child is punished if she correctly makes this distinction and feeds it back to the mother; however, she is also punished if she ignores her own capacity to make these important distinctions and responds only to the verbal message. She is punished in this latter situation because if she continues down this route she eventually doubts her own ability to make these essential distinctions. The child effectively has to deceive herself in order to support her mother's deception.

A double bind becomes a mindset which, irrespective of environmental conditions, means 'I cannot win whatever I do, so I might as well give up' ... and many people do just that.

The two keys to maintaining this double bind system are that the child is prohibited from commenting upon her internal distinctions, and also that she is trapped within the system with no way of being able to escape. Once these conditions have been met, a human being will begin to see the whole of their life in terms of double binds, even when they do not exist. This is a bit like the learned helplessness experiments which showed how when you punish an animal for trying to escape or trying to get food, eventually the animal will give up trying to do either, even when the punishment is blatantly no longer in force. For humans we can be caught in 'the poverty trap', or we can be a 'wage slave'. A double bind becomes a mindset which, irrespective of environmental conditions, means 'I cannot win whatever I do, so I might as well give up' ... and many people do just that.

If we and our coachee allow ourselves to give up on this amazing ability to make these distinctions through observation, we soon lose the capacity to make use of the unconscious mind and its enormous pattern-detecting capabilities. We live our life skimming the surface, never getting to the root of who we are, what we see and what we can do. We exist, rather than live. We reframe everything that is magical and wonderful as something that is banal and normal. When we get that excited rush in the viscera that tells us something is afoot, we become habituated to ignore it, in case we 'get into trouble'. And slowly and slowly, day by day, we become the living dead, who project their incapacity to live their life to the full onto others who have locked them into this claustrophobic hell, where there is no air to breathe, vision to see, word to express, nor space to move.

In NLP one of the reasons so much attention is paid to the unconscious mind is because it is believed to be wiser. It is wise because of its scope, it can take on so much more and its function is synthesis which brings things together rather than analysis which tends to take things apart. Whereas the conscious mind can only focus on small parts as it takes the larger system to pieces, the unconscious mind is in a much better position to apprehend larger portions of the system of which it is a part, and this information is often relayed to us through intuition or emotion as the APET model would predict. A nice piece of dialogue from the 1998 film *Ronin* illustrates the point. Sam, a CIA agent, is going to a rendezvous but is suspicious about the circumstances. He decides to leave with the following rationale:

> *Sam:* Whenever there is any doubt there is no doubt. That's the first thing they teach you.
>
> *Vincent:* Who taught you?
>
> *Sam:* I don't remember. That's the second thing they teach you.

This chapter is about how systems thinking in NLP coaching encourages a focus on the larger unconscious part of the system.

It is quite clear for Sam that conscious understanding and memory are over-rated, especially in life or death situations.

The rule of thumb for cognitive scientists, according to Lakoff and Johnson (1999: 13), is that 95 per cent of our thinking is unconscious; they tell us that even phenomenological introspection cannot come close to allowing us to know our own minds. NLP thus is famously utilitarian. The NLP coach seeks to provide a space where, through communication with the unconscious mind, a new system emerges and can generate the language and behaviour which moves the coachee to their well-formed outcome. This is often experienced as transformative and, as we will learn later, often necessitates a disruption of the current ineffective system.

This chapter is about how systems thinking in NLP coaching encourages a focus on the larger unconscious part of the system.

Theory

Tosey and Mathison (2009: 87) suggest Bateson is probably the most cited non-NLP author in the NLP literature. This is interesting because Bateson did not endorse NLP even though he may have influenced it. Nowhere in any writings about Bateson is there mentioned his involvement with Bandler, Grinder or NLP. All we have is one letter to Helen Kennedy of Kresge College in February of 1974 supporting Grinder and also the forward to *The structure of magic*. Tosey and Mathison ask the tantalizing question: if Bateson was really so supportive of Grinder and Bandler's NLP work, why did he not say more?

Another stream of systems thinking was supplied to NLP through Virginia Satir. Her influence seems to be more direct as Robert Dilts (1990) recounts early NLPers referring to her as 'mummy' as she took their hand in NLP workshop demonstrations. Satir served as the director of training at the Mental Research Institute (MRI) in Palo Alto from 1959 to 1966 and at the Esalen Institute in Big Sur beginning in 1966.

'Family sculpture' was one of Satir's well-known ways of transforming words into action, and depicting the family system. She would mould family members into a tableau that depicted family members' typical ways of interacting with each other – for instance, supporting, clinging, blaming, placating, including, excluding. Sometimes she added ropes to dramatize the ways in which members restricted or empowered each other. At other times the initial piece would become a moving sculpture, demonstrating a sequence of interaction (1988: 199).

Families, in this way, would become balanced systems where these types would play their part. Another way of making this system conscious would be to have a parts party. Here different aspects of people's personality within a group system are 'frozen', and brought into the open to understand how that 'part' affects not just the individual concerned, but also the system of which they are a part.

Another NLP coaching technique to assist in bringing an unconscious part to more conscious attention is to play polarities. The coach will model and then exaggerate the 'type' of behaviour which the coachee exhibits, yet denies. This has the effect of activating the opposite behaviour within the coachee thus demonstrating to them the flexibility they often deny having. So if a coach is overly placating to a coachee who is a placator, the coachee will eventually flip into a blamer. A computer type who prides themselves on their ability to think logically would flip over to become more of a distractor when faced with a 99th percentile computer type coach.

In NLP coaching, playing polarities is just one of many ways where we recognize the futility of engaging the coachee in a rational conversation about their ability to change, but rather engage dynamically in an interaction which taps into and activates the unconscious pattern-matching brain. In this case automatically the pattern matcher, when faced with a caricature of themselves

Figure 13.1   Placator, Blamer, Distractor and Computer type in a group system

that is unflattering, will switch to an alternative pattern in order to avoid a state of cognitive dissonance. This alternative pattern can then be modelled and used as evidence that the coachee in fact does have a capability they previously denied having. As the coachee throughout the coaching intervention experiences many of these phenomena, they begin to develop a belief about their ability to recognize when things are not going according to their blueprint and instantly adapt their behaviour to get them back on track. In this way the coachee who is lucky enough to have an NLP coach does not only go away with their problem fixed, but a new-found flexibility which means they never get stuck again.

Bateson's involvement in systems theory was developed through his work at the MRI and his decade of collaboration with John Weakland, Jay Haley, William Fry and Donald Jackson from 1952 to 1961. The purpose of the Institute was to use the principle of cybernetics in providing a frame for human communication and therapeutic change. Bateson was also a contributor to the Macey Conferences. It was Heinz Von Foerster who suggested Weiner's term cybernetics be applied to these conferences. Previously the rather long-winded term Circular Causal and Feedback Mechanisms in Biological and Social Systems had been used.

The long-winded term, however, does describe rather nicely what systems and cybernetics is all about. Let us look at some of the key elements of systems thinking:

1 Properties of systems emerge from the working of the whole system, not from one particular part of the system. You cannot predict the emergent properties of a system by analysis of its parts.

2 Although all parts of the system are essential for proper functioning, some parts have more leverage within the system.

3 Even though the parts of a system are essential, systems thinking is more attuned to the relationships *between* the parts. The whole in systems thinking is *much* more than the sum of its parts. This paradox is created through relationships between parts, not the intrinsic properties of the individual parts.

4 Systems thinking is the opposite to reductionism. In order to understand a small part, systems thinking will look at the whole of which that part belongs. Thus reductionism is more to do with analysis, and systems thinking is more to do with synthesis.

5 Systems thinking is about general rules of organization, not properties of parts.

6 Humans are open systems characterized by a continuous cycle of input, through-put, output and feedback. This is contrasted with a closed system, which is characterized by parameters that are pre-determined, for instance a clockwork toy. The more a human is characterized as though they were a closed system, the more predictable … like a clockwork toy … they are.

7 Systems thinking is always negative whereas causal (linear) thinking is always positive. In causal thinking we say this ball moved in this direction with a certain speed and hit that ball which caused it to move to point C. In systems thinking we think of all the other ways in which the ball could have moved and ask why it did not. Why did it choose to move in that particular direction at that speed? The course of events is subject to restraints and it is assumed that, apart from such restraints, the pathways of change would be governed only by equal probability. Homeostasis refers to the system's ability to maintain a steady state. The distinctness of any human being is a function of their homeostatic ability to control systems on the basis of *negative* feedback. This is where deviation from some norm or standard initiates actions to correct that deviation.

8 Open systems are characterized by negative entropy. Closed systems tend to run down (entropy) as they are closed and cannot interact with the environment. Open systems offset entropy by interacting with the environment and altering throughput so as to ensure relevance in the wider environment, thus maintaining energy and growth.

9 As mentioned in point 3 above, systems thinking is about looking at the relationship *between* parts. However, in living systems the danger is we generalize from mechanical systems and assume that these relationships are subject to reductionist analysis. They are not. The structure, function, differentiation and integration of any part are a manifestation of other parts of the system and can change as the system changes.

10 Any system must have within it, internal regulatory systems which are at least as diverse as the environment within which it interacts. If this is not the case then entropy and atrophy will occur. Having this internal diversity is known as having sufficient requisite variety.

11 In complex systems the principle of equifinality tells us there are many different ways to achieve an end state … or in NLP terms, a well-formed outcome. In closed systems there is no such internal flexibility and in order to get to a particular point fixed procedures must be followed. If these procedures are not possible or they are possible but irrelevant, then the system becomes stuck in an infinite loop of inefficient and irrelevant behaviour.

12 In NLP the patterns we seek to model are the most elegant patterns – that is, systems of operations where there is no redundancy. Occam's Razor, where within the system there is no 'dead wood', is the Holy Grail of any modelling project.

From these elements we can more fully appreciate that when we coach using NLP not only do we have to attend to the systemic relationship between the unconscious and the conscious mind, but we also need to attend to the wider systemic relationships between individuals, groups of individuals and organizations. From an NLP point of view when we adopt this perspective, however strange the particular limitation appears to be initially, it soon becomes very clear the person is not 'broken', but working very well according to the system within which they are currently operating. By finding out the key relationships within that system and making alterations at those points, one creates a new experience and from that experience flows choice, capability, self-belief, self-determination, energy and creativity.

Practice

When working as an NLP coach from a systemic perspective you soon realize that to approach the intervention in a linear cause-and-effect manner, where you attempt to 'correct' a fault, is futile. The thinking of Buckminster Fuller comes to mind, who suggested you never change things by fighting the existing reality, but rather to change you build a *new* model which makes the existing model obsolete. Systems thinking looks at the patterns of interactions *and* the underlying structures which are responsible for those patterns.

1. Analogue Marking and Logical Levels

A client once said this to me about her work: 'I hate working in *this place*; I can never get anything done'. I noticed that when she was talking she emphasized one part of the sentence: '*this place*'. Robert Dilts developed a model called logical levels, and it was based upon Gregory Bateson's use of logical types (Figure 13.2). It was called 'logical' levels because as Michael Hall would say, each level is meta to the level below it. Theoretically the meta level informs and modulates the level below it.

In fact this model does not necessarily flow downwards but upwards as well. Often people get stuck in a particular environment and there are many environmental anchors which *upwardly* trigger certain strategies, beliefs and a sense of who one is. We know this because we are usually very different people at work, at home or at play. If an individual changes their environment, often this has a knock-on effect upwards. All of a sudden the new environment triggers different behaviour which is generated by a different sense of who the individual is, what they believe, what they can do and how they can do it. This information is then fed back down the system to create a self-sealing loop of recursive validation.

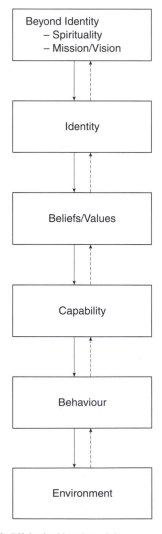

Figure 13.2   Robert Dilts's (1990: 56) logical level model

CASE HISTORY

In the above coaching conversation I agreed with Diana and said, 'I appreciate you can't get anything done in this place, however what happens when you are in a different place?' She began to explore how in different environments she actually had different identities, beliefs, capabilities and behaviours and was literally a totally different person. For instance, when at home she could stand up for herself to her husband and children, in a loving way which sought the best solution not just for herself but for them too. In the coaching conversation we simply modelled what these useful aspects of her were, and created a new set of associations with 'this place'. Diana recognized that her previous self had been a part of a larger system. In order for her to take control she needed to understand how that 'environment' was automatically triggering a host of internal systemic processes which were experienced as a rigid reality from which she could not escape. When in the coaching conversation we explored how each part of her internal system influenced each other part, she could begin to take control of her own phenomenological experience in 'this place' and make changes so she was in control and behaved in accordance with her own agenda … making sure that it ecologically fitted with the agenda of the organization in which she worked. This mainly entailed being assertive but not being aggressive, as she had experienced how aggression always seemed to snowball and leave a 'nasty' atmosphere. Because her new self in 'this place' accorded with the organizational values as well, when she returned to work she was perceived as very different, with more energy, being more in control and more assertive. Other people in the workplace had to make adjustments themselves to deal with this 'new' person. Diana told me she changed from being on the back foot to being on the front foot.

In this instance by noticing where the barrier to development was being placed by Diana, I worked with that part of the system (the environment) to remove the limiting aspect and reinvigorate the whole system. If I had attempted to work with Diana's beliefs, or her strategies, or her identity, or her values, or her language, the intervention would not have been nearly so effective or swift. The reason would have been that as soon as I accessed those parts of the system, they would have been anchored to 'this place' and I would have heard something like, 'I know it is stupid but I just can't change'. She was telling me where the barrier was – it was in the environment, in 'this place'. However, she was telling me this non-verbally, so I had to listen to the analogue marking of her voice to understand this. By initially taking her out of 'this place' to help her appreciate how effective she really was, then putting her back into 'this place' with a different set of beliefs, strategies and a new identity, the same environment was experienced as something totally different. In this sense the logical level model holds firm, because simply by changing how she saw her environment (new strategy/capability), based upon a different set of beliefs (new beliefs) which was generated by who she was in different places (new identity) which came from her personal mission in life (mission/vision), she was able to make an impact to such an extent that others recognized pressing hot buttons no longer worked on this person and they had to find alternative ways of working with her.

2. Secondary Gain

Secondary gain is an NLP term borrowed from psychodynamic psychology.

Firstly, primary gain 'hides' the main attractor within the mind–body system in a particular context and is entirely unconscious. For Freud the advantage of primary gain is that to the total system the discomfort of not being able to make the adjustments necessary to achieve a well-formed outcome is much more tolerable than the anguish caused by allowing the patterning of sensory representations and associated unconscious thalamic cognition into consciousness. In this way primary gain maintains the ineffective behaviour and language. What this sensory patterning, which is hidden through the process of primary gain, actually is, is simply a hurtful experience from which generalizations have been made. It is this sensory patterning, located in the unconscious mind and triggered within a particular context, which acts as an attractor for the whole mind–body system of the coachee and is resistant to change.

Secondary gain is simply the benefits which are associated with primary gain. For example, a coachee may feel they cannot obtain the confidence to go for a promotion. Secondary gains would be that in their current position they have less responsibility, pro rata get paid a better salary, are more invisible, meaning they can work within the organization more to their own agenda, do not take their job home with them in the evening, can choose when they go on holiday, etc., etc. All of these secondary gains support the coachee in not tackling the root cause of their problem: developing the confidence to go for a promotion. Individuals have often been using secondary gains for many years to justify why they do not develop themselves and move their life 'up to the next level'. When they come into a coaching environment of their own accord it is because, for whatever reason, the secondary gains no longer provide the satisfaction and fulfilment they used to. The individual knows something fundamental needs to change, however they do not know what that is. Whatever they do simply reinforces the problem. In Figure 13.3 you can see how the original expression of the mind–body system in the career dimension cannot express itself effectively because the mind–body system has assimilated negative beliefs, strategies, visions, identity, etc. in that context. These all sit, ready to be triggered whenever the coachee thinks about who they are and what they can do in the context of career. They intuitively know they are better than this ('core expression'), however somehow they cannot get past the 'negative' patterns which have been assimilated within. In Figure 13.3 we can see that in the dimension of health this particular coachee has no difficulties at all. They can express themselves well in the gym or within any other health-related environment, being who they are and knowing who they are. This coaching model (7 C's coaching) is explained further in the following chapter.

> A vision is something which an individual is 'connected' to through their belief, capability and strategy. A vision is consistently being realized and created each moment of the day through language and behaviour and flows through the viscera.

One can see that one of the consequences of not being able to express oneself along any life dimension authentically and congruently is the use of transference and fantasy. These too are secondary gains. Some individuals prefer rich internal fantasy lives and recognize that this is something they would lose if they systemically arranged their internal architecture so as to provide them with the results they wish for in 'real' life. In this instance the reader must appreciate the difference between a fantasy and a vision. A fantasy is an internal dynamic where the fantasist vicariously engages in the fable rather than engaging with internal demons encased in the black circle (Figure 13.3).

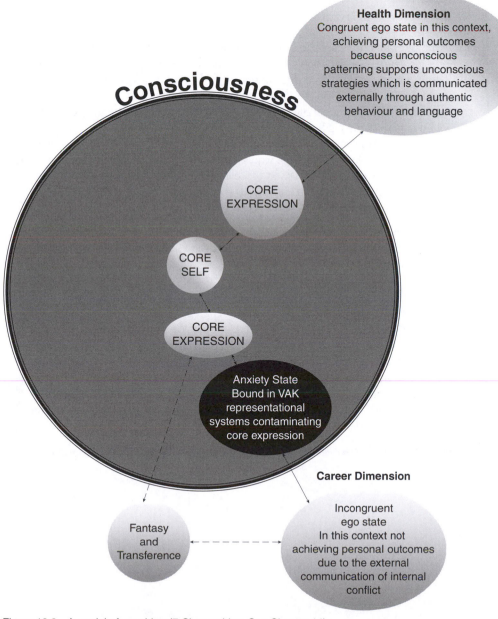

Figure 13.3   A model of coaching (7 C's coaching. See Chapter 14)

In this chapter we have put our toe into the water of systems thinking and its relevance to NLP coaching. Not only is systems thinking essential for coaching at an individual level but also at an organizational level. All that has been mentioned about blind spots, secondary gains and logical levels is also true of departments within organizations, and organizations within organizations. The key is not finding a solution, but rather modelling the system and changing key parts to produce a new system.

BRAIN TEASERS

1   A plumber was once asked to solve a complicated problem which had plagued a hotel for years. He went down to the basement and looked at the labyrinth of boilers, pipes, valves, taps and monitoring equipment. Every now and then he would stop and put his ear to one of the pipes. Sometimes he would touch a pipe. On other occasions, he would step back and almost go into a trance as he looked at how all the pipes were organized. Eventually he went over to a particular junction and took out a ball pein hammer. He hit the junction of the pipes quite hard three times. Immediately the whole system resumed proper functioning for the first time in many years. When the bill came in the hotel proprietors were amazed at the sum of £1,000 for only 10 minutes' work and they contacted the plumber for an itemized list of services and materials. He replied as follows:

 i Supplying one ball pein hammer and striking pipe junction three times: £1.00
 ii 10 minutes' analysis and knowing where to hit: £999.00
 iii Total invoice: £1000.00

Was the plumber justified in his bill? Discuss.

2   Adam Curtis, in his well-known documentary *The trap* (BBC2, 2007), suggests that the reason the state has been dismantled in many Western countries is because humans essentially are selfish and politicians, like all humans, essentially work to their own agendas and not those of the people who they represent. Paradoxically this was a view propagated by J.D. Laing, the psychotherapist who we came across in Chapter 3. It is argued that modern democracy is the marketplace where people 'vote' with their hard-earned money. From a systems perspective does the marketplace provide all with a fair vote? Discuss.

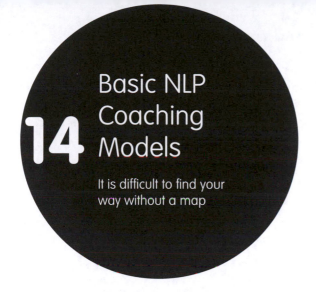

Basic NLP Coaching Models

14

It is difficult to find your way without a map

In this short chapter I would like to briefly look at three coaching models which have arisen from the practice of NLP practitioners. The first is one that first saw the light of day in 2002 and is a coaching model developed through modelling my own coaching practice. The second model arose from the modelling project by Michael Hall of how higher levels of thought and feeling govern primary experience. The final one developed from the modelling of a New Zealand psychotherapist, David Grove. What these models have in common is that in accordance with NLP their protocols were the product of modelling projects. What they also have in common is that they all inevitably involve eliciting conversations with the unconscious mind and facilitating change at that level in a process-oriented way.

Needless to say, in order to practice coaching using any of these models it would be most appropriate to contact the relevant trainers (Appendix 2), as this chapter simply puts a toe in the water.

1. The 7 C's of Courage

In 2002 I had been practicing as a coaching psychologist for six years and wrote an article in *Rapport* (2002) called 'Sexy variables'. This referred to six key coaching variables which resulted from modelling my practice to that time. The coaching variables which always needed to be addressed in any coaching intervention were:

Clarity

Climate

Capability

Congruence

Confidence

Commitment

By the summer of 2005 a further variable had been added, *Communication*, bringing the total to seven (Grimley, 2005). This part of the coaching model referred to the process. By 2005 a content part had also been added to the model. The content part asked, for instance, 'What does the coachee need to be clear about?'

The content part of the model fell into eight dimensions:

Relationship with self

Relationship with intimate others

Relationship with those at work

Interpersonal skills

Money

Career

Health

Relaxation

These eight dimensions were drawn from the challenges brought to me by coaching clients over 10 years (1995–2005).

An online questionnaire suggested that the key variable in the content part is that of 'Relationship with self'. An unrotated principle components analysis of 250 data sets from a 27-item questionnaire demonstrated that the only item to show in the main factor of a one-factor solution was 'Relationship with self'. What the research seemed to show was that if individuals have an excellent relationship with themselves, even if the other content variables are not going too well, they will not buckle, but will persevere with confidence, developing strategies that ultimately get them to where they want to go.

The five items which loaded (in brackets) most heavily into the one-factor solution were:

1 I feel very good about myself every day of the week. (0.72)

2 When I think of my future, I can see many exciting tasks to be accomplished. (0.74)

3 I often take corrective action when my life does not go according to plan. (0.71)

4 I am very sure of myself. (0.71)

5 I am confident I have what it takes to achieve my goals in life. (0.78)

This coaching model suggests that one of the content items unconsciously is acting as a disruptive attractor in the mind–body system. Within this dimension there is an interference preventing optimal performance. This is the reason the coachee is coming to see you.

The factor analysis above suggests that one of the content items will usually be 'my relationship with myself'. However, experience has shown this is always accompanied by at least one of the other content items. This may be my relationship with myself in the context of my intimate relationships ... my career ... my health, to be followed by one space, not two and so on.

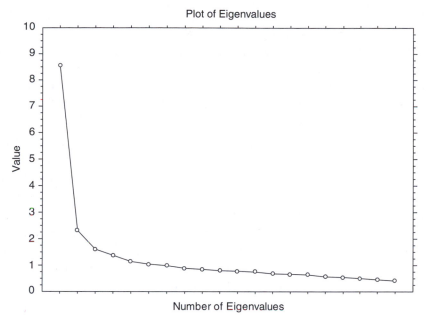

Figure 14.1   One-factor solution to 7 C's questionnaire: 8.6 Eigenvalue explaining 30.6% of total variance within the 27-item questionnaire

The key in this coaching model is to alter the unconscious attractor and thus remove the interference within the discovered context by developing the 7 C's using NLP presuppositions, design variables and methodology. In the previous chapter this unconscious attractor was represented by the grey circle within the unconscious mind (Figure 14.3). To start off using this model, the NLP coach develops rapport and, when appropriate, gently proceeds with Meta Model questions:

'How do you know that?'

'What is your evidence?'

'When does that happen?'

What happens during the coaching sessions is the conscious experience which has been created by the unconscious attractor is altered as the coachee learns to feed back into their personal system different pictures, sounds and feelings which they learn to anchor to commonly occurring contexts within their content dimension. This is known as active thinking rather than passive thinking. It is similar to what Dewey (1910) calls reflective thought where, rather than just accept the flow of consciousness generated by the unconscious attractor, one challenges it and also through this coaching process changes it when it is found to be at odds with the well-formed outcome. What NLP brings to the 7 C's model is a set of tools and a philosophy which recognizes the limitations of the conscious mind in usefully reflecting on the system of which it is a part and consequently makes much more use of the unconscious mind compared with more cognitively and behaviourally oriented coaching models.

By the end of the coaching session the coachee is *Clear* about their objective, believes now is the right time to address this as the *Climate* is right, has the *Capability* to address this, is *Congruent* in their *Confidence* and also *Committed* to operationalizing the solution uncovered in coaching. Finally they *Communicate* all of the above to both themselves internally through each of the sensory modalities and to others through language and behaviour using 'active language'. In this way a new generative system is triggered by the previous problem context which has been transformed into a lever for personal change. Passive thinking, which is the new conscious experience generated by the alterations within coaching, is experienced as a flow experience when the unconscious mind automatically works in accordance with the coachee's well-formed outcomes.

For coaches interested in this model there are examples of questions used to elicit each of the 7 C's in the notes in Appendix 2.

2. Meta Coaching

Meta Coaching was developed by Michael Hall (Hall & Duval, 2004) and its explicit frame is that humans are designed to grow into self-actualizing and self-empowered people. Coachees are people who operate from what Maslow (1968) called growth needs rather than deficiency needs. In this sense this coaching system was not developed from therapeutic frames such as Prochaska and DiClemente (2005), but designed explicitly for a 'healthy' population. According to Hall, this is why the third force in psychology never really took off, as despite its focus on positive psychology and growth needs, it was too tied down with therapeutic assumptions. It was also too vague and did not have a sufficient technical aspect associated with it. Hall seeks to correct this with what he regards as a methodology for the Human Potential movement. Thus Meta Coaching is truly associated with positive psychology and has a very definite technical aspect and an over-arching framework within which to house that technical aspect.

Meta Coaching is a coaching system which has eight primary models. These are explained in eight books, has outlined in Table 14.1.

At the heart of Meta Coaching is the concept of Meta States. This is because our Meta States create and set our frames of mind. For example, two people may both have a learning state. However, when asking each person how they feel about their learning state one may say, 'I feel great, it is easy to access and is useful' and the other may say, 'I feel terrible about it and get confused when in it'. Two people are in a learning state, however the Meta State is very different for both.

In order to create these Meta States we need language. Hall suggests what Maslow left out of his model was the mapping of the fluidity of human consciousness

Table 14.1   Eight primary models of the Meta Coaching system

Volume	Title	Model
I.	*Coaching Change*	Axes of Change
II.	*Coaching Conversations*	Facilitation Model
III.	*Unleashed: A Guide to Your Ultimate Self-Actualization*	Self-Actualization
IV.	*Self-Actualization Psychology*	Quadrants
V.	*Achieving Peak Performance*	Self-Actualization Volcano
VI.	*Unleashing Leadership: Self-Actualizing Leaders and Companies*	Meaning–Performance Axes
VII.	*The Crucible*	The Crucible Model
VIII.	*Benchmarking Intangibles*	Benchmarking Model

and also of how our meaning making transforms our basic needs. Thus we no longer eat to obtain strength and nutrition, as when we grow as children, but as adults we eat to feel loved, rewarded, comforted, etc. Hall calls this psycho-eating. Semantics thus are the meanings that we create through our symbol systems which we then embody. For Hall this is a tripartite process:

1   *Growing up.* This is when as children we develop along Maslow's hierarchy of needs and move out of deficiency need into growth need.

2   *Coping.* Having already moved from the lower parts of the Maslow triangle to the higher part, we now find we need to go back to the lower parts again as adults in order to satisfy these needs. However, now they are semantically loaded. We are no longer innocent. Having food of a certain type *means* something, having a car of a certain type to get to work *means* something, living in a house of a certain type *means* something, and these *meanings* become embodied and thus 'real'. These meanings also become the basis of the states we enter into when we think along those dimensions or act within them.

3   *Mastery.* At this stage we decide how we feel about our basic needs because we learn how to Meta State. At this level we can travel to our highest state and discover what is important to us and then take *that* meaning through our neurology out into the world of behaviour and language. This is very similar to the process which 'Diana' went through in the previous chapter. She recognized how her environment was triggering certain meanings within her which were experienced as states. However, when using the logical level model and travelling up to the very top in a different context she discovered what she really believed. She then modelled this and brought it back down through behaviour and language in the context of work.

In Figure 14.2 you can see how experience can be created by an interweaving of meanings and frames. Often we are not aware of these frames and are at their mercy. Meta Coaching helps untangle and unravel this meaning-making process in a structured way.

Michael Hall has developed this coaching system over the years and a short section in this chapter could not possibly do it justice. In Appendix 2 you can find out how you can contact Michael Hall and obtain training in this coaching system.

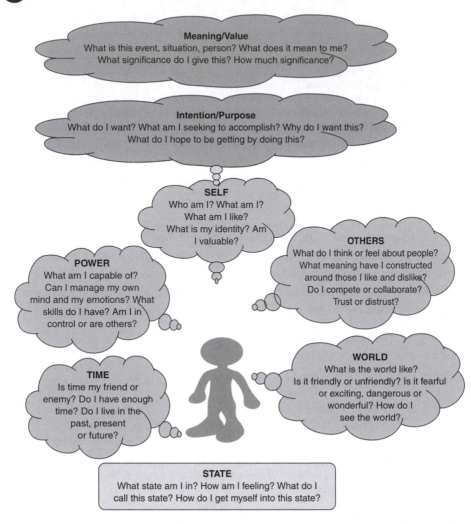

Figure 14.2   The 'Web of the mind' (Schwarzer, 2011). Adapted from Hall's 'Matrix of the mind'

3. Clean Language

The New Zealand therapist David Grove pioneered the technique of Clean Language while working with trauma victims during the 1980s. He first became involved with NLP in 1978 when, after seeking out business solutions, he became interested in the idea of experience having a structure; if you change the structure at some point you change the experience. After becoming involved at that time in Ericksonian hypnosis, he discovered that patients would often speak in metaphor when describing their pain and that the most effective way of alleviating the effects was to respect these metaphors using the patient's exact words in questioning to seek clarification of what the metaphors represented. This meant he avoided adding his own assumptions and refrained from contaminating the client's meaning with his own interpretation.

Throughout the 1980s and 1990s, Grove identified a set of questions that would least influence the client in their metaphorical journey and allow a clean unravelling of the deeper meanings and messages within the metaphor. The technique was modelled by James Lawley and Penny Tompkins (2000) and called symbolic modelling. It is an approach to modelling that uses Clean Language questions to explore personal metaphors so that the person can self-model their patterns.

All Clean Language questions start with 'and'. Grove originally came up with six basic neutral questions which did not interfere with the client's process. The key to these clean questions is that they directly address the client's experience and do not bring the client out of that experience.

In normal coaching a question is asked by the coach and the information is given back. The focus of attention moves backwards and forwards between coach and coachee. However, once a Clean Language question is asked the focus shifts from the coachee to where the information is sourced, without it having to be triangulated between the coachee's cognitive faculty and the coach. This is why the coachee does not have to think about answers to Clean Language questions, because the answers come from the source of the information. As soon as the question is asked, the client already knows. The effect of this is that sometimes the coachee's cognitive centres can be relegated to an amused onlooker as a conversation develops between their metaphor and the clean coach.

Grove found that the less he attempted to change the client's model of the world, the more they experienced their own core patterns, and organic, lasting changes *naturally* emerged from the mind–body system.

9 BASIC CLEAN LANGUAGE QUESTIONS

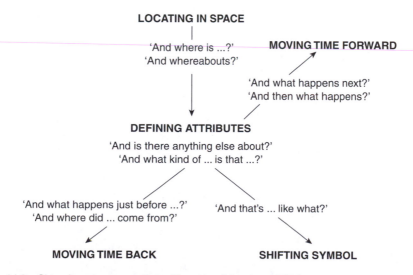

Figure 14.3   Clean Language questions (Tompkins & Lawley, 1997a)

Three further questions have since been developed and in Figure 14.3 readers can see for themselves how these questions map onto the metaphorical landscape.

The movement has been taken into the training and coaching sphere with various organizations offering training in clean coaching and certification for their graduates. These organizations develop their own coaching models such as *Clean language* (Sullivan & Rees, 2008), *The clean approach to leadership* (Watson, 2011) and *Clean coaching* (Wilson & Dunbar, 2011). Again, as with the above coaching models, in order to practice it is appropriate to contact the individual organizations which train coaches to coach from this perspective (see Appendix 2).

Summary

In this brief chapter we have looked at three coaching models that have emerged from NLP practice. There are of course many more, and potentially as many coaching models as there are NLP practitioners. If you are interested in the above models you can of course contact the relevant training associations. You can alternatively attend NLP practitioner training to develop NLP skills and design your own model. What would be useful if this strategy is adopted is that you make your model explicit and then find ways of testing it. In the autumn of 2011 the ANLP launched a series of research in practice articles edited by Associate Professor Suzanne Henwood. The purpose of these was to evolve the debate about research in NLP and to involve as many NLP practitioners as possible in this debate. We will discuss more about research and research findings in Chapter 16.

PART 3

The Evidence for NLP Effectiveness

15 Meeting Professional Coaching Standards

A standard is a benchmark against which performance can be compared. Without standards we never know where we stand

We discovered in Chapter 2 that it was a moot question as to whether the coaching industry could call itself a profession. The chapter concluded with the subjective evaluation that coaching is a maturing industry that can offer coaching to a professional standard. One of the pieces of evidence that allows anybody to say this is the existence of ethical codes, complaint procedures, competency frameworks and codes of conduct within the various coaching bodies. These have been in place for a considerable time now and the International Coach Federation (ICF) and European Mentoring and Coaching Council (EMCC) filed a common code of conduct for coaches and mentors with the European Union in 2011. This benchmark is designed to form the basis for self-regulation of the coaching and mentoring industry. It is drafted with regard to European law so as to be registered on the dedicated European Union database which lists self-regulation initiatives in Europe. It seems typical of the coaching industry that there is a move for membership organizations to seek collaboration in the interest of building a profession. Even though the Association for Coaching was not part of this professional initiative at the outset, it quickly became involved and there is now agreement in place to keep it informed and the Association for Coaching's voice has now been added to this EU initiative.

To meet professional coaching standards, one should be a member of one of the main coaching associations and conduct one's coaching business in accordance with those standards.

Does this mean that one cannot practice ethically and to a good standard without joining one of the main coaching associations? I would certainly challenge such a person. Why would you want to go it alone, when there is a host of professionally minded colleagues who wish to bring coaching forward through responsible dialogue and cross-fertilization of ideas and research?

There is an interesting discussion that 'accreditation' does not guarantee good practice. A bit like passing exams, it only provides evidence that a coach is sufficiently motivated to jump through the set of hoops put in front of them, has the basic mental ability to understand how to do this and behavioural flexibility to perform this activity. What this does not guarantee is that such a coach will practice in an ethical way, to a specific standard and according to a range of competencies.

Richard Mowbray (1995) argued the case in the mid-1990s that the call for registration and accreditation for psychotherapists did not come from the public or politicians but from psychotherapists themselves, aided and abetted by media horror stories. For Mowbray these calls for registration of psychotherapy were more usefully addressed as part of a political process concerned with power and control and the cure could well prove more fatal than the disease. For Mowbray psychotherapy, and we could argue here too, coaching, is so diverse that to regulate the activity would be to rob it of innovation, creativity and also growth. He argues that the evidence base for what does harm to people in a one-to-one discourse is so slim, and the evidence there is so hotly debated that the argument 'the public need to be protected' holds no water.

Mowbray makes the point that implicit in the word accreditation is the sense of authoritative sanction, and accreditation as such can therefore lull potential purchasers into a false sense of security. What he would prefer is a system of education where the purchasers of one-to-one work are educated concerning the important variables.

> We currently have a variety of self-regulating coaching organizations acting as educators and working together rather than in competition in order to promote a positive activity which is rapidly developing an evidence base.

Most of the current coaching associations do have this. I would indeed argue that they all see one of their main functions as that of educating the public concerning the coaching process. If this is indeed the case then maybe the coaching industry at present has the ideal solution: a variety of self-regulating coaching organizations acting as educators and working together rather than in competition in order to promote a positive activity which is rapidly developing an evidence base. It is within this scenario that the purchaser of coaching services is truly spoilt for quality choice. The purchaser of coaching services should be alerted to:

1　If the coach is not accredited, what are the reasons for not taking this route as a professional provider of coaching services? The potential buyer can decide for themselves whether the argument holds water or not.

2　What efforts has the coach made to educate themselves concerning the coaching process? At present there are post-graduate qualifications at both Masters and PhD level in coaching. A lack of coaching qualifications could mean a variety of things. Again, the potential buyer can determine for themselves whether the reasoning holds water.

3　How has the coach contributed to the coaching literature? As you would have gathered from this book, the coaching industry is a young industry and a part of the journey to full professional status is developing an evidence base for practice. If your coach is not actively contributing to this development process, why is this the case?

4 Does your coach have professional indemnity and public liability insurance? This is a must and if necessary the purchaser of coaching services has every right to view the certificate of insurance.

5 Is the coach an active member of a coaching association? If not why not?

6 What do you intuitively think concerning the *credibility* of your coach? If there is a *but*, see if you can surface what your unconscious mind is bringing to your conscious attention.

7 Are the premises from which your coaching provider practices suitable? Does the location provide sufficient access, confidentiality and comfort?

8 What evidence of continuing professional development does your coach have? Can they provide evidence of this continuing professional development?

9 Does your coach provide a clear and comprehensive contracting period where you can discuss, free of charge, how your coach operates, what their credentials are, the fee structure, and any questions which may arise as a result of your search for the appropriate provider? At the end of this period you should feel confident you know precisely what coaching involves, and you should have 100 per cent confidence in your selection of coach. You should be clear about what is expected of you and what you can expect of your coach.

10 Like number 6, but how do you *feel* about your coach as a person, as a human? You should feel 100 per cent comfortable this is the right person for you. There is a tremendous diversity of coaches and coaching styles available. You are about to embark on a journey that will take a portion of your time and your finance so it is important you take sufficient time to find just the right coach for you.

11 Does your coach have a supervisor and sufficient support to assist them in those areas which they find outside their level of competence?

12 Can your coach provide any references from previous customers? An effective and active coach should have no difficulty in being able to do this.

NLP Coaching

So if the above is the case for coaching in general, then how can we address the question about *NLP* coaching? Obviously the NLP coach will need to satisfactorily address all of the above 12 criteria. However, as an *NLP* coach there are *extra* ethical aspects which should be evident in the coaching practice.

Firstly, the NLP coach should be educated to at least practitioner level in NLP and should demonstrate a working knowledge of the basic presuppositions and models of NLP. The NLP course should be recognized by one of the main NLP organizations listed in Chapter 17, and the trainers running the course should be accredited by the NLP organization.

Secondly, the NLP coach should be adept at working at the level of process in their coaching and not comment either negatively or positively on the content which is brought into the coaching relationship. Freud, for instance, was aware that clients who came to him were highly suggestible to minimal cues offered by him and they would 'mind read' what these 'meant'. To overcome this he would sit behind the analysand and ask them to free associate. The NLP coach must be aware that they too can easily, and without being aware, influence the content of the coachee by minimally communicating their personal judgements. All NLP coaches should have sufficient emotional intelligence and personal awareness to minimize such counter-transference in coaching.

Thirdly, the NLP coach should not introduce their 'ideas' or 'beliefs' into the coaching process. Their work as an NLP coach is to work at a process level with the 'map' of their coachee. An example of this is given when, according to Bostic St Clair and Grinder (2001: 306), Virginia Satir suggested that behind a client's anger was hurt. This presupposition (behind anger is hurt), may have had a basis, based upon information gathering at some other part of the intervention; however, if not, it is an example of the coach's presupposition unconsciously and potentially becoming the coachee's presupposition. Clean Language, as discussed in the previous chapter, is an NLP model which is specifically very good at ensuring communication between coach and coachee is kept 'clean'.

Finally, NLP is believed to be especially rapid in assisting individuals in experiencing the change they seek in their life. The NLP coach should not therefore 'milk' any transference for financial gain within the coaching relationship. Just because overcoming anxiety may take four sessions using a different coaching paradigm, if it is within the scope of the NLP coach to jointly address this coaching outcome within one or two coaching sessions, this is what they should do. They should not extend the coaching intervention to four sessions just because this may be an acceptable professional norm using other coaching methods, or the coachee is overly impressed with the results and wishes to 'hang around'.

BRAIN TEASERS

1 Is coaching value for money? Having got this far in the book you will have some idea by now what coaching is, such as how it differs from talking to a friend over a pint of beer, or glass of wine. How would you assess whether or not you got value for money from a coaching intervention?

2 Just as the science of the material world is physics, the science of the psyche and related behaviours is psychology. Just as you would not have a medical operation carried out by someone who is not medically qualified, nor seek legal counsel from someone who is not legally qualified, why would you engage in a coaching conversation with someone who is not a qualified psychologist? Discuss this point of view.

Research: Who Says This All Works?

16

If in re-searching
what searching has discovered
we find little that has a significant
value, did searching
find anything in the
first place?

NLP as a discipline has been with us since the early 1970s, however a search on research databases returns very little in the way of good quality supporting evidence.

A search on Psyc Info, Psyc Articles, Psych Extra and Medline databases returned 774 hits for NLP compared with 9,120 for cognitive behavioural therapy (CBT), characterizing the present difference in research base concerning the respective paradigms. The NLP papers were a mixture of case studies and small-scale empirical studies (21 July 2011). A search through current coaching journals – *The Coaching Psychologist*, *Coaching*, *International Coaching Psychology Review* and *Coaching at Work* – provides no research into NLP, only sporadic discussions concerning its status and identity.

However, times are changing and within NLP circles some practitioners are recognizing NLP needs to be researched more comprehensively in order to convince those who like to enjoy the benefit of well-presented evidence before they make decisions on the value of anything.

For example, in 2007 the NLP research and recognition project (NLP R&R) was set up to demonstrate how effective NLP patterns are and to counteract exaggerated NLP claims, shoddy 'get rich' training programmes and unprofessional practices (www.nlprandr.org). To begin with 800 NLP practitioners, supported by 40 NLP institutions, focused research on the clinical area of Post-Traumatic Stress Disorder (PTSD). They put together a protocol to treat PTSD which they believe to be more effective than anything presently available and which produces results in hours or days rather than what is experienced at present – months and years. Frank Bourke, the NLP R&R Executive Director, makes the point that NLP works by adapting what you are doing to each individual person as they come along. Scientific psychology, however, asks us to design a protocol and rigidly adhere to it, irrespective of the characteristics of the

NLP works by adapting
what you are doing to
each individual person.

person who comes to us. When we have a 70 or 80 per cent success rate using this protocol we can then say with a 70 or 80 per cent probability that we can predict this protocol will work. How one translates the dynamic use of NLP design variables and the coaching context that triggers their use into a scientific frame which can be tested is the current challenge. Dr Bourke's outcome is for the NLP R&R to develop three NLP protocols established as the best in the world over the next three years. The relevance of this counselling research to the coaching world is that the majority of coaching paradigms in existence currently take their models from counselling psychology or psychotherapy.

Moving to other institutions, Surrey University School of Management (www.nlpresearch.org/) hosted the first International NLP Research Conference in July 2008. This was followed by the second conference in 2010 at Cardiff University, and the third conference at the University of Hertfordshire in 2012. At these conferences papers demonstrating the utility of NLP in such coaching-related areas as business, education, psychotherapy, stress management, expert performance, influence, creativity and personality were given. A constant factor at these conferences was the Association for NLP (ANLP). They partnered with Surrey in 2008, organized Cardiff in 2010 and hosted the 2012 conference in conjunction with the University of Hertfordshire. Many of the papers presented at these conferences are available in the ANLP publications *Current research in NLP*, Volume 1 (2009) and Volume 2 (2011) (www.anlp.org/).

Like Surrey University, the International Association of NLP Institutes (www.nlp-institutes.net/index.php) regularly holds research conferences and supervises NLP PhD research. The Association used Clare Graves's instrument as a model to structure their first world congress in Germany in 2006 with the second congress in Brazil (2009) focusing on the use of NLP in coaching, entitled 'Creating Solutions with NLP and Coaching'. The third congress in Croatia (2012) turned researchers' attention to the role of emotion in NLP and coaching.

Before we mention the role of other institutions such as the NLP University (www.nlpu.com), maybe we should ask whether or not NLP is subject to scientific verification and whether it should be taken seriously by the scientific community at this stage of its development.

Can NLP Be Reliably Researched?

Both co-founders, despite being aware of the nature of scientific enquiry, resist any suggestion that NLP should go down this route. John Grinder recognizes some aspect of NLP may be testable through statistical means, but generally believes NLP is subject, as systems theory is, to a subtractive paradigm rather than an additive one. What he means by this is that psychology, for instance, as a science will seek to *add* an experimental variable to demonstrate utility. The Null hypothesis will predict that there will be no significant difference between the experimental group and the control group. However, the experimental hypothesis is that there *will be* a significant difference due to the *addition* of a certain technique or process. Grinder points out that NLP is about modelling excellence and this essentially is a subtractive process. After the exemplar has been modelled and outputs replicated then at the coding stage the key to producing an elegant model is to *subtract* those elements of the model which are not needed to produce those outcomes. For instance, Milton Erickson used to sit with his left elbow on a pillow and lean over holding his right hand in his cupped left hand due to being partially paralyzed. He would also talk in a certain way due to missing upper teeth. Both Bandler and Grinder incorporated these postures and verbal tones into their original model of Erickson. However, during the coding phase they recognized that such posture and tones were not necessary to produce the outcomes Erickson created and so removed them from the final model.

Grinder categorically states that NLP is not interested in the scientific endeavour of prediction but is rather more interested in the endeavour of creation. He suggests that traditional scientific approaches are quite linear and thus pick the lowest hanging fruit. However, as chaos theory and dynamic open systems begin to become topical then different research paradigms become initiated. He points out, however, that the present state of NLP is so rudimentary that this exciting paradigm shift has little relevance to the ongoing discipline of NLP. What NLP needs to do in order for such research paradigms to become relevant is to stabilize its fundamental vocabulary and procedure for the investigation and coding of pattern.

> Traditional scientific approaches are quite linear and thus pick the lowest hanging fruit. However, as chaos theory and dynamic open systems begin to become topical then different research paradigms become initiated.

Key Research Challenges for NLP

1. Lack of Agreed Definition

The key challenge, then, is to start at the beginning and ask, what is NLP? Without stability here we really cannot proceed effectively. I have already provided my 'grassroots' definition in Chapter 1: 'An attitude with a methodology which leaves behind it a trail of techniques'. By the end of this chapter the reader might think this classic definition should be changed to: 'A trail of tested and validated techniques'.

However, we do not have stability here as many other people will criticize this definition and adopt their own. One popular current definition of NLP is 'Anything that works' … I ask you!

2. Fragmentation

The second challenge for NLP is to recognize that it has become fragmented and the idea of a unified field no longer really exists. The two co-founders of NLP have gone their separate ways. Bandler circumnavigates the planet promoting Design Human Engineering® while Grinder does the same with New Code. Other innovators promote their own 'brand' of NLP – for example, Dr Michael Hall heads up Neuro-Semantics, Tony Robbins has his Neuro-Associative Conditioning, Professor Graham Megson has Quantum Linguistic Patterning, and psychotherapy organizations such as NLPtCA and EANLPt tailor NLP to provide therapeutic outcomes. Branded approaches begin to emerge fully fledged as proprietary processes to assist in personal development of one kind or another, for example:

a **The LAB (Language and Behaviour) profile**. Shelle Rose Charvet builds upon the work of Rodger Bailey mentioned in Chapter 11.

b **Clean Language**. Penny Tompkins and James Lawley modelled the psychotherapist David Grove. We talk about this in Chapter 14.

c **Self Relations**. This is the work of Stephen Gilligan subsequent to his modelling of Milton Erickson.

d **Developmental Behavioural Modelling (DBM)**. This is John McWhirter's modelling of NLP to create a methodology and explanation of how NLP works.

e **Time Line**. This work is associated with Tad James who wrote *Time line therapy and the basis of personality* with Wyatt Woodsmall in 1988.

Pages could be filled, but what all of these innovations have in common is that they have successfully grown as a function of individual interest and predilection, yet have not done so according to any modelling project which has been properly written up and has demonstrably accorded with a protocol that demonstrates:

i **Selection of expert** and rationale as to why this person is regarded as an expert and how this person has demonstrated excellence over an extended period of time compared with other experts in the field.

ii **Unconscious uptake of the pattern.** How was this done? Methodologically, how is it possible? Even if, as Steve Andreas points out, it is not possible (Andreas, 2006), to what extent has 'unconscious uptake' been successful or not successful? If analytical modelling has been used, how explicitly is this related to the NLP literature? How were NLP design variables used in the modelling project? Why were these particular design variables chosen rather than others?

iii **Deployment of the pattern.** How has it been demonstrated that the modeller can now achieve the same outcome as the exemplar within the same context and time frame? How does this compare with a base measure of the modeller's competence and the competence of other experts in the field? How are these comparisons made and what is the evidence for any claim?

iv   **Codifying the pattern.** Where is this model written up in such a way that following the reduced set of elements others can now learn how to perform as well as the exemplar? What is the context for learning? Are any groups of people excluded from the learning process for this model? Can the model be refined into a design so as to include those who would ordinarily be excluded from learning?

v   **Testing of the model.** Where is the evidence that people who have been exposed to the model and who are motivated to learn the skills, perform as well as the exemplar in similar contexts and time frames? What is the nature of this evidence? How reliable is it? How valid is it? What methodological processes have been followed? What are the benefits and drawbacks of such a methodological approach? Do the learners now perform at a higher level compared with other experts in the field? What is the evidence for this?

From the examples on page 166, Clean Language and Self Relations probably come closest to the above process, but they are indeed a very far cry from what could be called a modelling project if we are to take the core discipline of NLP at face value and as described by the co-founders of NLP.

> Many people will call themselves NLP practitioners and simply do so on the basis of occasionally using Meta Model questions, perceptual positions or subscribing to *Rapport*.

The key question is, if we are not to take modelling as the core discipline of NLP, then can we still call it NLP? Many people will call themselves NLP practitioners and simply do so on the basis of occasionally using Meta Model questions, perceptual positions or subscribing to *Rapport: The Magazine for NLP Professionals* (ANLP). This is a bit like saying, I am a Christian because I live in England, or I support Chelsea because blue is a pretty colour.

I would suggest that if we take modelling out of NLP as we seem to have at present, we are left with an insipid form of eclectic pop psychology that would not look uncomfortable in the popular glossy magazines of airport terminals around the world.

3. Lack of Benchmarking and Agreed Standards in NLP Training ___

Following on from the Christians and Chelsea supporters, the lack of standardization concerning an NLP curriculum and quality control means any research will struggle to demonstrate internal validity. Internal validity demonstrates that we can reliably attribute outcomes in research to a particular independent variable, rather than some other intervening variable. It is for this reason we need to control research as much as possible for such variables as time, cohort of participants, location, etc. If we do not do this critics of the research could feasibly say the positive outcome was due to an intervening variable which was not controlled for. For example, they might say, 'Well, the reason this group got better results than the control group was the group consisted mainly of females and we believe females are generally better at naturally adopting the second perceptual position'. In this hypothetical case the outcome could have been influenced by an uneven distribution of gender rather than any specific NLP training.

So let us imagine two pieces of research. They both seek to test the hypothesis that a particular NLP model is more effective in developing communication skills compared with CBC. We run the two pieces of research and in one instance evidence is found that this is the case and in the other it is not found. In the wash-up the NLP trainers in the research which found evidence for NLP superiority say the trainers in the other experiment were not trained to an appropriate standard. They might say they did not fully understand the communication model or they omitted a crucial element. While we have this situation, as we do now, when NLP training is not standardized or quality controlled to any significant degree, we are not going to be able to do research that stands up.

4. Introduction of Non-NLP Literature

Tosey and Mathison (2009: 130) make the point that there is a growing tendency to introduce research findings from mainstream psychology and other disciplines into NLP literature. This is also the case concerning NLP training. For instance, in Train the Trainer the Kolb-based 4mat System of Bernice McCarthy is often used. Such non-NLP authors as Ken Wilber, Don Beck and Chris Cowan, and Peter Senge are routinely used to inform NLP trainings. Starting at the top of the Google listings for NLP trainers I found Michael Beale of PPI training. This led to a telephone conversation on 6 October 2011. Michael told me he readily makes use of the research conducted by neuro-scientists which supports NLP, for instance mirror neurons mentioned in Chapter 12. One of his favourite authors is the non-NLP author and psychologist Professor Richard Wiseman of Hertfordshire University in the UK.

While this tendency to 'import' material from other disciplines is to be applauded in terms of CPD and finding out 'what works', the key difficulty in terms of testing NLP is that such material, which is not derived from modelling projects, is then claimed as the domain of NLP, when it has clearly come from psychology, business studies, neuro-science or some other field. The NLP practitioner may throw their hands up in the air and say, 'So what, it works … let's make use of it'. However, my retort is, 'What works? How do you know it works consistently? And surely the best people to demonstrate whether or not it works and how it works are the people who put in the hard work in the first place and who probably understand it a lot better than you do?'

5. Who Does the Research?

In 1985 Einspruch and Forman published a paper in the *Journal of Counseling Psychology* stating that they had identified six categories of design and methodological errors within NLP research (39 empirical studies of NLP documented from 1975 through to April of 1984). They recommended that researchers into NLP be trained by competent NLP practitioners for an appropriate amount of time, and that NLP practitioners who are providing the therapy (*coaching*) have demonstrated mastery over the model and the associated techniques. They also recommended that dependent variables should be sensory based and objective and that research is conducted at an individual basis rather than a group basis so the therapist (*coach*) can appropriately calibrate to the patient (*coachee*) (my italics). Sharpley (1987) refuted the view of Einspruch and Forman (1985) that the efficacy of NLP interventions could not be determined, as current to that time methodological flaws invalidated the research. He suggested that if almost 86 per cent of controlled studies reliably failed to verify NLP[1] and that the non-supportive/supportive ratio of all research (including journals) to that time was 4.5:1, then it is hard to believe, as Einspruch and Forman claim, that this result is a function of methodological flaws.

It seems to me currently the answer is clear. The people who do research into NLP and NLP coaching are people who are versed both in research methodology and in NLP. Given that much criticism of NLP research is that it is only at the level of post-graduate dissertation, then the credibility of NLP can be enhanced even further when researchers such as Dr Frank Bourke, Professor Richard Gray, Dr Paul Tosey, Dr Jane Mathison, Professor Karl Nielsen, Professor Nandana Nielsen and Associate Professor Suzanne Henwood step up to the mark and accept the challenge. This indeed is exactly what these NLP practitioners and others like them are doing at present … and this is why it is a very exciting time to be involved in NLP and NLP coaching. What this does is provide a nice creative tension. It ensures that NLP does not fall into the trap of being unfalsifiable by ensuring qualified researchers adopt the appropriate methodology for the paradigm, and it also ensures that NLP practitioners are represented and the dynamic and systemic nature of NLP is fully represented in the research. In fact Sharpley (1987) makes exactly this point when he says in his paper, 'future research that can contribute new data on this issue via methodological advances or consideration of different aspects of NLP may be justified'. To this end Mathison and Tosey (2009), for example, have shown how the Meta Model and the concept of transderivational search are useful NLP tools and concepts to enhance the psychophenomenological explication interview. In terms of new paradigms which support NLP, they point to Lakoff and Johnson (1999) who propose a paradigm in cognitive science which recognizes that our conceptual system is grounded in, neurally makes use of, and is crucially shaped by our perceptual and motor systems. This of course is totally in accord with the APET model of Griffin and Tyrrell, which we discussed in Chapter 3.

---

[1]It should be noted that almost all of these studies tested only the NLP concept of primary representational systems.

6. How Is the Research Done?

Tosey and Mathison (2009: 139) point out that 70 per cent of organizational change strategies fail to deliver on outcomes, quoting Beer and Nohria (2000). However, these strategies do not come in for the vehement criticism that NLP appears to. This does not mean NLP has no need to be researched – it does. The question is, how can one do research in a way that accounts for the preceding five challenges? It might seem quite clear this is not an overnight job as the infrastructure to support such research will need to be put in place to start with. Just as we discovered in Chapter 15, the coaching associations are talking with each other and working in unison to develop a standard code of conduct for coaches working within the EU; so too NLP organizations really do need to work in a similar way.

> To what extent has *non*-NLP material been imported to NLP therapeutic and coaching practice which is *key* to efficacy and ethical practice?

In a very interesting radio programme broadcast by Radio 4 on 29 November 2010 William Little asked Lisa Wake the difference between NLP and NLP therapy. Although Wake pointed out that an NLP therapist would use NLP principles, attitudes and some of the tools within a therapeutic framework, being an NLP therapist *by itself* is not enough. She pointed out that well-meaning NLP practitioners and master NLP practitioners have provided interventions leaving individuals in even more uncomfortable and challenging places. A key question for the researcher then is as challenge 4 above: to what extent has *non*-NLP material been imported to NLP therapeutic and coaching practice which is *key* to efficacy and ethical practice?

In the same radio programme Richard Bandler points out that the type of research which Richard Churches of the CfBT Education Trust has done is typical of the research a good social psychologist would do, but is not the appropriate paradigm for research into NLP. Churches took as a base measure, results of a mathematics test for three different groups: (1) No training, (2) Innovative maths pedagogy and (3) NLP and innovative maths pedagogy. His team then took experimental measures for the three groups of learners after instruction and found only the NLP group had sufficient confidence levels to reject the Null hypothesis. Research hypothesis A was that adult learners whose teachers are trained in innovative maths pedagogy attain higher maths results than adult learners whose teachers have had no training. Research hypothesis B was that training in NLP influencing skills enhances the maths attainment of adult learners whose teachers have trained in innovative maths pedagogy.

When Bandler was asked how he would do the research, he said he would 'build a new school from the ground up, that's how I would test it and you know and I would take lots of the kids that are doing badly in school and lots of the kids that are doing good in school and I'd mix them all up together in a new formula, and I'd get rid of the grade level notion, and I'd make a race to the end of the educational system and find out how fast, how many of these kids could hit the cross line' (Little, 2010).

What Bandler seemed to omit in the interview is that a key characteristic of an NLP model is that the model is tested, so others who have been trained in the pattern of excellence can reproduce excellent results in the same context and within the same time frame as the exemplar. William Little seemed to appreciate this basic scientific process and suggested Richard Churches's approach is exactly the approach NLP should be taking. In the programme William Little did a little 'research' of his own. He disclosed a fear of swallowing pills and also difficulty in getting to sleep. He acknowledged a cramped BBC studio was probably not the best place to test the efficacy of NLP. However, after being taken through a well-known NLP pattern by one NLP practitioner to help with fear and a visualization exercise by a GP who was also an NLP master practitioner to help him sleep, he commented that he did not know for sure whether he had been cured of his fear of swallowing pills as he was still too anxious to try, and he made no comment concerning whether or not he could sleep any better on those occasions when previously he could not. Clearly Little's little experiment had not been favourable to NLP, despite recruiting two master NLP practitioners.

NLP by its very own admission is focused upon modelling what works and testing that comprehensively. To date no NLP model which accords with challenge 2 (i) to (v) above has been developed to my knowledge. Grinder acknowledges the Meta Model owes much of its incipience to Transformational Grammar, as does the methodology of modelling and the use of intuition as a key instrument in the modelling methodology. Concerning the Milton Model, in an email conversation with Bill O'Hanlon (2011) I was told:

> 'Erickson was once asked, several years after he met Bandler and Grinder, what he thought of their work. Bandler and Grinder spent four days with me and thought they got my techniques in a nutshell … What they got was the nutshell'. Bill continues, 'I had studied with Bandler and Grinder, obsessively read everything that they had written, did my Master's thesis on their work, and still I realized I was baffled by much of what Erickson was doing when I studied with him'.

Most NLP practitioners are well aware of Gregory Bateson's comment on the Milton Model … excellent patterning, shoddy epistemology![2]

How the research is done is still an open question and it is one NLP practitioners need to address. I would echo the sense of Tosey and Mathison (2009: 192). In my opinion if NLP is not tested using appropriate research methods that are current in science to date, it will only be of interest as a counter-culture social movement which provides no substantive contribution to human development. Like their contemporaries Carlos Castaneda, Ronnie Laing and Timothy Leary,

---

[2]This was the response of John Grinder to a direct question concerning what Gregory Bateson thought of the Milton Model at a three-day seminar on NLP modelling.

Bandler and Grinder are colourful and energetic personalities who in the 1970s attracted a following and still do, but do so on the basis of interesting ideas and challenging rhetoric which has yet to find substantial form, structure, process and content.

Conclusion

I have presented six challenges which NLP needs to address in order to get past the start line concerning research. It may be we discover NLP is just a self-help movement similar to Dale Carnegie's *How to win friends and influence people* (1936), or Norman Vincent Peale's *The power of positive thinking* (1952). Tosey and Mathison (2009: 161) point out that the leitmotiv of California in the early 1970s was not country, family and achievement, but love, peace and personal happiness. Forty years later post Enron and Lehman brothers, 9/11 and 7/7, Iraq and Afghanistan, tsunamis and earthquakes, maybe such a Zeitgeist has returned and the promise of autonomy, self-regulation and personal fulfilment are so enticing to many desperate souls that they sit wide-eyed and open-mouthed at the feet of NLP evangelists maxing out the Milton Model patterns.

Personally what attracted me to NLP was a course in the mid-1990s which was advertised as a module in a Masters degree at Derby University. What I found was a paradigm that had modelling at its centre and an appreciation of the unconscious which I had not experienced in my psychological journey to that time. The final convincer for me was the tremendous fun and enjoyment in learning. I personally believe that if we take NLP modelling out of NLP we are left with a Jackdoor epistemology that has no coherence and does not stand upon the shoulders of Giants, but simply misunderstands them, misquotes them and seeks to obtain credence by associating with them.

Professor Kinderman (Little, 2010) points out CBT would look very much like NLP if it had not been through the academic and scientific process to back it up. He said it would be a combination of placebo processes such as visualization and self-affirmation and scientifically validated processes such as graded exposure and possibly Socratic questioning of negative automatic thoughts. Whether you agree with Professor Kinderman or not, what is key is that the cognitive behavioural approach has subjected its claims to scientific investigation and discourse and consequently enjoys a far more credible status with key decision makers around the world.

Academic and scientific research does not have to be as Ulric Neisser experienced:

> In short the results of a hundred years of the psychological study of memory are somewhat discouraging. We have established firm empirical generalizations, but most of them are so obvious that every 10 year old knows them anyway. We have made discoveries, but they are only marginally about memory; in many cases we don't know what to do with them, and wear them out with endless experimental variations. (Neisser, 1982: 11)

NLP itself can contribute to methodological enquiry. I argued (Grimley, 2010) at the 2nd International NLP research conference in Cardiff that NLP enquiry is a viable form of action research. McNiff and Whitehead (2000), when talking about the theory–practice gap, quote Schon who argues for a new scholarship: a form of practical theorizing in action which is appropriate to all professional contexts.

'How do you do that?' is a really interesting question. Let us begin to answer in a scientific way so NLP can be all it can and start to attract funding and contribute in the only way such a dynamic paradigm can, with energy, enthusiasm, fun and enjoyment.

BRAIN TEASERS

1 Dr Anthony Grant says of Neuro-Associative Conditioning (NAC): 'The exaggerated claims made by Robbins as to the efficacy of NAC may well be harmful to individuals experiencing strong dysphoric states, and could increase their sense of failure when the promised results do not eventuate. Indeed, it could well be argued that Robbins' marketing of NAC comes close to breaking the Code of Ethics of the Australian Psychological Society (1997)'. Discuss how positive client expectation (Pygmalion effect) and supportive belief in a client's capability overstep the mark and wander into the unethical.

2 Discuss to what extent we can use predictive validity studies in coaching to 'promise' results to our prospective clients.

3 From a scientific point of view glowing testimonials are bound to skew the perception of our efficacy as coaches in a positive direction. To what extent is such a practice ethical?

4 Taking into consideration the Heisenberg uncertainty principle which tells us, *'The more precisely the position* is determined, the less precisely the *momentum* is known'*, to what extent can a positivist paradigm account for a dynamic social world?

5 If *you* were going to research NLP, how would you go about it?

EXERCISE 2

The embodied knowledge of taxi drivers would probably not be recognized by universities as valid knowledge. Taxi drivers would not get credits towards an MBA for getting an examiner to the station on time. The university expects excellence in abstract knowledge, not practical capacity. However, the reality of practice is the reverse: workplaces depend on practical capacity more than abstract knowledge (Fox, 1997: 52, cited in McNiff & Whitehead, 2000). To what extent is the nature of knowledge a political discourse with the concept of power being central? Examine the research you have developed consequent to Brain Teaser 5. Discover where it stands on the embodied–abstract knowledge continuum. What does this say about you politically?

17 NLP Resources

We all need a little help from our friends

As you probably are aware by now, even though the research that underpins the claims of NLP is in its very early stages, NLP activity around the world is exponentially increasing, testimony to 'something' within NLP which really resonates with twenty-first-century people. This chapter aims to help you, the reader, link up with professional NLP educators and groups so you can do the most important thing, and that is to start putting what you learn into practice. It is very important to recognize, as you choose an NLP provider to supplement your coaching credentials, that you need to keep in mind the 12 questions concerning coaching standards (Chapter 15). The range below can be from a five-day course with 500 other delegates to a 36-day course with a maximum of only 26 participants in the room and three trainers with intensive home and peer group work for the very same qualification of 'NLP Practitioner'. Of course, you can take your NLP coaching CPD further to post-graduate level and the gold standard offered by such coaching establishments run by Karl and Nandana Nielsen and Sally Vanson. In Australia, Chris and Jules Collingworth offer a vocational graduate certificate in NLP. If you still can't find the NLP answer you are looking for you can always contact me. I would be delighted to take your call.

NLP Organizations

There are not many truly independent NLP organizations. As we discovered in the previous chapter NLP has become fragmented and many well-marketed schools of NLP which claim to be special, unique or original for a host of reasons often find such speciality through association with a personality who was involved in the NLP movement during the 1970s or 1980s. Some NLP organizations seek to set independent standards for NLP training and those NLP trainers who wish to offer training under the relevant brand have to adhere to these standards. Understandably, and from an NLP perspective, these trainings will be in accord with the maps of the senior management team running such organizations and are far from 'objective'. The intention of such organizations is to step back from the 'this is how you do NLP camp', and recognize that though there are many ways to train in NLP, there is also a deeper structure which defines NLP and it is that which they seek to tap into as they represent NLP and provide NLP services to the public.

1. The Association of NLP (ANLP), www.anlp.org

A UK accrediting organization founded in 1985. ANLP's flagship publication, *Rapport* magazine, was joined by the first volume of *Current research in NLP*, which was published in 2009, and *Acuity*, a new anthology for shared findings and learning, in 2010. ANLP was set up as a Community Interest Company in 2008 and the MD is Karen Moxom. The strap line is 'ANLP – Informing the Public, Supporting our Members'.

2. The Professional Guild of NLP, www.professionalguildofnlp.com

A UK accrediting organization founded in 2003. What is characteristic about this organization is its enthusiasm to retain the 120 hours of direct training needed for an NLP practitioner certificate. In recent years it has become commercially attractive to certify NLP practitioners with less contact hours. Often hours are made up in these cases with video and audio materials. The Professional Guild of NLP believes that such materials from a pedagogical perspective are not as effective as the face-to-face contact with a certified trainer. All NLP training from this institution will therefore contain at least 120 hours of direct NLP training.

3. National Federation of Neuro-Linguistic Programming (NFNLP), www.nfnlp.com

The NFNLP is a US accrediting NLP organization set up by Dr William Horton in the early 1990s. Dr Horton believes the fact he is a *licensed* clinical psychologist compares with other NLP organizations which are led by doctors who are not licensed. He believes being licensed lends power to the argument of NLP as being legitimate. NFNLP was started because the majority of their students were already trained professionals and what they required was not extended training in their own field, but practical applications so they could enhance what they were already doing. He refers to social workers, alcohol and drug counsellors, psychologists and hypnotists. Dr Horton, when replying to the request for descriptions of NLP organizations for this chapter, pointed to the lack of recognition between NLP organizations, describing the field as very competitive and not at all accepting.

NFNLP has about 100 trainers worldwide, with a large presence in South East Asia and the Middle East.

4. The American Board of NLP (ABNLP), www.abh-abnlp.com

The American Board of NLP was founded in 1995 by Dr A.M. Krasner as an adjunct to the American Board of Hypnotherapy (ABH) and has functioned as its sister organization since then. ABNLP has a convention every February on President's Day weekend in Newport Beach with the ABH. The ABNLP has 500 institutions around the world certified to deliver NLP training. It recognizes that most NLP trainings around the world are quite similar, however it also recognizes that the style of delivery and the content may differ. It is for this reason it believes, like the other NLP organizations listed here, that its seal ensures training to a satisfactory standard.

5. John Grinder, www.johngrinder.com

John Grinder, the co-founder of NLP, together with Carmen Bostic St Clair, has joined up with the UK NLP trainer Michael Carroll to launch the International Trainers Academy of NLP (ITANLP) (www.itanlp.com). This too is an accrediting body and obviously accentuates the direction John Grinder has taken, which is New Code NLP. John Grinder also offers NLP training through his association with other NLP trainers around the world, many of whom have graduated from ITANLP.

6. Richard Bandler, www.richardbandler.com

Richard Bandler has branded many different NLP approaches, such as Design Human Engineering®, Persuasion Engineering® and Neuro-Hypnotic Repatterning™. He has teamed up with John LaValle to promote his training through the Society of NLP, which, like all of the above, is an accrediting body.

7. International NLP Trainers Association (INLPTA), www.inlpta.co.uk

INLPTA is an international co-operative association of aligned NLP trainers who have agreed to abide by and uphold INLPTA's standards of quality, professionalism and ethics in their NLP training and in the conduct of their NLP business. The association was started by Wyatt Woodsmall, an early NLP developer. Like other accrediting bodies, NLP trainers have been accredited through INLPTA from an international network of countries including the United Kingdom, the United States, Australia, New Zealand, South Africa, Germany, the Netherlands, Sweden and Slovenia.

8. NLP University, www.nlpu.com

Robert Dilts, an early developer of NLP, and his team offer NLP practitioner and NLP master practitioner certification. Understandably, like the organizations through which Bandler and Grinder train, Dilts has his own style of NLP. However, Dilts was at the forefront of the second wave of NLPers and is still playing a very active role.

9. International Association of Coaching Institutes (ICI), www.coaching-institutes.net/index.php

The International Association of NLP Institutes (IN) was founded in 2001 in Germany by Karl and Nandana Nielsen (www.nlp-institutes.net). It has more than 200 members in 33 countries. They work together with two universities in Nicaragua and in Mexico. Their NLP trainings can be recognized as credit points for studies (Lic., MA, PhD) in Psychology.

The IN offers as an option NLP with the P standing for Psychology. The IN works closely with the International Association of Coaching Institutes. They recognize Coaching as applied NLP – therefore the NLP qualifications of the IN are recognized as part of the Coaching qualifications of the ICI. The head of an IN Member Institute needs 252 days of training to be recognized. IN and ICI also organize the NLP & Coaching World Congresses

10. The Australian Board of NLP, www.abnlp.org.au

Founded in 1998, the ABNLP is the largest independent association in Australia. It is a non-profit organization run by volunteers from the NLP community. The Australian Board of Neuro-Linguistic Programming (ABNLP) Inc. was established to create a community of like-minded people who have a passion for NLP in Australia.

NLP Psychotherapy Organizations

The first exemplars for NLP were psychotherapists. It seems hardly surprising then that some NLP institutions specialize in psychotherapy.

1. The Neurolinguistic Psychotherapy and Counselling Association (NLPtCA), www.nlptca.com/

This is 'the home of NLP psychotherapy' in the UK. Set up 20 years ago it is within the College of Constructivist Psychotherapies of the United Kingdom Council for Psychotherapy (UKCP) as an accrediting member.

2. BeeLeaf Institute for Contemporary Psychotherapy, www.beeleaf.com

Pamela Gawler-Wright, a director of Beeleaf, describes her institute in the following way:

> BeeLeaf Institute for Contemporary Psychotherapy is a provider of NLP and Ericksonian Psychotherapy training to professional qualification, providing a direct route to UKCP registration as a psychotherapist. The school has been running since 1993 and is based in London, UK. The syllabus emphasizes Systemic NLP and combines this with a unique application of NLP as a meta science to integrate other models of psychotherapy influencing integrative outcome-oriented psychotherapy. As a UKCP accredited member organization, BeeLeaf Institute follows rigorous standards for application, assessment and monitoring of clinical practice which place the graduate in the best position for future employment in the field. Emphasis throughout the training is on effective, generative practice through the development of the personhood of the therapist, as expressive of their clinical excellence. Accredited Prior Learning (APL) may be awarded for elements of NLP training, research studies, mental health familiarization and practice experience. APL is calculated during the application process in respect of equivalent and diverse past learning.

3. Awaken School, www.awakenschool.co.uk

The Awaken School of outcome-oriented psychotherapies provides NLP practitioner and master practitioner programmes as part of a four-year comprehensive training pathway to UKCP accreditation as a psychotherapist. The pathway includes extensive clinical supervision of substantial clinical hours, personal therapy and personal development for therapists, and allied studies such as research methods, advanced patterns in psychotherapy, psychopathology, mental health placement, ethics and sociological perspectives on psychotherapy.

Awaken Consulting and Training Services Ltd also offers NLP training courses at diploma, practitioner and master practitioner level for coaching which has been recognized by the ANLP and the Association for Coaching. Awaken provide tailored specialist NLP coach programmes that provide a diploma in behavioural safety coaching. Each of the practitioner and master practitioner programmes is recognized through The Performance Solution as part of the MA in Applied Coaching at the University of Derby.

4. Lifetide Training, www.lifetidetraining.co.uk

Lifetide Training has developed a programme which meets the requirements of the NLPtCA to ensure that successful participants meet the accreditation requirements and so can be registered with the UKCP.

5. Austrian Training Centre for Neuro-linguistic Psychotherapy, www.nlpzentrum.at

Neuro-Linguistic Psychotherapy is described by Peter Schutz as a systemic imaginative method of psychotherapy with an integrative-cognitive approach. Peter runs a Ministry of Health accredited curriculum for the psychotherapeutic special training in Neuro-Linguistic Psychotherapy.

NLP Practice Groups

Once you have completed your NLP practitioner training you are encouraged to *practice* the patterns you learn on a regular basis. One of the best places to do this, especially if you are faint-hearted, is in NLP practice groups. The ANLP magazine *Rapport* has lists of these groups in the UK in its back pages. You will find after your internet search for an appropriate provider that most NLP training providers will be more than happy to point you in the right direction. Sometimes if there is no practice group near you, you will be encouraged and supported to set up an NLP practice group in your area.

NLP in Academia

There are some organizations which are actively interested in testing scientifically the claims of NLP and also exploring NLP in a structured way and systematically reporting their findings.

1. University of Surrey, School of Management, www.nlpresearch.org

Paul Tosey and Jane Mathison are both NLP trainers and have successfully supervised many PhD students who have included elements of NLP in their research.

2. NLP Research and Recognition Project (NLPR&R), http://nlprandr.org

Since its incorporation as a not-for-profit organization in 2008 the NLP Research and Recognition Project has accrued, in addition to the leadership necessary for a corporate Board of Directors, an advisory board of 40 leaders from the field of NLP, academia and business. Among them are Professor Emeritus Bill McDowell from Marshall University; International NLP consultant and trainer Shelly Rose Charvet from Toronto; Dr Paul Tosey from Surrey University; Professor Richard Gray from Fairleigh Dickenson University; and Provost Rosalyn Templeton from Montana State University. Its membership, from around the world, has swelled to 800. For its first large project, it has developed a researchable protocol for treating PTSD from NLP materials, which it is attempting to get certified in the USA as 'evidentiary medicine' by completing gold standard, university-sponsored research. Among its other current projects, its members will also be publishing the first comprehensive review and evaluation of existing NLP clinical research, as well as recommendations for future research based upon the comprehensive critical review.

3. Richard Churches @ CfBT Education Trust, www.cfbt.com

CfBT offers a Certificate of Professional Practice in Coaching and Mentoring which includes a lot of NLP. Richard holds a PhD from Surrey University and was supervised by Paul Tosey. It is his research that William Little referred to in the Radio 4 interview mentioned in the previous chapter. Richard is leading the charge concerning the use of NLP within education.

NLP in Coaching

As we discovered in Chapters 1 and 2, NLP is an unregulated activity and coaching is a new and emerging industry. What this means is despite there being the occasional post-graduate qualification with modules containing elements of NLP, there is no definitive route to becoming a professional coach in the way there is a well-defined route to becoming a professional psychologist, doctor or lawyer.

The gold standard in NLP coaching, for example, is offered by the training organizations which bear the seal of the International Association of NLP Institutes run by Karl and Nandana Nielsen in Germany, who, like Peter Schutz in Austria, offer MSc programmes for NLP coaching through their centres: www. coaching-institutes.net/index.php and www.nlpzentrum.at.

The gold standard at the time of writing is also offered by Sally Vanson, CEO of The Performance Solution, and Jules and Chris Collingwood from Inspiritive in Australia. Even though not university-based the competency-based Meta Coaching programs run by Michael Hall are probably equivalent to post-graduate level.

However, the majority of NLP coaches at present are not qualified at these gold standards and will settle for an NLP practitioner certificate and a coaching certificate from one of the many coaching training organizations which are members of one of the coaching associations listed in the next section.

1. The Performance Solution, www.theperformancesolution.com

The Performance Solution offers a Master's degree which culminates in a traditional research-based dissertation that both encompasses and extends the breadth of NLP. Students have to get their hours in for ICF (International Coaching Federation) qualifications and do practical as well as academic assessments so double loop learning continues throughout. The degree programme is now in its third iteration and running at the University of Derby. Successful students are now progressing to Doctoral studies in 2012, providing a much needed and current research base where they both challenge and integrate the concepts of the various personalities who have informed and dominated the field so far.

2. Inspiritive, www.inspiritive.com.au

Jules and Chris Collingwood from Inspiritive in Australia have gone to the trouble of developing their vocational graduate certificate in NLP.

Inspiritive offers comprehensive NLP training in a New Code design. As an Australian Registered Training Organization, it has a Vocational Graduate Certificate in NLP and a suite of five-day Nationally Recognized Training Short Courses in NLP applications. The Vocational Graduate Certificate is an accredited post-graduate qualification equivalent to post-graduate certificates offered by universities around the world. It is a 40-day programme with eight units of five days each and can be accessed via the Inspiritive website.

Coaching Associations

1. Association for Coaching, www.associationforcoaching.com/home/index.htm

Katherine Tulpa is the CEO and co-founder with Alex Szabo who is the COO of the Association for Coaching. Launched in July 2002 as a UK organization, it is now an international membership organization which provides accreditation for coaches.

2. European Mentoring and Coaching Council (EMCC), www.emccouncil.org

The EMCC sees itself as a unifying coaching body. Its key focus is to develop European standards, ethics and a professional code with a view to assure quality in the industry.

3. International Coach Federation (ICF), www.coachfederation.org

A coaching organization formed in 1995 and providing independent certification for coaches, the ICF defines coaching as partnering with clients in a thought-provoking and creative process that inspires them to maximize their personal and professional potential.

4. The Special Group in Coaching Psychology (SGCP), www.sgcp.org.uk

A subgroup within the British Psychological Society (BPS), the SGCP is dedicated to supporting coaching psychologists. Its aim is to promote the development of coaching psychology as a professional activity and clarify the benefits of psychological approaches within coaching practice.

5. The Australian Psychological Society's Interest Group for Coaching Psychology (IGCP), www.groups.psychology.org.au/igcp

IGCP was created in August 2002 to facilitate the theoretical, applied and professional development of coaching psychology as an emerging sub-discipline of psychology. The interest group, in collaboration with the SGCP, launched the *International Coaching Psychology Review* in 2006. This peer-reviewed academic and professional publication focuses on the theory, research and practice of coaching psychology.

6. Association for Professional Executive Coaching and Supervision (APECS), www.apecs.org

APECS is the professional body for executive coaching and for the supervision of executive coaches. Executive coaching differs from other forms of coaching in that it is primarily concerned with the development of the executive in the context of the needs of their organization. APECS defines 'executive' as a person who has a level of leadership responsibility (financial/operational/ people) and/or responsibility for policy formulation and/or who makes a senior level individual contribution to the organization.

NLP Books and DVDs

Anglo American Books (www.anglo-american.co.uk) is a specialist booksellers covering NLP, hypnosis, coaching and personal growth. They distribute a free newsletter and new book review called *Changes* and also run the NLP Conference.

A Selection of 11 NLP Coaching Books to Get You Started

1 Angus McLeod, *Performance coaching*, Crown House Publishing (2003). A very good NLP handbook with great linguistic tips inside. What is especially great is that NLP is hardly ever mentioned.

2 Curly Martin, *The life coaching handbook*, Crown House Publishing (2001). A really good straightforward NLP coaching text.

3 Jeremy Lazarus, *Ahead of the game*, Ecademy (2006). An NLP coaching book which looks at the application of NLP coaching to sport.

4 Phil Hayes, *NLP coaching*, Open University Press (2006). A part of the Coaching in Practice series. A book on the application of NLP in executive coaching.

5 Suzanne Henwood and Jim Lister, *NLP and coaching for health care professionals: developing expert practice*, John Wiley and Sons (2007). An excellent NLP coaching book in a specialist sector.

6 Joseph O'Connor and Andrea Lages, *How coaching works*, A&C Black (2007). The authors integrate other coaching models such as The Inner Game and GROW model into this coaching book by one of NLP's most prolific authors. Robert Dilts provides a contribution in the chapter on NLP coaching and there is a useful reflection on coaching psychology by Anthony Grant.

7 Michael Hall and Michelle Duval, *Meta-coaching*, Volume 1 and Volume 2, Neuro-Semantics Publications (2004). Michael Hall, another prolific NLP writer who we looked at in Chapter 14, along with Michelle Duval (one of the expert coaches he modelled), explains his transformative Meta Coaching system consisting of the Meta States model, the Matrix model and the Axes of Change model.

8 Susie Linder-Pelz, *NLP coaching*, Kogan Page (2010). An excellent book that has the academic rigour of Tosey and Mathison, yet also a practical texture which will assist any NLP coach wishing to understand how NLP coaching really works.

9 Joseph O'Connor and Andrea Lages, *Coaching with NLP*, Element (2004). Another coaching book by Joseph O'Connor with Andrea Lages. This time they focus more specifically on NLP coaching.

10 Robbie Steinhouse, *How to coach with NLP*, Pearson Education Limited (2010). A really good little NLP coaching paperback.

11 Ian McDermott and Wendy Jago, *The NLP coach*, Piatkus (2001). A good comprehensive NLP coaching book.

18

Conclusion: Where NLP Goes From Here?

A journey of a thousand miles starts with the first step. That step needs to be in the right direction

Congratulations if you are still with me on this epic journey through the jungle of NLP. By now you know something of the deep structure of NLP, so when you see the tremendous variety within the surface structure you understand there is a common deeper link that holds NLP practice together. This deep structure concerns an appreciation of the unconscious and a desire to be the best you can by utilizing the fantastic resource of the unconscious mind in partnership with the conscious mind. The word psychology is derived from the Greek word 'logos' meaning *word*. For NLP coaches what lights their fire is not *talking* about psychology, it is *doing* it. I feel, as a passionate psychologist myself, sometimes in the psychology profession we get this wrong – we do a bit too much *talking* and *systemizing* and not enough *doing* and *experiencing*. As Ian McGilchrist (2009) points out, in twenty-first-century Western living, we need to balance our left-brain activity a little more with some extra right-brain activity. NLP is most definitely the model to help you do this.

I think at this juncture it might be a good idea to remind ourselves of Tosey and Mathison's six faces of NLP (2009: 14). The NLP coach will firstly encounter the surface structure of framework, techniques, consumables and coaching products. However, the deep structure and the substance of NLP is in the practical magic, methodology and underlying philosophy.

1　Practical magic: communication in action.
2　Methodology: modelling core of the practice.
3　Philosophy: epistemology and presuppositions.
4　Technology: framework techniques.
5　Commodities: consumables, self-help products.
6　Professional services: coaching, consulting and psychotherapy.

Another useful chunking-up exercise was found in Chapter 10 where Bostic St Clair and Grinder sum up the whole gamut of every NLP coaching strategy as a function of five Meta strategies (2001: 198–9). Each of these strategies has nothing more than the manipulation of unconscious representations as their core objective:

- The Meta Model, designed to verbally challenge the mapping between first access to the outside world through our senses (F^1), and our linguistically mediated mental maps (F^2).

- Operations defined over representational systems and their sub-modalities, for example the Swish technique.

- Reframing patterns, where representations are placed in a different cognitive structure.

- Anchoring, where undifferentiated groupings of representations are brought together for purposes of integration.

- The Milton Model, where representations at F^1 (first access through our senses to the world) are shifted by using F^2 (linguistically mediated maps) patterning without the need to map those representations into the client's conscious understanding.

Of course one needs to add to these five the core methodology of NLP which is that of modelling.

Even though I may not have cleared the jungle for you in this book, hopefully what I have done is put some signposts up so that as you hear the language and see the practice you too now have a map of the NLP world, which you can intelligently add to and make use of.

Based upon the map *I have*, below I provide some subjective pointers as to what I think NLP and NLP coaching needs to do in order to develop into what it should be already.

1. Modelling Other Successful Paradigms

I think one lesson NLP practitioners need to learn is from the lessons of the past. CBT[1], which started at about the same time as NLP, is only more widely accepted and used within mainstream clinical practice than NLP because it has been validated using positivist methodology. NLP coaching now has the opportunity to ensure during the next 30 years this mistake is not replicated. If NLP coaching practitioners begin to gather evidence that NLP when used as a coaching paradigm is more effective than other paradigms or at least equivalent, they and their associated institutions can begin to make the business case more effectively

While many NLP 'experts' have historically either ignored the need for research evidence for the effectiveness of NLP techniques or maintained the 'un-measurable nature' of NLP techniques, 'knowing' IS 'measuring' and useful knowledge must have standardized measures.

---

[1]CBT actually started in the late 1950s and early 1960s under the name of Rational Emotive Therapy (RET) with Albert Ellis at the helm. Aaron Beck who developed CBT later drew heavily on the work of RET.

in the future. This may appear to be a paradox given I have just said that NLP can help us make more use of our right hemisphere, but it is not. If a coachee comes to you because they are over muscling an activity and making too much use of their conscious mind they will not be effective in that activity. This lack of efficiency is something which can be quantified in some way. At the end of the coaching intervention when they have learned to make more use of their own unconscious resources in the context of that activity their performance will be markedly improved. This measurement provides the evidence that NLP, when used in coaching, works. This state of affairs is put nicely by the executive director of the NLP Research and Recognition Project, Dr Frank Bourke:

> I believe strongly that a 'statistical system of analysis' that develops validation and replication measures for outcome measures of psychotherapy research based upon individual clients' outcomes will be able to be developed. While many NLP 'experts' have historically either ignored the need for research evidence for the effectiveness of NLP techniques or maintained the 'un-measurable nature' of NLP techniques, 'knowing' IS 'measuring' and useful knowledge must have standardized measures. (Bourke, 2011)

2. More Science Less Marketing

NLP practitioners need to learn to be more honest about the extent to which their interventions can assist people in obtaining their outcomes. We discovered in Chapter 16 that Tony Grant suggested it could be argued that Tony Robbins's marketing of NAC comes close to breaking the code of ethics of the Australian Psychological Society. NLP needs to focus less on marketing and more on science.

3. Better Collaboration and More Discipline

NLP associations and institutes around the world need to start communicating and collaborating more effectively in order to develop common standards of practice. NLP also needs to develop protocols to explicate clearly how such standards are evidenced.

NLP needs to throw off the chaos of the past and concentrate on a more disciplined future if it is to move up to the next step. Seasoned practitioners of NLP know of the associated court cases: the murder of Corine Christensen, after which Richard Bandler was arrested in the winter of 1986 (Clancy & Yorkshire, 1989) and the release and covenant not to sue signed between Bandler and Grinder on 3 February 2000 (Bostic St Clair & Grinder, 2001). The two co-founders of NLP still do not talk to each other and while this lack of collaboration is modelled, NLP will never become a coherent discipline which can add to our knowledge.

4. Putting Modelling Back into the Heart of NLP

NLP as a discipline needs to start acting 'as if' it does believe modelling is at the heart of its practice. If we take the format in Chapter 16 (section 2, i–v) as the NLP modelling format which it is, then to date we do not have one NLP model in existence. I give my reasons why this is the case in that chapter. It may well be that the coding and testing of any NLP model is indeed at present a vague art, and if it is, NLP practitioners should come clean about this and develop a Meta Model to increase the efficacy of this aspect of modelling rather than harp on about modelling being the core of NLP. Grinder himself recognizes that there is no known useful algorithm for modelling. This is despite the digitalization of analogue processes being an issue of supreme importance to NLP in his opinion. As I point out in previous chapters, if NLP cannot begin addressing this conundrum, it is then reduced to an insipid form of eclectic pop psychology.

> If coding and testing of any NLP model is a vague art, NLP practitioners should come clean about this and develop a Meta Model to increase the efficacy of this aspect of modelling rather than harp on about modelling being the core of NLP.

5. More Critical Analysis, Less Personality

NLP needs to pay less attention to personalities and more attention to critical analysis. I watched a programme on TV one evening (ITV4, 28 October 2011) where millionaire evangelical pastors in Nigeria were telling an ITV reporter (Seyi Rhodes) that they are raising people from the dead on a regular basis. When going to an evangelical meeting the reporter pointed out among all the injured people who had come for a miracle cure the only difference he could see was a dustbin that was empty at the beginning of the meeting was full of money at the end of the meeting. Mfonobong Nsehe (2011), who blogs for *Forbes* business magazine, put the joint wealth of five Nigerian pastors at £121 million. I could not help but think of the present state of NLP and the similarities. However, to date NLP, to my knowledge, has not claimed the ability to raise people from the dead. This capability by personality trend in NLP is very similar to what Malcolm Gladwell has coined the Warren Harding error, where we make the wrong decision very quickly, yet with great certainty, based upon an unuseful map of the world. Warren Harding was regarded as one of the worst ever US presidents. His speeches were described as 'an army of pompous phrases moving over the landscape in search of an idea' (Gladwell, 2005: 73).

6. Good Quality Science Which Is Appropriate to the NLP Paradigm

Given Dr Bourke's comment above contrasted with the acknowledgement that NLP is anti-positivist in orientation, a scientific way of measurement must be developed to address this issue. Many other paradigms have done this. For instance, EMDR which was developed from NLP (Shapiro, 1985) has done this very effectively and is constantly requested when insurance companies need an evidence-based approach to assist people. Standard randomized control methods are often criticized based upon the premise that human life is too dynamic and complex. Jonah Lehrer (2010) points to the decline effect, which shows many perfectly good randomized controlled studies in psychology, medicine and biology, which cost millions of pounds/dollars, when replicated produce declining results. He points to such well-known effects as the experimenter effect, publication bias, regression to the mean and just sheer randomness which cannot be controlled for. He concludes that just because an idea can be proved doesn't mean it's true, and the converse. When the experiments are done, we still have to choose what to believe.

Despite these well-documented criticisms of positivist science, a much more critical appraisal and a higher quality of research needs to become established before NLP practitioners can ethically and professionally talk about NLP in the manner that they do.

If NLP truly does believe, as I suggest it does, that we live in a world of individual and collective constructs then an ideographic methodology needs to be pursued. NLP needs to develop robust protocols for unconscious uptake, deployment of pattern, coding of pattern and testing of pattern. I would suggest it is this aspect of NLP at present which is most ambivalent, yet it is also this aspect of NLP that needs the closest attention, as it is at the heart of NLP practice. Both Robert Dilts (1998) and Gordon and Dawes (2005) have made good attempts, and Bostic St Clair and Grinder (2001) through New Code NLP endeavour to assist people in accessing the 'know nothing' state, which is good for modelling as well as the application of New Code NLP. However, these efforts are very much the exception rather than the rule.

Modelling of course can be accomplished at an organizational level as well as an individual level. Dilts modelled leaders at Fiat in the late 1980s. However, currently there seems little consistency in how these projects flow, and they do not seem to flow in the way modelling is described in the NLP literature. Dilts's model (Dilts, 1998) sounds more like a psychology project with phrases such as 'needs analysis', 'survey of current literature', 'interviews with selected top managers', and even the recognition that NLP modelling does employ questionnaires. Dilts recognizes NLP needs to make use of active engagement with the exemplar, however he goes on to suggest it is this mix of conscious cognitive data with data obtained from the modelling that provides the 'highest quality information' (Dilts, 1998: 46).

This brings us back to the key difficulty in NLP: the lack of an agreed definition. Without this we actually have nothing to research from either a positivist or non-positivist perspective.

7. Clear Definition

It would be excellent in my opinion if some of the bodies mentioned in Chapter 17 could put their heads together and come up with an NLP coaching definition that is clear and precise. If it does use words like modelling in the definition, it would also be most helpful if they could agree among themselves specifically what type of modelling and how that modelling is accomplished.

Such a state of affairs would then set the ball in motion for good quality courses in NLP coaching (which can be accredited by those organizations) and then good quality research into the interventions provided by those coaches.

What If?

What if NLP could do all the above? If it could ... it would match all that the CBT paradigm has done and more. If it does not ... it will remain a somewhat jaded but popular pop psychology driven by marketing and personality, rather than innovative new ideas, critical analysis and scientific dialogue. In my opinion it is as simple as that. Only the next 20 years will tell us which direction NLP is going to take.

Does this mean one needs to put the equivalent of the Belo Monte Dam through our jungle and call this progress? I believe it does not. It means, as section 6 above suggests, we need to look at this jungle we call the human race and without imposing our paradigms and statistical tests upon it too readily, observe and record accurately using all means possible the patterns of excellence which emerge and are distinguished at the 99.9 percentile. NLP believes the unconscious human mind is the best instrument for this job. Ok then, let us start to put that to the test.

Tosey and Mathison (2009: 182) say NLP techniques have been over-sold and under-tested. They provide eight research avenues which could take NLP forward and are abbreviated below (2009: 195):

a Action research by practitioners.

b Case studies and evaluations.

c Modelling projects.

d Review and testing of specific NLP models and techniques.

e Surveys of the incidence and use of NLP.

f Elaboration and critique of the underpinning philosophy and epistemology of NLP.

g Studies of NLP as a social phenomenon.

h Use of NLP to enhance existing research methods.

I would totally agree with Tosey and Mathison *if* NLP had actually got past the start post concerning serious research into its efficacy. However, I believe NLP is not yet at that stage; rather, it has got its running gear on and is limbering up. Maybe the NLP Research and Recognition Project will be the first major piece of research into NLP techniques ever?

I think we still need firstly to understand and agree on what NLP is (f), and this will pave the way for modelling (c) and then testing of those techniques (d). This provides us with the simple answer to the question that most people want to know: 'What is NLP and does it work?'

If NLP had already done this and we found it did work, then the other areas of research would be interesting. If we engage in those other areas of research *before* we know what NLP is and whether it works there is the likelihood the fog of NLP will continue. It will then be supported by interesting and good quality qualitative research which investigates a social phenomenon that has no evidence of utility in specific contexts and is very similar to the evangelical movement in Nigeria (see section 5 above).

Put Up or Shut Up

> The shining stars of NLP thus are tagged with the buzzword 'genius' and become the sum of their anecdotes. Brown points out that within NLP the subject of testing is generally mocked.

NLP has had a good run and has many interesting stories to tell. Derren Brown, the well-known TV magician, calls NLP the Frankenstein grandchild of Milton Erickson (Brown, 2007: 128). He goes on to tell us the permissive approach of Erickson, which NLP has modelled, puts NLP into a tricky situation. Often the permissive approach will make use of fictitious anecdotes to indirectly produce the desired change in someone. Brown goes on to explain how similarly anecdotes are told about the miraculous changes created by the founders of NLP with little importance paid to how accurate the facts are. The shining stars of NLP thus are tagged with the buzzword 'genius' and become the sum of their anecdotes. He points out that within NLP the subject of testing is generally mocked. I think he has a very good point. At least when Derren Brown does his amazing tricks on TV he tells us they are a function of magic, misdirection, showmanship and psychology. He does not tell us the proportion each of these variables enjoy, however we are left in awe at someone who can appear to do miraculous things, simply because he is honest about the fact he is going to be dishonest with us, as all magicians are. Brown, who himself has attended an NLP practitioner, talks with delight when he experienced two instances of modelling providing no better outcome than that of traditional teaching in the skill of sharp shooting and juggling. For Brown, NLP's exaggerated claims in an unchecked and sprawling industry that affects personal lives and business is concerning. He seems quite unequivocal when he says, 'spending those few days in the company of hundreds of would-be NLP'ers had put me off ever practicing it as a profession' (Brown, 2007: 186).

If NLP is to gain any traction in the world of people who think critically, it needs to address the points concerning what it is precisely, and what it can do.

We know NLP has credibility because it links itself with well-known paradigms within traditional psychology. However, we have absolutely no evidence to date that the techniques which flow from NLP are any better than those parallel techniques in other disciplines.

For example, is the Meta Model any more effective than Socratic questioning? Is the Milton Model any better than clinical hypnosis? Are rapport, matching and pacing techniques any better than those taught in a sales seminar or a Rogerian workshop? Can NLP leverage gains using perceptual positioning and time line any better than a Gestalt therapist? Are NLP well-formed outcomes any more effective than goal setting in CBC? Is NLP emotional state management any better than positive psychology? We do not know the answer to any of these questions. The list could go on and on. Until NLP practitioners show us good quality evidence for their case, NLP will remain an amusing anecdote of the face of the planet. Maybe the answer concerning NLP to date has been staring us in the face all along on the cover of the very first volume, *The structure of MAGIC*. Let us hope the next 40 years can make use of science to take us out of that double bind.

BRAIN TEASERS

1 Now you have finished this book, which path are you going to follow in the NLP jungle to supplement your coaching? Will it be modelling? Will it be Meta Programs? Will it be well-formed outcomes? Why is it that you have chosen to follow this particular signpost in the NLP jungle?

2 The next two questions are known in NLP as the Outcome Sequitur and the Meta Outcome:

Now you have finished this book what is going to happen next? If you achieved what happens next, what would that mean for you? Whatever it is I wish you every success in the jungle of life.

Appendix 1

Examples of some Meta Programs*

Appendix Table 1.1   Proactive–Reactive Meta Program

Style	Description	Influencing language
Proactive	Proactive people initiate, make things happen; act with little or no consideration. They are motivated by doing; can bulldoze. Short crisp sentences; active verbs; body language show signs of impatience; pencil tapping; inability to sit for long periods.	*Go for it; just do it; jump in; why wait; now; right away; get it done; take the initiative; take charge; run with it; what are you waiting for; let's hurry.*
Reactive	Reactive people wait for others to initiate; might analyse without acting; need to fully assess before acting; believe in chance and luck; are good analysts. Incomplete, long sentences, subject or verb missing; passive verbs; lots of infinitives; conditionals *would, could, might, may;* believe in chance or luck; talk about *thinking about, analysing, understanding;* willing to sit for long periods.	*Let's think about it; now that you have analysed it; you'll really understand; this will tell you why; consider this; this will clarify it for you; think about your response; the time is ripe; luck is coming your way; wait until ...*

There is no traditional question to ask. These styles are determined by observing body language and the way in which people talk.

---

*From Rose Charvet (1997)

Appendix Table 1.2   Internal–External Meta Program

Style	Description	Influencing language
Internal	People with an internal pattern provide their motivation from within themselves. They decide about the quality of their work. They may have difficulty accepting other people's opinions. They gather information from the outside then make a decision based on internal standards. Sitting upright, minimal gestures, point to self. Outside information is taken as information to be weighed internally.	*Only you can decide; you might consider; it's up to you; I suggest that you think about it; here's some information so that you can decide.*
External	People with an external pattern derive their motivation from other people, and need outside feedback to know how well they have done. They will compare their work with outside norms; outside information is taken as an order.	*You'll get good feedback; others will notice; it has been approved by; well respected; you'll make quite an impact; so-and-so thinks; I would strongly recommend; the experts say; give references; scientific studies show.*

Traditional Question: *How do you know when you've done a good job?*

Appendix Table 1.3   Options–Procedures Meta Program

Style	Description	Influencing language
Options	Options people are motivated by opportunities and possibilities to do something in a different way, even break the rules. There is always another better way to have things. They create procedures and systems but have difficulty following them. They like to start new ideas and new projects but not necessarily complete them.	*Use words like opportunities; variety; unlimited possibilities; lots of choice; options; break the rules.*
Procedures	These people like to follow set ways. They believe there is a right way to do things. They learn a procedure and can follow it over and over again. They are interested in how to do things. As they are motivated to get to the end of a procedure once started, they will always complete what they start. They are interested in how people do things, not why.	*The right way; how to; tried and tested; tell me about the process; first ... then ... lastly; reliable; proven; how to use this.*

Traditional Question: *Why did you choose ... (e.g. your present job)?*

Appendix Table 1.4   Sameness–Difference Meta Program

Style	Description	Influencing language
Sameness	Sameness people want their situation to stay the same. They do not like the idea of change, even if they can manage it. Change is acceptable every 10 years but they will only provoke change once every 15–25 years.	*Highlight the sameness; same as; in common; as you always do; like before; unchanged; as you already know; maintaining; totally the same; exactly as before; identical.*
Sameness with Exception	These people like things mainly the same but will accept non-drastic change once a year. Show how the new is the same as before but then point out a difference.	*More; better; less; the same except; advanced; upgrade; progression; gradual improvement; similar but even better; moving up; growth; improvement.*
Difference	Difference people love change; they thrive on it and it has to be constant and major. They need change about every 1–2 years.	*New; totally different; unlike anything else; unique; one of a kind; completely changed; unrecognizable; shift; switch; a complete turnaround; brand new; unheard of; the only one.*

Traditional Question: *What is the relationship between your job this year and last year?*

Appendix Table 1.5   Towards–Away From Meta Program

Style	Description	Influencing language
Towards	Towards people stay focused on their goal. They are motivated to have, get, achieve, attain, etc. They sometimes miss what should be avoided. They talk about achieving their goals. Body language: pointing towards something, nodding, gestures of inclusion. They find it difficult to motivate themselves when they do not have a goal.	*Attain; obtain; have; get; include; achieve; benefits; advantages; accomplish.*
Away From	Away From people notice what should be avoided, got rid of and otherwise not happen. They are motivated by solving a problem – moving away from something that is happening. They are energized by threats. They find it difficult to motivate themselves when everything is OK.	*Avoid; prevent; eliminate; solve; get rid of; won't have to; let's find out what's wrong.*

Traditional Questions: *What is important to you (at work)?*
(Take one from the list or take the single answer)
Why is that important? (After next answer)

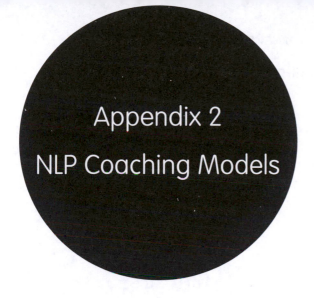

Appendix 2

NLP Coaching Models

7 C's Coaching Model (www.achieving-lives.co.uk)

Bruce Grimley
Achieving Lives NLP Training
185 Ramsey Road, St Ives, Cambridgeshire, PE27 3TZ
Tel: 01480 359108
www.achieving-lives.co.uk

7 C's Coaching Questions

- **Clarity:** *specific, measurable.* 'What specifically do you want to happen?' (ensure sensory-based and well-formedness). 'How would you know you have achieved this?' 'How would you test your outcome achievement?'

- **Climate:** *ecology, timeframe.* 'Is this the right time to do this?' 'How long are you giving yourself?' 'Does any part object?'

- **Capable:** *achievable.* 'Is there anybody else who could achieve this?' 'What would they do to achieve this?' 'Do you have the necessary training to achieve this?'

- **Communicate:** *confidence, ecology, congruence.* 'Tell me about your outcome' and 'How will you achieve it?' (use Meta Model questions: what, when, where, who, how? Then calibrate).

- **Confidence:** *stated in positive, preservation of positive, chunk size.* 'Tell me about your outcome' (ensure it is not 'away from'). 'In obtaining this outcome is there anything you are leaving behind of value?' (if yes, reframe outcome to include that of value). 'Given the time you have given yourself, is this the right chunk size for you?'

- **Congruence:** *ownership, future pace.* 'Do you own each aspect of this outcome?' 'I would like you to imagine yourself achieving this goal in the future' (calibrate). 'When do you know it is time to start this?' (anchor strategy to external or internal trigger).

- **Commitment:** *motivation, future pace.* 'Do you *really* want this?' (calibrate congruence and ecology). 'I actually don't think you do want this' (again calibrate congruence and ecology). Future pace as for congruence.

Meta Coaching (www.meta-coaching.org)

USA

The Meta-Coach Training System
PO Box 8
Clifton, Colorado, 81520, USA
Tel: 877-686-2867; +1-970-523-7877
Email: usa@meta-coaching.org

Europe

Germaine Rediger
Rood Kruisstraat 48
1500 Halle
Belgium
Tel: 00 32 2 3053545 – gsm 0474/719469
Email: germaine@indialogue.eu
Website: www.indialogue.eu
Skype: germainered

South Africa

Cheryl Lucas
Tel: 012 362 6542
Mobile: 083 267 1412
Fax: 088 012 362 3167
Email: cheryl@peoplesa.co.za
Website: www.psacoaching.co.za
Skype: Meta Coach

Australia

Martin Urban
Urban Trainings
Gold Coast, Australia
Tel: 1300 660 175; 61 7 5530 6652
Mobile: 61 411 388 318
Email: martin@UrbanTrainings.com
Website: www.UrbanTrainings.com
Skype: martinurban1

Heidi Heron
Australasian Institute of NLP
Level 9, 143 York Street
Sydney NSW 2000
Australia
Tel: +61 2 9264 5418

Email: heidi@nlpworldwide.com
Website: www.nlpworldwide.com

Joseph Scott
The Leadership Coach
PO Box 19
Blackmans Bay 7052
Tasmania, Australia
Tel: 0437 121 121
Email: joseph@theleadershipcoach.com.au

Mexico

Omar Salom
Email: omar@salomchd.com or emilia@salomchd.com

New Zealand

Lena Gray
Tel: 027 4774 561
Email: lena@ignition.org.nz
Website: www.ignition.org.nz

Clean Language (www.cleanlanguage.co.uk)

To contact either Penny Tompkins or James Lawley, go to the contact page of
the above website or email:
james@cleanlanguage.co.uk
penny@cleanlanguage.co.uk

Clean Change Coaching (www.cleanchange.co.uk/cleanlanguage)

Clean Change Company Ltd
18 Byfield Road, Isleworth, Middlesex, TW7 7AF
Tel: +44 (0)20 8400 4832

Appendix 3
NLP Design Models

As mentioned in Chapter 12 the difference between a model and a design is that a design takes the patterns which have been found in modelling projects and puts them together to create another model. There are many NLP coaching models which seek to address the complex systemic relationships between the conscious and the unconscious. They take many of the NLP design variables and put them together in a comprehensive and coherent way to address each aspect of human functioning as seen from the NLP perspective. The reader can readily access these models by looking up the relevant entry in the NLP encyclopedia online or putting the acronym into their web browser. Below are some of the more well-known NLP designs.

BAGEL (Body posture, Accessing cues, Gestures, Eye movements, Language patterns)

A design created by Robert Dilts which puts together all the NLP variables that help a coach calibrate the internal state of a coachee through that which is observable in the outside world.

RESOLVE (Resourceful state for the practitioner, Establish rapport, Specify outcome, Open up the coachee's model of the world, Leading to desired state, Verify change, Ecological exit)

This is a design which, even though it is a model of therapy, applies equally to NLP coaching. The author is Dr Richard Bolstad (2002) and his book goes by the name of the model.

ROLE (Representational systems, Orientation, Links, Effect)

This design looks at how we orientate our representational systems and how this orientation is linked to other representations to create an effect of some kind – for example, a feeling or behaviour.

SCORE (Symptoms, Causes, Outcomes, Resources, Effects)

This model arose from a self-modelling project of Dilts and Epstein when they recognized that there was a difference in problem solving between themselves and their advanced NLP students. It illustrates nicely that being an NLP coach is not just about delivering NLP models, but it is an orientation to life which has observation at its heart, and the purpose of that observation is to notice what is different between that which works and that which does not work in a specific context.

SOAR (State, Operator And Result)

This design is borrowed from computer modelling. It is based upon the assumption that intelligent systems can learn on the basis of feedback from the environment. Similarly people ideally will move from a problem space to a solution space through a series of transitions. The problem space is defined by the jungle gym which we visited in Chapter 11. It is a goal-oriented model which is similar to the three-minute NLP seminar. Outcome (know what you want) … Acuity (understand the problem space as it is in the present) … Flexibility (identify and execute the necessary operations to move to what you want).

References

Andreas, S. (2006) Modeling modeling. *The Model Magazine*, spring. www.steveandreas. com (accessed 27 June 2011).

Andreas, S. & Andreas, C. (2000) Selecting a resource to anchor. www.steveandreas.com/ articles/resource.html (accessed 23 April 2011).

ANLP (2009) *Current Research in NLP*. Volume 1. Proceedings of the 2008 conference. Ed. Paul Tosey. ANLP International CIC.

ANLP (2011) *Current Research in NLP*. Volume 2. Proceedings of the 2010 conference. Ed. Paul Tosey. ANLP International CIC.

Arnold, M.B. (1960) *Emotion and personality*. New York: Columbia University Press.

Association for Coaching (2004) *Summary report: UK coaching rates*. www.association forcoaching.com/memb/UKcrs104.pdf (accessed 12 June 2012).

Babiak, P. & Hare, R.D. (2006) *Snakes in suits: when psychopaths go to work*. New York: HarperCollins.

Bachkirova, T. & Cox, E. (2004) A bridge over troubled water: bringing together coaching and counseling. *The International Journal of Mentoring and Coaching*, 2 (1), July. http://old. emccouncil.org/eu/public/international_journal_of_mentoring_and_coaching/volume_ ii_issue_1_072004/a_bridge_over_troubled_water/index.html (accessed 12 June 2012).

Bandler, R. (1985) *Use your brain for a CHANGE*. Moab, UT: Real People Press.

Bandler, R. & Grinder, J. (1975a) *Patterns of the hypnotic techniques of Milton H. Erickson, M.D.* Volume 1. Capitola, CA: Meta Publications.

Bandler, R. & Grinder, J. (1975b) *The structure of magic: a book about language and therapy*. Palo Alto, CA: Science and Behaviour Books.

Bandler, R. & Grinder, J. (1979) *Frogs into princes: neuro linguistic programming*. Moab, UT: Real People Press.

Bateson, G. (1972) *Steps to an ecology of mind*. Chicago and London: University of Chicago Press.

Battino, R. & South, T.L. (1999) *Ericksonian approaches: a comprehensive manual*. Carmarthen, Wales: Crown House Publishing.

Beck, J. (1995) *Cognitive therapy: basics and beyond*. New York: Guilford Press.

Beck, D.E. & Cowan, C.C. (1996) *Spiral dynamics: mastering values, leadership and change*. Oxford: Blackwell.

Beer, M. & Nohria, N. (2000) Cracking the code of change. *Harvard Business Review*, 78 (3), May–June, 133–41.

Bem, D.J. (1965) An experimental analysis of self-persuasion. *Journal of Experimental Social Psychology*, 1, 199–218.

Berger, P. & Luckmann, T. (1966) *The social construction of reality: a treatise in the sociology of knowledge*. London: Penguin.

Berglas, S. (2002) The dangers of executive coaching. *Harvard Business Review*, June.

Bolstad, R. (2002) *Resolve: a new model of therapy*. Carmarthen, Wales: Crown House Publishing.

Bostic St Clair, C. & Grinder, J. (2001) *Whispering in the wind*. Scotts Valley, CA: J&C Enterprises.

Bourke, F. (2011) Personal email to bruce@achieving-lives.co.uk (7 November 2011).

Bowers, K.S. (1976) *Hypnosis for the seriously curious*. New York: Norton.

Bresser, F. & Wilson, C. (2006) What is coaching? In J. Passmore (ed.), *Excellence in coaching: the industry guide*. London: Kogan Page, 9–25.

Briggs Myers, I. & Myers, P. (1980) *Gifts differing: understanding personality type*. Palo Alto, CA: Davies-Black.

Brock, V. (2006) Key influences on the field. *Choice: The Magazine of Professional Coaching*, 4 (2), 26.

Brock, V. (2008) Grounded theory of the roots and emergence of coaching. A dissertation submitted in partial fulfilment of a PhD in coaching and human development. International University of Professional Studies, Maui.

Brown, D. (2007) *Tricks of the mind* (2nd edn). London: Channel 4 Books.

Business Wire (2011) www.n2growth.com/quotes-coaching.html (accessed 23 January 2011).

Cannon, W.B. (1920) *Bodily changes in pain, hunger, fear and rage*. New York and London: D. Appleton and Co.

Caplan, P.J. (1995) *They say you are crazy: how the world's most powerful psychiatrists decide who's normal*. Reading, MA: Addison-Wesley.

Carlson, N.R. (1994) *Physiology of behaviour* (5th edn). Boston: Allyn and Bacon.

Carmichael, L., Hogan, P. & Walter, A. (1932) An experimental study of the effect of language on the reproduction of visually perceived forms. *Journal of Experimental Psychology*, 15, 73–86.

Carnegie, D. (1936) *How to win friends and influence people*. New York: Simon and Schuster.

Carroll, M. (2003) The new kid on the block. *Counselling Psychology Journal*, December. www.supervisioncentre.com/docs/kv/New%20Kid%20on%20the%20Block.pdf (accessed 12 June 2010).

Castaneda, C. (1970) *The teachings of Don Juan: a Yaqui way of knowledge*. London: Penguin.

Cavanagh, M., Grant, A.M. and Kemp, T. (eds) (2005) *Evidence based coaching*. Volume 1. Queensland: Australian Academic Press.

Clancy, F. & Yorkshire, H. (1989) The Bandler Method. *Mother Jones*, 14 (1), February/March, 23–64.

Cox, E., Bachkirova, T. & Clutterbuck, D. (2010) *The complete handbook of coaching*. London: Sage.

Csikszentmihalyi, M. (1990) *Flow: the psychology of optimal experience*. New York: Harper Collins.

Danziger, K. (1997) The varieties of social construction. *Theory & Psychology*, 7 (3), 399–416.

DeLozier, J. & Grinder, J. (1987) *Turtles all the way down*. Scotts Valley, CA: Grinder and Associates.

Dewey, J. (1910) *How we think*. Boston: D.C. Heath & Co. Publishers.

Dilts, R. (1983) *Roots of neuro-linguistic programming*. Capitola, CA: Meta Publications.

Dilts, R. (1990) *Changing belief systems*. Capitola, CA: Meta Publications.

Dilts, R. (1998) *Modeling with NLP*. Capitola, CA: Meta Publications.

Dilts, R. & DeLozier, J. (2000) *Encyclopedia of systemic neuro-linguistic programming and NLP new coding*. Scotts Valley, CA: NLP University Press.

Dilts, R., Grinder, J., Bandler, R. & DeLozier, J. (1980) *Neuro-linguistic programming. Volume 1. The study of the structure of subjective experience*. Capitola, CA: Meta Publications.

Dilts, R. & Hallbom, T. (1990) *Early days of NLP* (DVD). Smart Dreamers Productions Ltd. www.smartdreamerspublishing.com.

Dryden, W. (1990) *The essential Albert Ellis: seminal writings on psychotherapy*. New York: Springer Publishing.

DSM-III™ (1980) *Diagnostic and statistical manual of mental disorders* (3rd edn). Washington, DC: American Psychiatric Association.

DSM-IV-TR™ (2000) *Diagnostic and statistical manual of mental disorders* (4th edn), text revised. Washington, DC: American Psychiatric Association.

Edelstien, G. (1990) *Symptom analysis: a method of brief therapy*. New York: Norton.

Einspruch, E.L. & Forman, B.D. (1985) Observations concerning research literature on neuro-linguistic programming. *Journal of Counseling Psychology*, 32 (4), 589–696.

Ellenberger, H.F. (1970) *The discovery of the unconscious: the history and evolution of dynamic psychiatry*. London: Fontana.

Erikson, E.H. (1950) *Childhood and society*. New York: W.W. Norton.

Fauconnier, G. & Turner, M. (2002) *The way we think: conceptual blending and the mind's hidden complexities*. New York: Basic Books.

Festinger, L. (1957) *A theory of cognitive dissonance*. New York: Harper and Row.

Festinger, L. & Carlsmith, J.M. (1959) Cognitive consequences of forced compliance. *Journal of Abnormal and Social Psychology*, 58 (2), March, 203–10.

French, W.L. & Bell, C.H. (1995) *Organization development: behavioural science interventions for organization improvement*. Englewood Cliffs, NJ: Prentice Hall.

Gallwey, T. (1986) *The inner game of tennis*. London: Pan (first published 1975).

Garcia, J. & Koelling, R.A (1966) Relation of cue to consequence in avoidance learning. *Psychonomic Science*, 4, 123–4.

Gergen, K.J. (1997) The place of the psyche in a constructed world. *Theory & Psychology*, 7 (6), 723–46.

Gilligan, S. (2011) An interview with Dr Stephen Gilligan by Chris & Jules Collingwood. www.stephengilligan.com/interviewA.html (accessed 21 January 2011).

Gladwell, M. (2005) *Blink: the power of thinking without thinking*. London: Penguin.

Goleman, D. (1996) *Emotional intelligence: why it can matter more than IQ*. London: Bloomsbury.

Gordon, D. (1978) *Therapeutic metaphors*. Capitola, CA: Meta Publications.

Gordon, D. & Dawes, G. (2005) *Expanding your world: modeling the structure of experience*. Tucson, AZ: Desert Rain.

Gordon, P. (2009) RD Laing in context. *The Psychotherapist*, 43, 10–12.

Grant, A.M. (2001a) Neuro-associative conditioning. *Australian Psychologist*, 36 (3), November, 232–8.

Grant, A.M. (2001b) Towards a psychology of coaching. Coaching Psychology Unit, University of Sydney.

Grant, A.M. & Cavanagh, M.J. (2004) Toward a profession of coaching: sixty-five years of progress and challenges for the future. *International Journal of Evidence-based Coaching and Mentoring*, 2 (1), 1–16.

Green, J. (1986) *Language understanding: a cognitive approach*. Milton Keynes: Open University Press.

Greer, S. (1997) Nietzsche and social construction. *Theory & Psychology*, 7 (1), 83–100.

Griffin, J. & Tyrrell, I. (2000) *The APET model: patterns in the brain*. Chalvington, East Sussex: HG Publishing for the European Therapy Studies Institute.

Griffin, J. & Tyrrell, I. (2001) *Hypnosis and trance states: a new psychobiological explanation*. Chalvington, East Sussex: HG Publishing for the European Therapy Studies Institute.

Grimley, B. (2002) Sexy variables. *Rapport: The Magazine for NLP Professionals*, autumn.

Grimley, B. (2005) Sailing the 7 C's of courage. *The Bulletin of the Association for Coaching*, summer, 5, 2–4.

Grimley, B. (2008) Goal setting at the 1st European Coaching Psychology Conference, Westminster, London, 17–18 December. Presentation given with Dr H. Law.

Grimley, B. (2010) NLP: a viable form of action research? Presentation at the 2nd International NLP Research Conference, Cardiff University, Wales.

Grinder, J. (2012) Two interviews with John Grinder. www.empoweredtolearn.com/GrinderInterview2005.htm (accessed 28 September 2012).

Grinder, J. & Bandler, R. (1976) *The structure of magic 2: a book about communication and change*. Palo Alto, CA: Science and Behaviour Books.

Grinder, J., DeLozier, J. & Bandler, R. (1977) *Patterns of the hypnotic techniques of Milton H. Erickson, M.D.* Volume 2. Capitola, CA: Meta Publications.

Grinder, J. & Elgin, S.H. (1973) *Guide to transformational grammar: history, theory, practice*. New York: Holt, Rinehart and Winston, Inc.

Gross, R.D. (1987) *Psychology: the science of mind and behaviour*. London: Hodder Arnold.

Hall, M.L. (2011a) Meta-reflections on the history of NLP. www.neurosemantics.com/nlp/the-history-of-nlp/nlp-history-and-self-actualization (accessed 16 February 2011).

Hall, M.L. (2011b) Meta Reflections #16. Challenging, provoking, teasing, and mastering the experience of stuttering. www.neurosemantics.com/wp-content/uploads/2012/01/2011-Meta-Reflections-1.pdf (accessed 6 April 2011).

Hall, M.L. (2011c) How meta-states enriches logic levels in NLP. www.neurosemantics.com/meta-states/how-meta-states-enriches-logical-levels-in-nlp-2 (accessed 10 December 2011).

Hall, M.L. (2011d) Meta reflections #5. The art of mapping Alfred Korzybski, series #2: Neurons. www.neurosemantics.com/wp-content/uploads/2012/01/2011-Meta-Reflections-1.pdf (accessed 28 September 2012).

Hall, M.L. & Bodenhamer, B. (2003) *The user's manual for the brain*. Volume 2. Carmarthen, Wales: Crown House Publishing.

Hall, M.L., Bodenhamer, R.G., Bolstad, R. & Hamblett, M. (2001) *The structure of personality: modeling 'personality' using NLP and neuro-semantics*. Carmarthen, Wales: Crown House Publishing.

Hall, M., Bodenhamer, R. & Min, D. (2003) *Figuring out people: design engineering with meta-programs*. Carmarthen, Wales: Crown House Publishing.

Hall, M.L. & Duval, M. (2004) *Meta-coaching. Volume 1. Coaching change*. Clifton, CO: Neuro-Semantics Publications.

Hamlin, R.G., Ellinger, A.D. & Beatti, R.S. (2009) Toward a profession of coaching? A definitional examination of coaching, organization development, and human resource development. *International Journal of Evidence Based Coaching and Mentoring*, 7 (1), 13–38.

Hayley, J. (1985) *Conversations with Milton H. Erickson, M.D. Volume 1. Changing individuals*. New York and London: W.W. Norton/Triangle Press.

Hayley, J. (1986) *Uncommon therapy: the psychiatric techniques of Milton H. Erickson*. New York: W.W. Norton.

Heap, M. (1988) Neuro-linguistic programming: an interim verdict. In M. Heap (ed.), *Hypnosis: current clinical, experimental and forensic practices*. London: Croom Helm, 268–80.

Jackendoff, R. (2002) *Foundations of language: brain, meaning, grammar, evolution*. Oxford: Oxford University Press.

James, T. & Woodsmall, W. (1988) *Time line therapy and the basis of personality*. Capitola, CA: Meta Publications.

James, W. (1884) What is an emotion? *Mind*, 9 (34), 188–205.

Jung, C. (1923) *Psychological types*. London: Kegan Paul.

Jung, C. (1960) *The structure and dynamics of the psyche. Volume 3. The collected works of Carl G. Jung* (trans. R.F.C. Hull). Bollingen Series XX. Princeton: Princeton University Press.

Kinsbourne, M. (1972) Eye and head turning indicates cerebral lateralization. *Science*, 176, 539–41.

Klass, A. (1961) What is a profession? *Canadian Medical Association Journal*, 85, *September*, 698–701. www.ncbi.nlm.nih.gov/pmc/articles/PMC1848216/pdf/canmedaj00909- 0027.pdf (accessed 27 December 2010).

Köhler, W. (1929) *Gestalt psychology*. New York: Liveright.

Korzybski, A. (1994) *Science and sanity: an introduction to non-Aristotelian systems and general semantics* (5th edn). New York: Institute of General Semantics.

Kroger, W.S. (1963) *Clinical and experimental hypnosis*. Philadelphia: Lippincott Williams and Wilkins.

Lakoff, G. & Johnson, M. (1999) *Philosophy in the flesh: the embodied mind and its challenge to western thought*. New York: Basic Books.

Lawley, J. & Tompkins, P. (2000) *Metaphors in mind: transformation through symbolic modelling*. London: The Developing Company Press.

LeDoux, J. (1996) *The emotional brain: the mysterious underpinnings of emotional life*. New York: Touchstone.

Lefcourt, H.M. (1976) *Locus of control: current trends in theory and research*. Hillsdale, NJ: Lawrence Erlbaum Associates.

Lehrer, J. (2010) The truth wears off: is there something wrong with the scientific method? *The New Yorker*, Annals of Science, December 13. www.newyorker.com/reporting/2010/12/13/101213fa_fact_lehrer (accessed 12 June 2012).

Lewin, K. (1951) *Field theory in social science: selected theoretical papers* (edited by D. Cartwright). New York: Harper & Row.

Lewis, B. & Pucelik, F. (1990) *Magic of NLP demystified: a pragmatic guide to communication and change*. Portland, OR: Metamorphous Press.

Lilly, J.C. (1967) *Programming the human biocomputer*. Berkeley, CA: Ronin.

Linder-Pelz, S. (2010) *NLP coaching: an evidence-based approach for coaches, leaders and individuals*. London: Kogan Page.

Linder-Pelz, S. (2011) Questions about meta programs. *Acuity*, 2, 78–91.

Linder-Pelz, S. & Hall, M. (2007) Let the research begin: a reply to Bruce Grimley. *The Coaching Psychologist*, 3 (3), December, 145–7.

Little, W. (2010) Power to persuade: the story of NLP. BBC Radio 4, 29 November.

Mansi, A. (2009) Coaching the narcissist: how difficult can it be? Challenges for coaching psychologists. *The Coaching Psychologist*, 5 (1), June, 22–5.

Marks, L.E. (1975) On coloured hearing synaesthesia: cross-modal translations of sensory dimensions. *Psychological Bulletin*, 82, 303–31.

Marks, L.E. (1982) Bright sneezes and dark coughs, loud sunlight and soft moonlight. *Journal of Experimental Psychology: Human Perception and Performance*, 8, 177–93.

Maslow, A. (1968) *Towards a psychology of being*. New York: Van Nostrand.

Mathison, J. (2007) Mirror neurons: a neurological basis for making sense of the words, feelings and actions of others. Centre for Management Learning & Development, University of Surrey.

Mathison, J. & Tosey, P. (2009) Exploring moments of knowing: neuro-linguistic programming and enquiry into inner landscapes. *Journal of Consciousness Studies*, 16 (10–12), 189–216.

McClelland, D. (1961) *The achieving society*. Princeton, NJ: D. Van Nostrand Company Inc.

McClendon, T.L. (1989) *The wild days: NLP 1972–1981*. Capitola, CA: Meta Publications.

McCrone, J. (1999) *Going inside: a tour round a single moment of consciousness*. New York: Fromm International.

McGilchrist, I. (2009) *The master and his emissary: the divided brain and the making of the western world*. New Haven, CT and London: Yale University Press.

McNiff, J. & Whitehead, J. (2000) *Action research in organisations*. London: Routledge.

Merleau-Ponty, M. (1962) *Phenomenology of perception*. London: Routledge and Kegan Paul.

Michalko, M. (2011) The tale of five monkeys. www.creativity-portal.com/articles/michael-michalko/tale-five-monkeys.html (accessed 18 November 2011).

Miller, G.A. (1955) The magical number seven, plus or minus two: some limits on our capacity for processing information. *Psychological Review*, 101 (2), 343–52.

Miller, G.A., Galanter, E. & Pribram, K.H. (1960) *Plans and the structure of behaviour*. New York: Holt, Rhinehart & Winston.

Morris, C.W. (1932) *Six theories of mind*. Chicago: University of Chicago Press.

Morris, C. (2010) www.nlpconnections.com/forum/16114-frank-pucelik-early-days-nlp.html (accessed 26 October 2010).

Mowbray, R. (1995) *The case against psychotherapy registration: a conservation issue for the human potential movement*. London: Trans Marginal Press.

Nagle, G. (1999) *Focus on geography: development and underdevelopment*. Cheltenham: Thomas Nelson.

Neenan, M. & Dryden, W. (2002) *Life coaching: a cognitive behavioural approach*. London: Routledge.

Neisser, U. (1982) *Memory observed*. San Francisco: W.H. Freeman and Co.

NLP Academy (2001–2003) Real NLP modelling. www.nlpworld.co.uk (accessed 24 August 2010).

NLP Academy (2010) The early days of NLP with Frank Pucelik. www.nlpacademy.co.uk/videos/view/the_early_days_of_nlp_with_frank_pucelik (accessed 27 January 2011).

NLP World (2012) NLP practitioner standards. www.nlpworld.co.uk/nlp-affiliation-aip-anlp-abnlp-inlpta (accessed 7 June 2012).

Nsehe, M. (2011) Nigeria's pastors 'as rich as oil barons'. www.bbc.co.uk/news/world-africa-13763339 (accessed 29 October 2011).

Nunn, J.A., Gregory, L.J., Brammer, M., Williams, S.C.R., Parsloe, D.M., Morgan, M.J., et al. (2002) Functional magnetic resonance imaging of synaesthesia: activation of V4/V8 by spoken words. *Nature Neuroscience*, 5, 371–5.

O'Connor, J. & Seymour, J. (1990) *Introducing NLP: psychological skills for understanding and influencing people*. London: Thorsons.

O'Hanlon, B. (2011) Personal email to bruce@achieving-lives.co.uk (1 February 2011).

Packard, V. (1991) *The hidden persuaders: the classic study of the American advertising machine*. London and New York: Penguin (first published 1957).

Parsloe, E. & Wray, M. (2000) *Coaching and mentoring: practical methods to improve learning*. London: Kogan Page.

Passmore, J. (2006) *Excellence in coaching: the industry guide*. London: Kogan Page.

Perls, F. (1973) *The Gestalt approach and eye witness to therapy*. Palo Alto, CA: Science and Behaviour Books.

Piaget, J. (1955) *The child's construction of reality*. Trans. M. Cook. London: Routledge and Kegan Paul (first published 1936).

Prochaska, J.O. & DiClemente, C.C. (1984) *The transtheoretical approach: crossing traditional boundaries of therapy*. Homewood, IL: Dow Jones Irwin.

Prochaska, J.O. & DiClemente, C.C. (2005) The transtheoretical approach. In J.C. Norcross & M.R. Goldfried (eds), *Handbook of psychotherapy integration* (2nd edn). New York: Oxford University Press, 147–71.

Pucelik, F. (2010) Personal notes from workshop (22 September 2010).

Ramachandran, V.S. (2005) *Phantoms in the brain*. London: Harper Perennial.

Ramachandran, V.S. & Hubbard, E.M. (2001) Synaesthesia: a window into perception, thought and language. *Journal of Consciousness Studies*, 8 (12), 3–34.

Redler, L. (2001) Remembering Ronnie. In L. Redler, S. Gans & B. Mullan, *Janus Head*. www.janushead.org/4-1/index.cfm (accessed 30 May 2012).

Ritter, D.J. (2002) *LabVIEW GUI: essential techniques*. New York: McGraw-Hill.

Robbins, A. (1986) *Unlimited power: the new science of personal achievement*. New York: Free Press.

Rogers, C. (1961) *On becoming a person: a therapist's view of psychotherapy*. London: Constable.

Rose Charvet, S. (1997) *Words that change minds: mastering the language of influence* (2nd edn). Dubuque, IA: Kendall/Hunt.

Rossi, E.L. & Cheek, D.B. (1988) *Mind-body therapy: ideodynamic healing in hypnosis.* New York: W.W. Norton.

Rotter, J.B. (1954) *Social learning and clinical psychology.* New York: Prentice-Hall.

Rowan, J. (1990) *Subpersonalities: the people inside us.* London: Routledge.

Rowan, J. (2008) NLP is not based on constructivism. *The Coaching Psychologist,* 4 (3), December, 160–2.

Sanders, R.S. & Reyher, J. (1969) Sensory deprivation and the enhancement of hypnotic susceptibility. *Journal of Abnormal Psychology,* 74, 375–81.

Sargent, N. (2010) What's happening in the coaching conversation with an executive at risk of derailing? Dissertation submitted to Oxford Brookes University for the partial fulfilment of the requirement for the degree of MA Coaching and Mentoring Practice, September.

Satir, V. (1988) *The new peoplemaking.* Palo Alto, CA: Science and Behaviour Books.

Schachter, S. & Singer, J.E. (1962) Cognitive, social and physiological determinants of emotional state. *Psychological Review,* 69 (5), 379–99.

Schilpp, P.A. (1979) *Albert Einstein: autobiographical notes.* La Salle, IL: Open Court Publishing.

Schwarzer, M. (2011) Web of the mind. www.mikeschwarzer.com

Senge, P.M. (1990) *The fifth discipline.* London: Century Business.

Shapiro, F. (1985) Neuro-linguistic programming: the new success technology. *Holistic Life Magazine,* summer, 41–3.

Shapiro, J.L. & Diamond, M.J. (1972) Increases in hypnotizability as a function of encounter group training. *Journal of Abnormal Psychology,* 79, 112–15.

Sharpley, C.F. (1987) Research findings on neurolinguistic programming: nonsupportive data or an untestable theory? *Journal of Counseling Psychology,* 14 (1), 103–7.

Smith, C.H., Morton, J. & Oakley, D. (1998) An investigation of the 'State-Dependency' of recall during hypnotic amnesia. *Contemporary Hypnosis,* 15 (2), 94–100.

Sperry, R.W. & Gazzaniga, M.S. (1967) *Language following surgical disconnection of the hemispheres in brain mechanisms underlying speech and language.* Ed. R.L. Darley. New York: Grune and Stratton.

Spitzer, R. (1992) Virginia Satir and origins of NLP. *Anchor Point,* 6 (7), July.

Stober, D.R. & Grant, A.M. (eds) (2006) *Evidence based coaching handbook: putting best practice to work for your clients.* Hoboken, NJ: John Wiley and Sons.

Stone, F. (1999) *Coaching, counselling and mentoring.* New York: American Management Association.

Sullivan, W. & Rees, J. (2008) *Clean language: revealing metaphors and opening minds.* Carmarthen, Wales: Crown House Publishing.

Swingle, J. (2006) Interview with David Gordon. *Noneuclidean Café,* 1 (2), spring. www.noneuclideancafe.com/issues/vol1_issue2_Spring2006/gordon.htm (accessed 30 May 2012).

Tart, C.T. (1970) Increases in hypnotizability resulting from a prolonged program for enhancing personal growth. *Journal of Abnormal Psychology,* 75, 260–6.

TFL (Team Focus Ltd) (1997) *Foundation course for personality.* Version 1.1. Maidenhead: Team Focus Ltd.

The Therapist (1998) Part of quote on back cover. 5 (4), autumn.

Tompkins, P. & Lawley, J. (1997a) Less is more … the art of clean language. *Rapport: The Magazine for NLP Professionals,* 35, February, 36–40.

Tompkins, P. & Lawley, J. (1997b) Symbolic modelling. *Rapport: The Magazine for NLP Professionals,* 38, winter, 3–13.

Tosey, P. & Mathison, J. (2009) *Neuro-linguistic programming: a critical appreciation for managers and developers.* Basingstoke: Palgrave Macmillan.

Tulving, E. & Thompson, D.M. (1973) Encoding specificity and retrieval processes in episodic memory. *Psychological Review,* 80, 352–73.

Vaihinger, H. (1924) *The philosophy of as if.* London: Routledge and Kegan Paul.

Valins, S. (1966) Cognitive effects of false heart-rate feedback. *Journal of Personality and Social Psychology*, 4 (4), 400–8.

Vincent Peale, N. (1952) *The power of positive thinking*. New York: Simon and Schuster.

Wagstaff, G.F. (1998) The semantics and physiology of hypnosis as an altered state: towards a definition of hypnosis. *Contemporary Hypnosis*, 15 (3), 155.

Walker, W. (1996) *Abenteuer Kommunikation Bateson, Perls, Satir, Erickson und die Anfange des Neurolinguistischen Programmierens (NLP)* (4th edn). Stuttgart: KlettCott.

Ward, J. (2003) State of the art synaesthesia. *The Psychologist*, 16 (4), 196–9.

Watson, A. (2011) *The clean approach to leadership* (e-book). Angela Watson Consulting.

Whitmore, J. (1997) *Need, greed and freedom*. Shaftesbury: Element Books.

Wilber, K. (2000) *A brief history of everything*. Boston: Shambhala.

Willis, P. (2011) Coaching psychology explained. www.coachingpsychologist.net/WhatIs/index.php (accessed 23 January 2011).

Wilson, C. & Dunbar, A. (2011) www.cleancoaching.com.

Yapko, M.D. (2003) *Trancework: an introduction to the practice of clinical hypnosis* (3rd edn). New York: Brunner/Routledge.

Index

Page references to Figures or Tables will be in *italics*